Child Welfare in Canada

The Role of Provincial and Territorial Authorities in Cases of Child Abuse

Federal-
Provincial
Working
Group on
Child and
Family
Services
Information

```
362
.828
0971
C536
```

JUL 4 1995

Copies available from:

National Clearinghouse on Family Violence
Family Violence Prevention Division
Health Programs and Services Branch
Health Canada
Ottawa, Ontario
Canada K1A 1B5

Tel.: 1-800-267-1291

 TDD line: (Telephone Device for the Deaf)
1-800-561-5643

Fax: 613-941-8930

Information contained in this report was compiled by the Federal/Provincial Working Group on Child and Family Services Information in cooperation with provincial and territorial Directors of Child Welfare. Contents may not be commercially reproduced but any other reproduction, with acknowledgements, is encouraged.

Également disponible en français sous le titre
Bien-être de l'enfance au Canada : le rôle des autorités provinciales et territoriales en matière d'enfance maltraitée

©Minister of Supply and Services Canada 1994
Cat. H72-21/99-1994E
ISBN 0-662-21454-4

Preface

This is the report of the Provincial[1] Child Welfare[2] Systems data collection project under the Federal Family Violence Initiative. The project is one of six data collection projects coordinated by the Canadian Centre for Justice Statistics on behalf of the Family Violence Prevention Division at Health Canada. The project was undertaken by the Federal-Provincial Working Group on Child and Family Services Information. The Secretariat to the Working Group, which is part of the Social Program Information and Analysis Directorate at Human Resources Development Canada (formerly Health and Welfare Canada), produced the report in cooperation with the provincial/territorial Directors of Child Welfare. This co-operative effort is an important first step in providing information on child and family services available at the provincial level for children who have been abused or neglected.

---

1. The term "provincial" refers to provincial/territorial.
2. The term "child and family services" is often used in this report instead of "child welfare".

Table of Contents

		Page
Chapter 1 –	Introduction	5
Chapter 2 –	Newfoundland	17
Chapter 3 –	Prince Edward Island	27
Chapter 4 –	Nova Scotia	37
Chapter 5 –	New Brunswick	53
Chapter 6 –	Quebec	69
Chapter 7 –	Ontario	83
Chapter 8 –	Manitoba	99
Chapter 9 –	Saskatchewan	117
Chapter 10 –	Alberta	129
Chapter 11 –	British Columbia	145
Chapter 12 –	Yukon	161
Chapter 13 –	Northwest Territories	173

Appendices	187
List of Tables	195
List of Figures	199

Chapter 1 – Introduction

Purpose and Scope

The mandate for this project was to produce a report outlining the roles and responsibilities of provincial and territorial child welfare authorities in cases of child abuse and neglect and present available statistics on abused and neglected children as identified by child welfare authorities. As current child protection programs and services stress the provision of services to both the child and the child's natural family, the term "child and family services" is often used in this report instead of "child welfare".

This report, which reflects each jurisdiction's provisions as of July 1, 1992, was written based on existing policy and legislation, supplemented by information provided by each jurisdiction[1]. It should be noted that actual practice may vary somewhat from the principles stated in legislation and policy. The report is an information document only; no analysis of the material is provided.

The report consists of an Introduction (Chapter 1), individual chapters for each jurisdiction and two appendices. The Introduction provides a general overview of the philosophy and goals of child and family services legislation, the service delivery systems, and the process for dealing with reports of alleged or suspected child abuse or neglect. Each jurisdictional chapter presents specific provisions as of July 1, 1992 with respect to: administration and service delivery; legislative and working definitions; mandatory reporting of a child in need of protection; investigation of reports of alleged or suspected child abuse or neglect; voluntary agreements and court-ordered protection; descriptions of child abuse registers where they exist; and child abuse and neglect protocols. Each jurisdictional chapter concludes with available statistical data in the form of tables and graphs and a list of resource material. The appendices contain supplemental data on the child population in Canada and a list of contacts for further information.

Although it is recognized that some child and family services cases may involve elements warranting parallel criminal investigation, criminal proceedings are not described in this report.

Limitations

While a framework was used to provide consistency in topics covered in the descriptive sections of the jurisdictional chapters, it was not possible to use standard definitions or terminology. Although some generalizations are presented in this chapter, each jurisdiction has its own legislation, definitions, policies, and services; it is these specific approaches which are described in the subsequent chapters. A summary of the case management process starting from the original receipt of information about suspected or alleged abuse

---

1. The terms "jurisdiction" and "jurisdictional" refer to "province/territory" and "provincial/territorial" respectively.

or neglect of a child through to case closure is included in the Overview of Child and Family Services in Canada which follows. Although the actual process may vary among jurisdictions, the summary attempts to reflect the common elements.

It was not possible to identify common statistical data elements on child abuse and neglect which would permit the generation of national estimates. There are several reasons for this. The definitions of abuse and neglect differ among jurisdictions. Statistical data are extracted from data systems developed to meet the administrative and case management needs of each jurisdiction; as such, there are extensive variations in the types of data collected and the manner in which they are reported. For instance, some data may relate to all allegations and others to investigations only. Actual client data may represent the number of families or children. The periodicity of the data varies from monthly to annual: the data reported may include all activity during the month, snapshot data as at the end of the month, or cumulative data during the year (calendar or fiscal). In addition, few jurisdictions report the reason(s) a child requires services; for those which do, there may be problems with data consistency and quality, since few guidelines for standard coding of data exist within jurisdictions. As an example, where there is a court application to remove a child from the family home, it may be easier to prove neglect than it is to prove any other form of abuse; consequently, data based on reason for coming into care may underestimate actual cases of abuse. Because of the many data inconsistencies, readers are advised to consult the footnotes which accompany each jurisdiction's data.

As a result of these data limitations, data from the statistical graphs and tables for a given province or territory cannot and should not be compared with data from other jurisdictions.

Definition of Child Abuse and Neglect

For the purpose of this report, child abuse and neglect are considered to be the physical, sexual, or emotional abuse or physical or emotional neglect of a child which causes the child to be in need of protection or at risk of being in need of protection.

The legislation in each jurisdiction defines a "child in need of protection" or comparable term. These definitions provide the legal basis for government intervention where a child's well-being is at risk. Although these definitions vary across Canada, each one references child abuse and neglect as reasons for a child being in need of protection. In addition, detailed definitions of "child abuse" are contained in the legislation for Nova Scotia, Manitoba, Alberta and the Northwest Territories. Most jurisdictions have working definitions of child abuse or neglect which are used by workers when investigating alleged or suspected cases. Because of the variation in the definitions, a more detailed one is not presented here; rather, the specific definitions are included in each jurisdictional chapter.

Overview of Child and Family Services in Canada

Child and family services in Canada come under the jurisdiction of the provincial and territorial governments, with funding of most services shared by the federal government; the rate of cost sharing depends on the jurisdiction. Each province and territory has legislation providing for the protection of neglected and abused children.

Although the goals and philosophies of child and family services legislation vary somewhat across jurisdictions, they generally reflect the notion that families are the basic units of society and should be supported and preserved. Families are responsible for the care, nurturing, supervision and protection of their children. However, the various pieces of legislation recognize that children have certain basic rights, including the right to be protected from abuse and neglect, and that governments have the responsibility to protect children from harm. Child and family services authorities across Canada carry out this role of protecting children. Their primary responsibilities are to investigate alleged or suspected child abuse or neglect and, where appropriate, to provide relevant services to ensure the well-being and safety of the child. If a family is unable, despite the provision of support services, to adequately protect a child, the authorities may temporarily or permanently assume responsibility for the child; this involves court action and is referred to as "taking a child into care"[2]. All jurisdictions recognize that the best interests of the child must be a primary consideration in all aspects of child and family services, and that the least intrusive form of intervention should be adopted.

The design and delivery of child and family services are the responsibility of the department of social services, or its equivalent, in each province and territory. Each department has a central child and family services division or section which develops policies and programs necessary for the delivery of services. Most jurisdictions have a network of regional, area and/or district offices responsible for the delivery of services. In Ontario, children's aid societies deliver services, whereas services in Nova Scotia and Manitoba are delivered by a combination of mandated non-government agencies and government offices. All jurisdictions also make use of the services of various non-government/community-based agencies. Because of the diversity of services required by families and children, services of other government departments such as health and education are also often requested. In addition, First Nations and other native organizations are becoming increasingly involved in the design and delivery of native child and family services.

Mandatory Reporting and Investigation

It is required by child protection law in all jurisdictions except the Yukon that persons must report cases of alleged or suspected child abuse or neglect to a child and family services authority. In the Yukon, cases may be reported but it is not mandatory. Reports include self referrals and referrals made by the police, hospitals or schools, among others. The national Kids Help Phone[3] is also an important referral source in some provinces.

There is no liability for a person making a report, as long as it is not made maliciously. Failure to report alleged or suspected abuse or neglect is an offence in Newfoundland, Prince Edward Island, Nova Scotia, Manitoba, Saskatchewan, Alberta, British Columbia and the Northwest Territories. Conviction may result in a fine and/or imprisonment. In New Brunswick and Ontario, only the failure of a

---

2. In Quebec, child protection authorities assume responsibility for the child's situation, not for the child. This may be done by agreement or order.

3. The Kids Help Phone is a national, toll-free, confidential helpline for children and adolescents. It is funded by the Canadian Children's Foundation, and provides bilingual services, 24 hours a day, seven days a week. Professionally trained counsellors with extensive backgrounds in social work, psychology, nursing, child care and the law respond to calls for help, offering advice and often making referrals to other agencies. The Kids Help Phone number is 1-800-668-6868.

professional to report is an offence; this may result in a fine and/or imprisonment upon conviction. In Quebec, the failure of a professional to report child abuse or neglect is also an offence; moreover, the failure of any person to report suspected sexual or physical abuse is an offence which again may result in a fine. In some locations, protocols or guidelines describing signs and symptoms of child abuse and/or neglect and reporting procedures have been developed for professionals such as teachers and physicians.

Child and family services authorities investigate reports of alleged or suspected child abuse or neglect; however, the degree of involvement varies according to the legislation and policy within each jurisdiction[4]. All jurisdictions investigate allegations of intra-familial abuse or neglect; most investigate allegations of extra-familial abuse by someone known to the child. This may include babysitters, day care workers or teachers. Cases of abuse by strangers are generally dealt with by the police under criminal law, although family support services may be provided to victims through the department of social services or its equivalent. Generally, the role of child and family services authorities is to determine whether an alleged or suspected child victim is in need of protection. In situations where abuse occurred outside the family home, it must be determined whether or not the parent is willing or able to adequately protect the child and whether or not other children may be at risk.

With the exception of Quebec[5], cases of alleged or suspected child abuse or neglect which may have grounds for criminal investigation are referred to the police. Criminal and child protection investigations may be carried out simultaneously. In most cases, the worker and police officer work together during the information gathering phases of their respective investigations. This cooperation is often formalized in a protocol or guideline, setting out standard procedures to ensure consistent practice. Protocols regarding the cooperation of various other professionals such as physicians, nurses, or teachers during the investigation may also apply.

During the investigation, the worker must assess the case by applying the legislated definition of a child in need of protection to determine if the child requires services. In order to provide a guide to assist workers in making clinical assessments and judgements and to provide a means to document and justify case decisions, Newfoundland, Nova Scotia, Manitoba, Saskatchewan and several Ontario Children's Aid Societies have formally adopted risk management models. Various factors may be used, but they all help to identify the risk-causing aspects of a case and to assess the severity of these elements. A risk management model is used in conjunction with the professional assessment of the investigating worker, colleagues and supervisors to determine if a child is in need of protection and/or what level of services to provide.

---

4. It should be noted that each jurisdiction's legislation identifies the maximum age up to which the child and family services authorities must investigate a report and provide services. The age varies from 16 to 19 years. (See Table 1.1 at the end of this chapter.) A case involving a child over the specified age is referred to the police, unless younger siblings may be victims.

5. There is no requirement in Quebec for the Director of Youth Protection to report such cases to the police. However, in cases of alleged abuse in either a school or a health and social services establishment, the Director and police, along with other involved parties, work cooperatively.

All jurisdictions have policies concerning the investigation of allegations of abuse in placement resources[6] for children in care. In addition, provisions exist in most jurisdictions for the investigation of the injury or death of a child receiving services under child protection legislation.

Support Services and Agreements

Support Services

Support services may be provided as a preventive measure in all jurisdictions to families and children considered to be at risk or potential risk; they may also be provided under the terms of a voluntary agreement or court order where the order deemed a child to be in need of protection. The intention of support services is to strengthen the family and resolve problems to enable the child to either remain in the natural home or return home. Services may be provided at the request of the family, on the recommendation of a social worker, or under the provisions of a court order. Although support services are provided on a relatively informal basis, formalized agreements are used in Quebec, Manitoba, Saskatchewan and Alberta.

The types of support services available include parenting skills, counselling, respite care, day care, homemakers, life skills, drug and alcohol treatment or rehabilitation programs, and specialized treatment programs for child victims and/or perpetrators of abuse. The nature and extent of services vary across jurisdictions, with most services developed and delivered at the community level. For example, most departments of social services purchase treatment services for abuse victims or perpetrators from non-governmental or community organizations, agencies and private practitioners. In addition, churches, hospitals and schools may offer services to victims of abuse. Transition homes and safe houses also provide short-term accommodation and support to victims of family violence, including child abuse.

Some child and family services authorities operate or fund programs geared exclusively towards victims of child abuse and/or their families. Examples include: foster parents helping natural parents, in both Prince Edward Island and New Brunswick; Regina's Integrated Family Treatment Program for Sexually Abused Children; British Columbia's Sexual Abuse Interventions Project, an inter-ministry project which contracts with community agencies to provide services to sexually abused children and youth; and Yukon's Child Abuse Treatment Services (CATS), which provide individual/group counselling and treatment for abused children and the non-offending parent.

In each jurisdiction, health authorities play an important role in delivering mental health services to victims of abuse and neglect. In addition, most provincial justice departments fund victim assistance programs when criminal charges have been laid. These programs, which are usually offered through the police or community agencies, provide services ranging from referrals and support services to witness preparation and support to child abuse victims required to testify in criminal court.

---

6. This could include foster homes, group homes or residential treatment facilities.

Although not technically a support service, most jurisdictions have informal, community-based child abuse teams or committees. These are often composed of professionals from the health, education, legal and social service fields. The roles of these teams vary from public education and advocacy to the development of protocols.

Agreements

There are several options for services if, following the investigation of a report of alleged or suspected abuse or neglect, it is believed that a child is in need of protection. The provision of services with the agreement of the parent, and without going to court, is the least intrusive option and generally includes family support or placement services. The parent agrees voluntarily to the provision of services and/or placement of the child. The placement of a child in the home of a friend or relative, or the supervision of a child in the natural home by a departmental or agency worker are other examples of voluntary services which may be available. The home situation may be further improved if an alleged abuser agrees to leave the child's home.

Placement agreements[7] allow the parent to voluntarily give up care/custody (but, in most cases, not guardianship) of the child to the child and family services authority for a temporary period of time. The placement agreement, signed by the worker and the parent, sets out the terms of the child's care, including goals, services required and their duration. Many agreements also address parental financial contributions and access to the child. Because these agreements are voluntary, either party may terminate the agreement upon providing appropriate notice.

With the exception of the Northwest Territories, placement agreements may be used when the child is in need of protection, but it is expected that the provision of short-term services will improve the family situation. They may also be used when the child has special needs (i.e., mental and/or physical handicap) and the parent is unable to provide the support and services the child requires[8]. It is recognized that there may be additional stress placed on a parent caring for a special needs child which could potentially lead to a protection situation.

In protection situations where the family situation does not improve with the provision of support services or under a placement agreement, the worker reviews the case and may consider renegotiating the agreement, applying for a protection hearing, or apprehending the child (i.e., removing the child from the care of the parent).

Apprehensions and Court Hearings

In non-emergency situations, workers in most jurisdictions who believe a child is in need of protection and should be removed from the home, may apply to the court for a warrant to apprehend the child. In Nova Scotia and Saskatchewan, a child can be apprehended if at risk of incurring serious harm and the department's assessment is that provision of in-home services will not be sufficient to protect the child. In Quebec, a child may not be apprehended in a non-emergency situation. When a child is in immediate danger, an

---

7. All jurisdictions have provisions in legislation for the voluntary relinquishment of a child, usually an infant, for adoption purposes. These provisions are not discussed in this report.

8. In Quebec, services for special needs children are outlined in the *Act Respecting Health Services and Social Services*, not the *Youth Protection Act*.

emergency apprehension may be carried out to remove the child from the home. In all jurisdictions, this may be done without a warrant. The assistance of the police may also be requested.

Following an apprehension, or when the provision of voluntary services is not feasible or successful, the worker applies to the appropriate court for a child protection hearing. (In Quebec, the worker may attempt to negotiate an agreement.) After reviewing the material presented by the worker and the testimony of all relevant witnesses, the judge determines whether or not the child is in need of protection.

Criminal Court Proceedings and Child Protection Hearings

As indicated earlier, the police are required to investigate cases of alleged or suspected child abuse or neglect referred by child welfare authorities to ascertain whether an offence may have been committed under the *Criminal Code*[9]. These usually include cases of serious physical abuse, sexual abuse and serious neglect. If the police lay charges, it is the role of the criminal court to protect society and punish offenders; no decision is made with respect to the child[10]. In criminal court, various techniques for lessening the stress on a child witness may be employed. In sexual abuse cases, a video of the child's testimony (the contents of which have to be adopted by the child in court) or a screen to block the child from the alleged abuser during the questioning may be used[11] if the judge or justice is of the opinion that the exclusion is necessary to obtain a full and candid account of the acts complained of by the victim.

The role of the judge presiding over the child protection hearing, on the other hand, is to determine if the child is in need of protection and to remove the child from the home if necessary. Based on the worker's recommendations, the judge may also specify that services be provided to the child and/or family to improve the situation. The hearing does not determine if anyone is guilty of an offence.

The criminal and child protection investigations may proceed simultaneously and there may be a relationship between the two. For example, the question of whether the criminal prosecution or the protection hearing should proceed first may be important.

Court Orders

If, as a result of the protection hearing, the judge finds that a child is in need of protection, the judge will consider the child's best interests before making an order. Where possible, the judge will attempt to keep the family intact. All jurisdictions have appeal processes with respect to child protection orders.

---

9. See footnote 5.
10. It should be noted that several jurisdictions have provisions in their child protection legislation for an alleged offender to be charged with child abuse as a provincial offence if a criminal trial has not resulted in a conviction or is unlikely to do so.
11. Bill C-15, which amended the *Criminal Code* and the *Canada Evidence Act*, provides for these techniques and other changes regarding child witnessing in criminal trials of child sexual abuse cases. Some of these are being implemented by Family Courts for child protection hearings. Bill C-15 came into effect in January 1988; its implementation is to be reviewed by Parliament four years after the proclamation of the Act. In June 1993, the Supreme Court of Canada ruled against a Manitoba challenge that the use of videotaped child testimony as evidence in sexual assault cases violated the *Canadian Charter of Rights and Freedoms*.

The three most commonly made orders are: an order for supervision of the family in the home (the child remains at or is returned home or to the person who had custody prior to the apprehension); an order for the child to be brought into the temporary care of the child and family services authority; or an order for the child to be brought into the permanent care of the authority. Orders to prevent a specific person from having access to a child in need of protection may be made under child protection legislation in Nova Scotia, New Brunswick, Ontario, Manitoba, Saskatchewan, Alberta, and British Columbia. If a criminal charge has been laid under the federal *Criminal Code*, a "no contact order" as a condition of bail is another means of preventing access.

When a child is brought into care through a permanent order of the court, the parent loses all custody and guardianship rights. Under a temporary order, the parent loses custody of the child for the duration of the order; provisions for guardianship vary between provinces. Under a supervision order, the parent generally retains custody and guardianship. Terms of any order may include mandatory provision of family support services to the family and, where appropriate, the type and frequency of access between the child and family. Child and family services authorities must prepare a service or case plan for each child in care outlining provisions such as the services required and placement objectives. The long-term goal for a child under a permanent order, particularly for a younger child, is usually adoption; other alternatives such as preparation for independence may be more appropriate for an older child.

Placement of a Child

When a child comes into the care of the child and family services authority through an apprehension, placement agreement or court order, the child is placed in an appropriate living arrangement. Placement possibilities include the home of a relative, neighbour or other person known to the child, a foster home, or a group home. Children with severe emotional and behaviourial problems may sometimes be placed in structured residential treatment facilities equipped to meet special needs. These facilities range from group homes with specially trained staff to psychiatric hospital settings.

Closure of a Case

When family support services are provided and/or a child is in care under a placement agreement, services may be withdrawn and/or the child returned home once it is determined by the child and family services authority that the child is no longer in need of protection. Services provided at the request of a family or through a voluntary agreement may be discontinued at the request of the family.

When a court order regarding the care of a child has been made, the case is generally closed once the order expires. In the case of temporary or supervision orders, authorities generally review the case prior to the expiry of the order to determine whether there are ongoing protection concerns; where there are, the worker will return to court for a further order. A case may also be closed before the order expires if circumstances have changed; however, it must be brought back to court to determine if the child is still in need of protection. In Newfoundland, an order can only expire when a child turns 16; otherwise, the order must be terminated by the court. Returning a child in care home may be done initially under the supervision of the child and family services authority or with the provision of support services.

Generally, children who are permanent wards remain in care until they reach the jurisdiction's maximum age with respect to child protection services (see Table 1.1). Some jurisdictions may review a permanent order where the child's family's situation has improved. Permanent orders also expire if a child marries (except in Quebec and British Columbia), dies, or is adopted. Care and maintenance of permanent wards may be extended for up to several years beyond the maximum age in certain circumstances (see Table 1.1); at the end of this period the case is closed.

Table 1.1 Age of Child as Defined in Child Protection Legislation

Province or Territory	Age	Extension Provisions
Newfoundland	under 16	• wardship to age 19 (subsequent to Order of Temporary Wardship, Order of Permanent Wardship) • services to age 21 (under an agreement or following extension of wardship to age 19)
Prince Edward Island	under 18	• services to age 21 (subsequent to Permanent Guardianship Order)
Nova Scotia	under 16	• wardship to age 21 (subsequent to Permanent Care Order)
New Brunswick	under 19[1]	• *Post Guardianship Services Agreement*[2] : services – age varies[3] (subsequent to Guardianship Order)
Quebec	under 18	• compulsory foster care may be extended to age 21 by Court Order
Ontario	under 16[4]	• wardship to age 18 (subsequent to Society Wardship Order [temporary], Crown Wardship Order [permanent]) • services to age 21 (former Crown wards)
Manitoba	under 18	• services to age 21 (subsequent to Permanent Guardianship Order)
Saskatchewan	under 16[4,5]	• wardship to age 18 (Permanent Committal Order) • care and custody to age 18 (Temporary Committal Order, Long-Term Order to Age 18) • services to age 21 (subsequent to Permanent Committal Order, Long-Term Order to Age 18)
Alberta	under 18	• *Care and Maintenance Agreement*[2]: services to age 20 (subsequent to Temporary or Permanent Guardianship Order, Support or Custody Agreements entered into with the child)
British Columbia	under 19	• *Post Majority Services Program*[2]: support and/or maintenance to age 21 for current and former permanent wards (Permanent Order)
Yukon	under 18	• wardship to age 19 (Order for Temporary Care and Custody, Order for Permanent Care and Custody)
Northwest Territories	under 18	• wardship to age 19 (subsequent to Permanent Guardianship Order)

(cont'd)

Table 1.1   Age of Child as Defined in Child Protection Legislation (cont'd)

1. Regulations stipulate mandatory provision of child protection services applies only to a child under age 16 (under 19 for a disabled person). Mandatory reporting of a child in need of protection applies only to children under 16 and disabled children under the age of 19.
2. Formal agreement signed by the youth and department.
3. There is no upper age limit if services are provided to a child who has been continuously enrolled in an educational program since reaching age 19. An upper age limit of 24 applies to a disabled child.
4. 16 and 17 year olds can enter into an agreement for services until age 18.
5. In Saskatchewan, a 16 or 17 year old may be apprehended in extraordinary circumstances.

Chapter 2 – # Newfoundland

Administration and Service Delivery

Under the *Child Welfare Act*, the Director of Child Welfare in Newfoundland's Department of Social Services is responsible for providing care to children who are in need of protection. This includes children who have been abused or neglected.

The Child Welfare Division of the Department of Social Services, headquartered in St. John's, is responsible for the development of policy, programs, and legislation in the areas of family support services, child protection, and adoption. Services are delivered through a system of five regional offices and 53 district offices. The five regional directors report to the Assistant Deputy Minister of Client and Community Services. Child protection services are delivered by departmental social workers. Family support services may be provided by staff of the Department of Social Services or Health or non-governmental workers in local agencies.

In order to better coordinate services, the Interministerial Committee on Family Violence has a mandate to develop a strategic plan to respond to family violence. The committee is composed of representatives from five departments – Education, Health, Social Services, Justice, Municipal Affairs – and the Women's Policy Office which reports to the Executive Council (Provincial Cabinet).

One of the subcommittees is Violence Against Children which is chaired by the Director of Child Welfare.

Definitions

For the purposes of investigating allegations of child abuse or neglect and initiating child protection proceedings, Sub-section 2(a) of the *Child Welfare Act* defines a **child** to be an unmarried boy or girl under the age of 16. Under Paragraph 19(13)(a) of the Act, a child who is in the Director's care at age 16 may have wardship extended to age 19. Paragraph 19(13)(b) allows financial and other services to be extended to age 21. Adoption provisions are specified in the *Adoption of Children Act*; under Sub-section 2(f), a **child** under the age of 19 years may be adopted.

Sub-section 2(b) of the *Child Welfare Act* defines a **child in need of protection** to mean:

"(i)   a child who is without adequate care or supervision;

(ii)   a child who is without necessary food, clothing or shelter, as may be available with the level of financial assistance given in relation to that child under the laws of the province;

(iii)   a child who is living in circumstances that are unfit or improper for the child;

(iv)   a child in the care or custody of a person who is unfit, unable or unwilling to provide adequate care for the child;

(v) a child who is living in a situation where there is severe domestic violence;

(vi) a child who is physically or sexually abused, physically or emotionally neglected, sexually exploited or in danger of that treatment;

(vii) a child who is in the care and custody of a person who fails to provide adequately for the child's education or attendance at school;

(viii) a child who has no living parents and who has no person willing to assume responsibility or with a legal responsibility for the child's maintenance;

(ix) a child who is in the care or custody of a person who refuses or fails

(a) to provide or obtain proper medical or other recognized remedial care or treatment necessary for the health or well-being of the child, or

(b) to permit such care and treatment to be supplied to the child when it is considered essential by a qualified medical practitioner;

(x) a child who is brought before the court with the consent of the parent, guardian or person with actual control for the purpose of transferring the guardianship of the child to the director;

(xi) a child who is beyond the control of the person caring for the child;

(xii) a child who by his or her behaviour, condition, environment or association, is likely to injure himself or herself or others;

(xiii) a child taken into a home or otherwise in the care and custody of a person contrary to subsection 3(3) or (5) of the *Adoption of Children Act* (i.e., without the written approval of the Director of Child Welfare); and

(xiv) a child actually or apparently under the age of 12 who performs an action that contravenes a provision of an Act or a regulation made under that Act or a municipal regulation or by-law or an Act of the Parliament of Canada."

Paragraph 2(b)(vi) of the definition of a child in need of protection provides the definition of **child abuse and neglect** which is used by the Department – "a child who is physically or sexually abused, physically or emotionally neglected, sexually exploited or in danger of that treatment". A protocol between the police and the Department of Social Services elaborates that "Such situations as lack of supervision or control and failure to provide the basic necessities of life constitute neglect...". Although not defined as abuse, under Paragraph 2(b)(v), a child who is living in a situation where there is severe domestic violence is included in the definition of a child in need of protection.

Mandatory Reporting of a Child in Need of Protection

Section 38 of the *Child Welfare Act* specifies that anyone (including lawyers) having information concerning the abandonment, desertion, physical ill-treatment or need for protection of a child must report the information to the Director of Child Welfare or a departmental social worker in a regional or district office[1]. This is a requirement even if the person makes a report to an agency such as the police or to a school. Unless the information is given with malicious intent or without reasonable cause, the person making the report is protected under the law. A person who fails to report or who does so maliciously or without reasonable cause, is guilty of an offence and is liable, upon summary conviction, to a fine of up to $1,000[1] or to imprisonment of up to six months, or both.

---

1. Section 38 of the Child Welfare Act was amended in December 1992. Reports may be made directly to a police officer. The maximum fine for failure to report was increased to $10,000.

Investigation of an Allegation of Child Abuse or Neglect

All reports that a child may be in need of protection, including allegations of abuse or neglect by a family member, caregiver, acquaintance or stranger, must be evaluated by a social worker. Investigations of alleged child abuse or neglect must be initiated within 24 hours. The social worker, in consultation with the supervisor, determines whether police intervention is warranted. The social worker must inform the police of cases of sexual abuse and serious physical abuse where there may be grounds for criminal charges to be laid. The police must inform the Department immediately of any report of alleged child abuse. In cases of non-familial abuse, the social worker reviews the situation with the parent to determine if lack of parental supervision or negligence was a contributing factor to the abuse to ensure that the child will be protected in future and to offer services if required. If the alleged offender is employed as a caregiver, such as a teacher or day care worker, the employer is advised and risk to other children is assessed. When both the police and the Department are investigating a case, the investigation is to be carried out jointly wherever possible, including interviewing the alleged victim together to reduce the number of interviews.

When a social worker believes that a child is in need of protection and a suitable voluntary arrangement cannot be made to protect the child, the worker may apprehend the child. In an emergency, the apprehension may be done without a warrant, although it is recommended that a warrant be obtained. Except in an emergency, the worker must consult with the supervisor prior to apprehending the child. A police officer may also apprehend a child but must involve a social worker in the case as soon as possible. In some cases, the arrest or voluntary removal of the alleged offender may eliminate the need for apprehension.

In all cases where physical injuries are visible or suspected, and in cases of alleged sexual abuse, a medical examination must be arranged as soon as possible. The parent or caregiver is to accompany the child. If the parent cannot be located or will not consent, the child must be apprehended before a social worker can give consent for a medical examination.

Investigations of reports of abuse or neglect of native children follow the same procedure as outlined above.

To assist them in carrying out their responsibilities, social workers take a one week orientation course when they join the Child Welfare Division. Social workers are also trained in a Risk Assessment process and how to use risk assessment tools where appropriate. In addition, social workers also receive a two week training course on the detection of child sexual abuse, the investigation of allegations and treatment for victims. Police and social workers also receive joint training regarding the investigation of child abuse.

Voluntary Agreements

Working with the parent when a child is at risk is the preferred option for the Department of Social Services. Voluntary supervision allows the child to remain at home. It involves regular visits from a social worker, plus provision of other family support services. A formal contract may be drawn up outlining the terms of the supervision. Voluntary supervision may be possible in an abuse situation if the alleged abuser is no longer in the home or in a neglect situation when the parent is cooperative. Placement with relatives with or without support services may be an alternate arrangement. A child welfare allowance is available through the Child Welfare Division to enable relatives without sufficient resources to care for a child who would otherwise be taken into the care of the Director of Child Welfare.

A Voluntary Care Agreement may be used in cases of neglect and some cases of abuse to allow a parent to voluntarily give up care and custody of a child to the Director of Child Welfare for a short period of time. These agreements are also used when a parent is temporarily unable to care for a child for other reasons or is unable to meet a child's special needs. The parent retains guardianship rights and must be making a sincere effort to provide a safe, stable environment for the child. The term of the agreement is generally three months; indefinite extensions are possible with the proper approvals. Unless an extension is approved, the agreement ends at age 16. With extensions, the agreement may be continued until age 21.

Court-Ordered Protection

When a social worker believes on reasonable or probable grounds that a child is in need of protection and voluntary arrangements to assist the family are not felt to be appropriate, have not been successful, or the child has been apprehended, a court hearing is held. The case is heard by the Unified Family Court in St. John's or the Provincial Court in other areas.

The judge may make one of several orders if, as a result of the information presented at the hearing, the child is found to be in need of protection. Under a Supervision Order, the child may remain with, or be returned to, the parent or be placed with another adult, usually a relative or friend. In the case of placement with another adult, that person may be granted temporary guardianship as well as custody. Such arrangements must be supervised by the Director of Child Welfare. Under an Order of Temporary Wardship, custody and guardianship of the child is temporarily transferred to the Director of Child Welfare. The initial maximum term of a Supervision Order or an Order of Temporary Wardship is 12 months. Either order may be renewed for a total term of up to 36 months following reviews by the court at least every 12 months. An Order of Permanent Wardship permanently transfers custody and guardianship to the Director. Permanent wardship may be requested by the worker; however, it becomes a legal requirement when a child has been in continuous temporary care under an order for 36 months.

Temporary or permanent wardship may be extended to age 19 if approved by the social worker prior to the child's 16th birthday. For a youth who is a temporary or permanent ward at age 19, guardianship is terminated but financial and support services may continue to age 21 if the youth is disabled or continuing his/her education.

Child Abuse Register

Newfoundland does not have a child abuse register.

Child Abuse and Neglect Protocols

A protocol entitled "RNC/Department of Social Services" outlines a coordinated approach by the Royal Newfoundland Constabulary and the Department of Social Services to the reporting, investigating, and managing of cases of child abuse. It emphasizes a team approach and identifies the roles and responsibilities of each partner. The protocol is used in the several centres, including St. John's, which are policed by the RNC.

Development of an interdepartmental protocol on child abuse investigation is being coordinated by the Working Group on Child Sexual Abuse of the St. John's Community Services Council under contract to the Department of Social Services. The protocol will include working definitions of child abuse. It is to be ready early in 1993.

A pamphlet entitled "The Child, Everyone's Responsibility: A Message to the School Principal and Teachers about Child Abuse" is distributed to schools by the Department of Social Services. It covers mandatory reporting provisions, signs that a child may have been abused, and what to do if abuse is suspected. Many school boards have also developed protocols for responding to abuse within their school system.

Statistics

The following tables include available data provided by the Child Welfare Division of the Department of Social Services. The data on investigations are for the fiscal year April 1, 1991 to March 31, 1992. The children in care data are as at March 31, 1992. Native children are included in the data.

Children in care are in need of protection under the *Child Welfare Act* and are in care under the following legal statuses: Voluntary Care Agreement, pending disposition (those who have been apprehended and are waiting for the child protection hearing plus those under interim orders waiting for the judge's decision), consent to adoption, temporary wards (Order of Temporary Wardship), permanent wards (Order of Permanent Wardship), and over 16 (youth under extended care who were in care on the day before their 16th birthday under an order or agreement).

Not all children deemed to be in need of protection are taken into care. Many receive services in the home of a parent or other adult either voluntarily or under a Supervision Order. These children are not included in the data presented in this section.

Due to the limitations noted in Chapter 1, Introduction, these data should not be compared with data for other jurisdictions.

Table 2.1 Investigations[1] by Type, April 1, 1991 to March 31, 1992

Type	Number	Percentage
Child Abuse		
Physical	953	21.0
Sexual	1,407	31.0
Emotional	431	9.5
Subtotal	**2,791**	**61.5**
Other[2]	1,747	38.5
Total	**4,538**	**100.0**

1. Data represents the number of allegations of child abuse and/or neglect which are investigated plus the number of incidents of abuse and/or neglect which subsequently become identified through an investigation. Data does not represent the number of allegedly abused or neglected children because each investigation of abuse or neglect is counted; more than one investigation may be carried out with respect to a child. Only the primary abuse is identified.
2. All investigations other than child abuse, including neglect.

Table 2.2 Children in Care[1] by Legal Status as at March 31, 1992

Legal Status	Number	Percentage
Temporary Ward[2]	182	25.0
Permanent Ward[3]	227	31.1
Voluntary Care Agreement	44	6.0
Pending Disposition[4]	70	9.6
Consent to Adoption[5]	42	5.8
Over 16[6]	164	22.5
Total	**729**	**100.0**

1. Children in care represents children under the legal statuses shown.
2. Children under an Order of Temporary Wardship.
3. Children under an Order of Permanent Wardship.
4. Includes children who have been apprehended and are waiting for the child protection hearing plus those under interim orders waiting for the judge's decision.
5. Voluntary surrender of a child for adoption.
6. Youth under extended care who were in care on the day before their 16th birthday under an order or agreement.

Figure 2.1   Children in Care[1] by Legal Status as at March 31, 1992

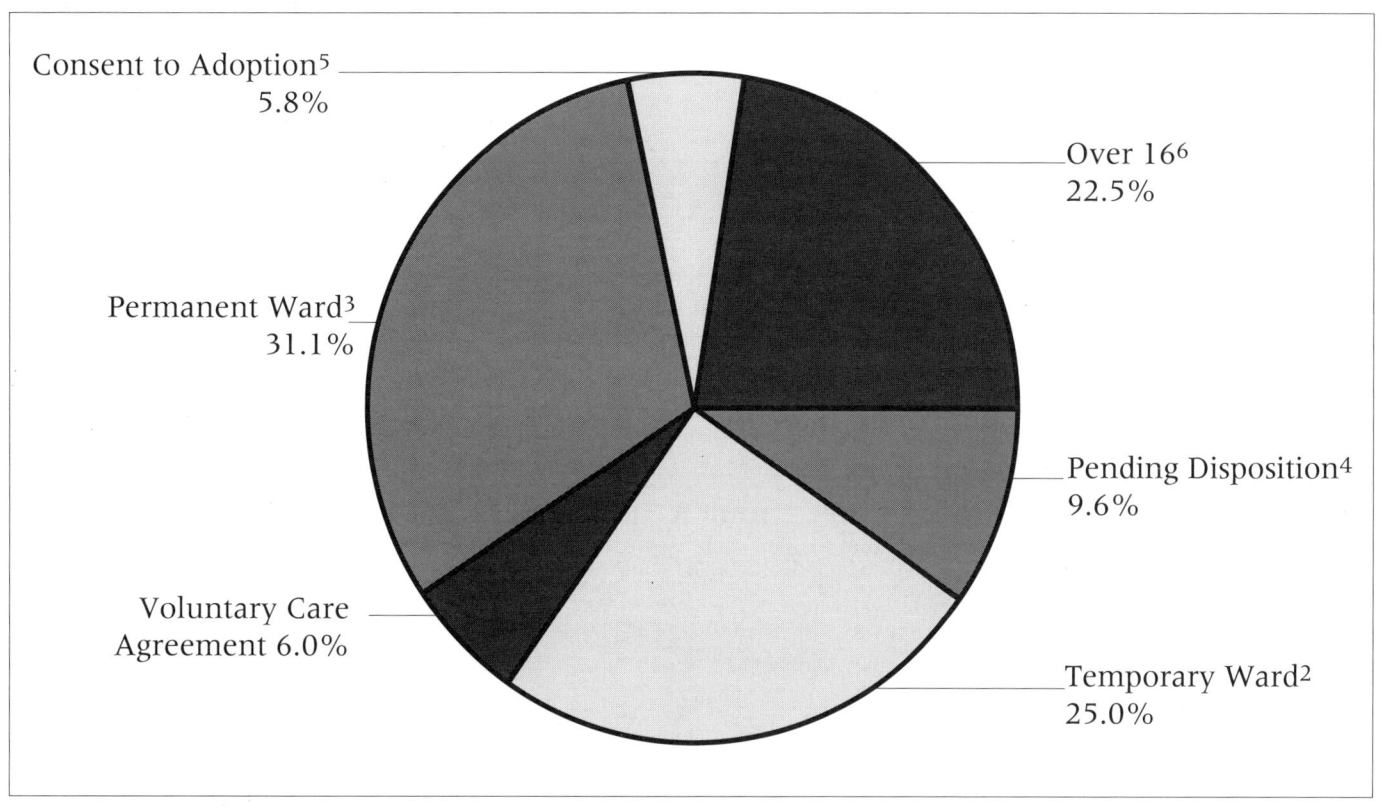

Children in care: 729

1. Children in care represents children under the legal statuses shown.
2. Children under an Order of Temporary Wardship.
3. Children under an Order of Permanent Wardship.
4. Includes children who have been apprehended and are waiting for the child protection hearing plus those under interim orders waiting for the judge's decision.
5. Voluntary surrender of a child for adoption.
6. Youth under extended care who were in care on the day before their 16th birthday under an order or agreement.

Table 2.3   Children in Care[1] by Sex as at March 31, 1992

Sex	Number	Percentage
Male	389	53.4
Female	340	46.6
Total	**729**	**100.0**

1. Children who are in need of protection under the *Child Welfare Act* and are in care under the following legal statuses: Voluntary Care Agreement, pending disposition (those who have been apprehended and are waiting for the child protection hearing plus those under interim orders waiting for the judge's decision), consent to adoption, temporary wards (Order of Temporary Wardship), permanent wards (Order of Permanent Wardship), over 16 (youth under extended care who were in care on the day before their 16th birthday under an order or agreement).

Figure 2.2   Children in Care[1] by Age Group as at March 31, 1992

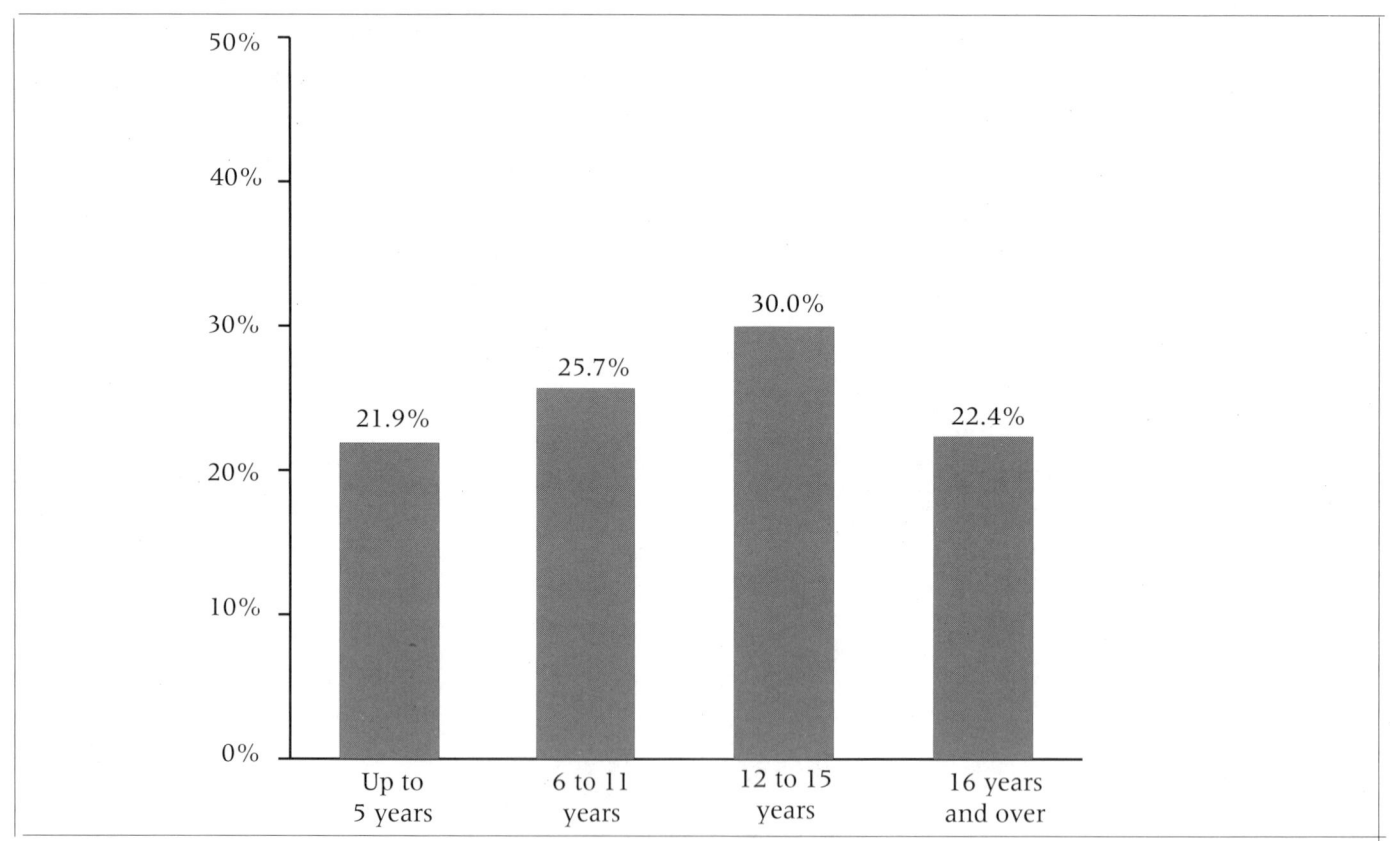

Children in care: 729

1. Children who are in need of protection under the *Child Welfare Act* and are in care under the following legal statuses: Voluntary Care Agreement, pending disposition (those who have been apprehended and are waiting for the child protection hearing plus those under interim orders waiting for the judge's decision), consent to adoption, temporary wards (Order of Temporary Wardship), permanent wards (Order of Permanent Wardship), over 16 (youth under extended care who were in care on the day before their 16th birthday under an order or agreement).

Figure 2.3   Children in Care[1] by Placement Type as at March 31, 1992

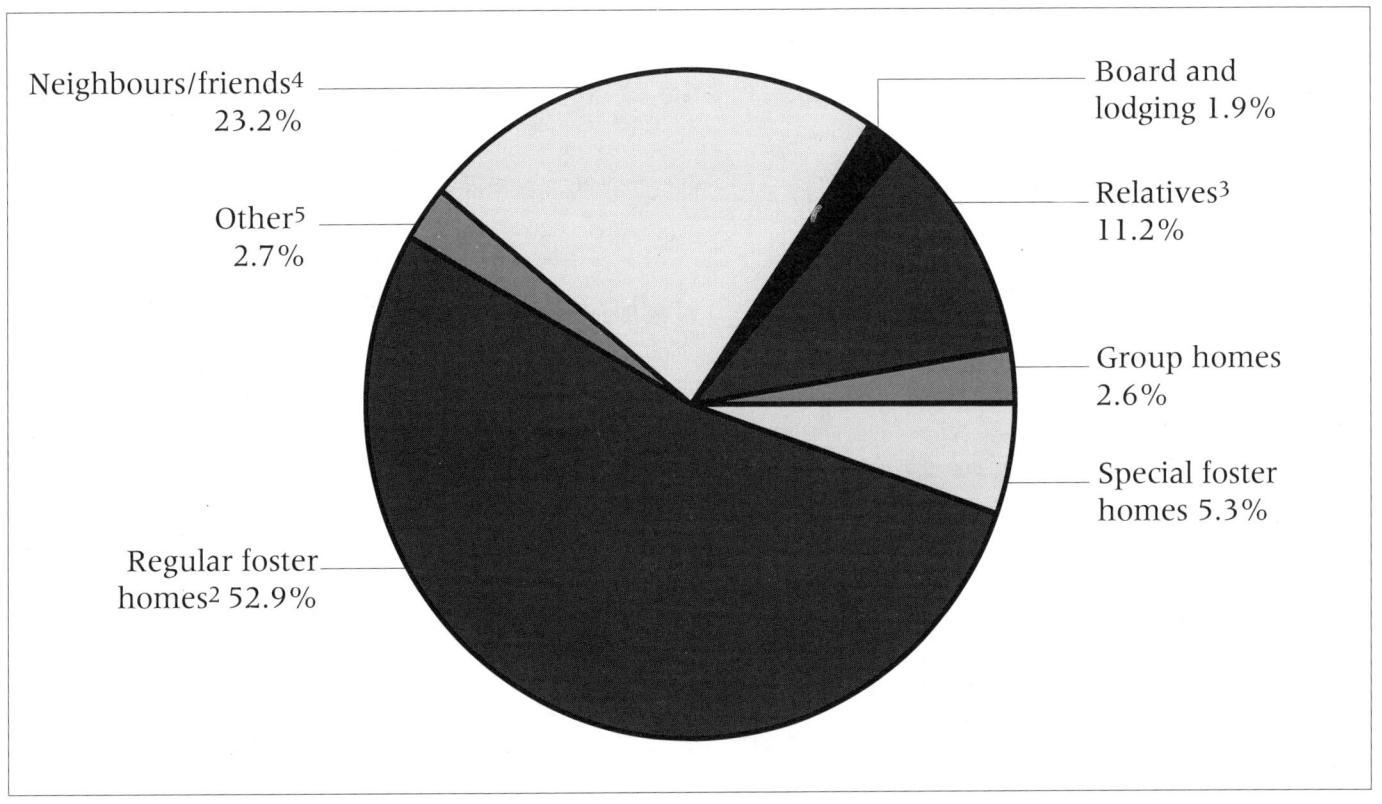

Children in care: 729

1. Children who are in need of protection under the *Child Welfare Act* and are in care under the following legal statuses: Voluntary Care Agreement, pending disposition (those who have been apprehended and are waiting for the child protection hearing plus those under interim orders waiting for the judge's decision), consent to adoption, temporary wards (Order of Temporary Wardship), permanent wards (Order of Permanent Wardship), over 16 (youth under extended care who were in care on the day before their 16th birthday under an order or agreement).
2. Includes six children in free foster homes, not receiving payment.
3. Relatives receiving a child welfare allowance from the Department of Social Services.
4. Homes certified under Section 34 of the *Child Welfare Act* and receiving foster care payments. Two children are in homes not receiving payment.
5. Includes children in hospital, in correction facilities still receiving some assistance, in alternate living arrangements such as staffed apartments which do not qualify as group homes, in placements outside the province, or in placements not receiving financial assistance.

Resource Material

Legislative Material

Consolidation of the Child Welfare Act, Revised Statutes of Newfoundland 1992, c. C-12.

Consolidation of the Adoption of Children Act, Revised Statutes of Newfoundland 1992, c. A-3.

Reports

Hanrahan, Colleen A. *A Trilogy of Discussion Papers on the Voluntary, Multi-Disciplinary Child Protection Teams operating within Newfoundland and Labrador*, prepared for the Working Group on Child Sexual Abuse, Community Services Council, St. John's, March 1991.

The Working Group on Child Sexual Abuse. *A Guide to Services and Resources – Child Protection Services, Child Victim Services, Adult Survivors programs, Offender Services, Resources for Education and Training*, Community Services Council, St. John's, October 1990.

Other Material

Government of Newfoundland and Labrador, Department of Social Services. "Child Welfare Policy Manual", St. John's.

"Protocol – RNC/Department of Social Services", November 1988.

Pamphlets, Department of Social Services

"The Child – Everyone's Responsibility: A Message to the School Principal and Teachers about Child Abuse".

"Every Person having information of the abandonment, desertion, physical ill-treatment or need of protection of a child, shall report the information to the Director of Child Welfare or a Social Worker".

Chapter 3 – Prince Edward Island

Administration and Service Delivery

The Director of Child Welfare, as designated by the Minister of Health and Social Services, administers and enforces the provisions of the *Family and Child Services Act*. The Director is responsible for ensuring that allegations of child abuse and neglect are investigated accordingly. This responsibility is further delegated to authorized employees involved in the implementation of child protection services.

The Child and Family Services Division of the Department of Health and Social Services is responsible for protection services, adoption, family support services, substitute care placement, and general counselling. The central office in Charlottetown is involved in program development, provides overall direction to the Division and coordinates services to ensure provincial consistency. Services are delivered on a decentralized basis through five regional offices located in Charlottetown, Montague, O'Leary, Souris and Summerside. Central office also performs support functions for regional office operations such as policy development, human resource planning and development, quality control activities and case consultation. Services assisting abused or neglected children and their families may be provided directly by the Department of Health and Social Services or in conjunction with private agencies and community organizations. The Department's Division of Mental Health provides counselling and psychiatric support to children and families in situations of abuse and neglect.

Various committees have been established to further explore the issue of violence against women and children, such as the Community Consultation Committee on Family Violence Prevention (CCCFVP) and the Inter-Ministerial Committee on Family Violence Prevention (IMCFVP). These are both involved in making recommendations and developing prevention strategies to reduce family violence, including that against children. The Department of Health and Social Services is active on the Child Sexual Abuse Interagency Committee in Charlottetown. This committee is made up of about fifty members from various community, government and private agencies, who work toward enhancing service delivery for child sexual abuse victims, their families and offenders. A similar committee has been set up in the Montague and Souris regions that also draws agencies together to mobilize a shared response to child sexual abuse intervention.

Definitions

According to Paragraph 1(1)(e) of the *Family and Child Services Act*, a **child** is defined as actually or apparently under the age of majority (18 years). However, under Sub-section 37(7) the Director of Child Welfare may provide care and maintenance to a child up to the age of 21. For the purposes of adoption, Sub-section 1(b) of the *Adoption Act* states that a person who is over twenty-one years of age is also considered to be a **child**; in this sense child is used to describe an individual in terms of his or her relationship to others (i.e., parent/child) rather than to define someone by age.

The definition of a **child in need of protection** is found under Paragraph 1(2)(e) of the *Family and Child Services Act* and refers to a child:

"(a) who is not receiving proper care, education, supervision, guidance or control;

(b) whose parent is unable or unwilling to care for the child, or whose behaviour or way of life creates a danger for the child;

(c) who has been physically abused, neglected or sexually exploited or is in danger of consistently threatening behaviour;

(d) who is forced or induced to do work disproportionate to his strength or to perform for the public in a manner that is unacceptable for his age;

(e) whose behaviour, condition, environment or associations is injurious or threatens to be injurious to himself or others;

(f) for whom the parent or person in whose custody he is neglects or refuses to provide or obtain proper medical or surgical care or treatment necessary for his health and well-being where it is recommended by a duly qualified medical practitioner;

(g) whose emotional or mental health and development is endangered or is likely to be endangered by the lack of affection, guidance and discipline or continuity of care in the child's life;

(h) for whom the parent or person in whose custody he is neglects, refuses or is unable to provide the services and assistance needed by the child because of the child's physical, mental or emotional handicap or disability;

(i) who is living in a situation where there is severe domestic violence;

(j) who is beyond the control of the person caring for him;

(k) who is living apart from his parents without their consent; or

(l) who is pregnant and refuses or is unable to provide properly and adequately for the health and welfare needs of herself and her child both before and after the birth of her child."

Within the legislation, under Paragraph 1(1)(a), **abuse** in relation to a child is defined as "physical, mental, emotional or sexual mistreatment of the child by a person responsible for his care and well-being." While formal definitions of neglect, physical, emotional or sexual abuse are not provided in the *Family and Child Services Act*, the "Child Sexual Abuse Protocol: Guidelines and Procedures for a Co-ordinated Response to Child Sexual Abuse in Prince Edward Island", describes child **sexual abuse** as "any sexual activity (intercourse, molestation, fondling, exhibitionism, sexual exploitation, harassment) that involves a child". Furthermore, the Child Protection Services Policy Manual provides the following as indicators of **abuse**:

— "where a non-accidental injury or condition is identified which requires immediate medical attention, e.g., bruises, burns, etc.

— whenever non-accidental injuries or conditions result in hospitalization of the child, e.g., broken limbs, lacerations, etc.

— when there is evidence of repeated physical violence committed against the child, or where it is established that a child has been deprived of necessary and essential care over a substantial period of time

— when a child has been subjected or exposed to unusual or inappropriate sexual activity, or harassment

– when a child's life has been endangered by being abandoned."

Mandatory Reporting of a Child in Need of Protection

Under Sub-section 14(1) of the *Family and Child Services Act*, any person who has knowledge of, or reasonable and probable cause to suspect that a child has been abused, deserted, or abandoned, must report this information to the Director of Child Welfare, or to a police officer who shall in turn report it to the Director. Failure to comply with this provision is an offence under Section 49 of the Act, punishable by a maximum fine of $1,000. This includes all professionals with the only exception being lawyers withholding such information on the basis of lawyer/client privileges. An individual who files a report is not liable to civil action for anything contained in the report or for anything done in good faith when assisting in an investigation.

The Department of Health and Social Services operates a provincial, toll-free child abuse line that deals with both reporting and counselling. This service, which is advertised on the inside cover of the provincial telephone directory, becomes available to the public immediately following working hours and includes full weekend coverage.

Investigation of an Allegation of Child Abuse or Neglect

The validity of all child abuse and neglect allegations, both intra-familial and extra-familial, is assessed by an intake worker. If there is reasonable cause to believe that a child is in need of protection, an investigation is undertaken. The intake worker determines the urgency and seriousness of the situation, and mobilizes an immediate response if the child is in immediate danger. When a non-urgent report is received outside of normal working hours, an investigation may be postponed until a convenient time in the next working day.

If, during the investigation, it becomes apparent that there may be grounds for criminal charges to be laid, it is the responsibility of the worker (or supervisor) to report this to the police. Upon completion of the tandem investigation by the Department and the police, the worker consults with the supervisor, determines an appropriate case plan and follows up with the parent. The worker may then refer the family to the necessary services, enter into an agreement or apprehend the child, depending on the case and circumstances.

Where it is believed that a child has been physically abused, undernourished or maltreated, the child should be seen immediately by a physician. A parent who is unwilling to accompany the child and worker to the doctor, is asked to sign a consent to treatment form. If the parent refuses to sign the form, the worker apprehends the child and subsequently seeks medical treatment. In cases of sexual abuse, an immediate medical examination should be arranged if recent intercourse or violence has occurred, or where there are any specific medical concerns. Medical guidelines indicate that forensic evidence should be taken within 24 hours.

If it is determined, during a child abuse or neglect investigation, that circumstances are serious enough to consider apprehension of the child, a consultation is held with two Child Welfare Supervisors and other relevant divisional staff. In this situation, the child care worker, Director, or police officer is expected to obtain a warrant from a judge before apprehending the child. However, warrants are available only during working hours, and in some cases it is impossible to obtain a warrant before apprehending a child. If time is a factor and a delay would create serious risk to the child, a warrant is not required.

In accordance with the *Family and Child Services Act*, only designated child care workers are authorized to apprehend a child or enter into a voluntary care agreement. To be designated, workers are required to have received orientation on all aspects of child protection services. They must also display a certain knowledge and skill level, and must have the recommendation of both the immediate supervisor and the director of the regional office. Training requirements are being formalized for designated workers, which address the principles, philosophy, treatment, interventions, self-awareness, development and administration components of abuse or neglect situations.

Workers also participate in workshops delivered by the Department's staff training officer, the Maritime School of Social Work, contracted professionals, and sessions sponsored by other agencies and organizations. While training is considered optional by the Department, the province's Social Work Registration Board considers the level of a worker's training when processing that worker's yearly application for registration.

In situations of extra-familial abuse, allegations are most often received by the police, who in turn advise the Department of Health and Social Services. The Department is involved in all cases of abuse or neglect regardless of the alleged perpetrator's relationship to the child. All cases are investigated following the same procedures regardless of where the abuse or neglect occurred (i.e., in the home, foster care, institution, etc.).

No specific provisions exist in the legislation for the investigation of suspected abuse or neglect of native children; investigations are undertaken in the same manner as for non-native families. However, at the service level the Department involves the native community when taking a child into care and in trying to find a placement resource.

Voluntary Agreements

While the least disruptive and intrusive approach to protection is desirable, efforts to provide in-family services may fail or be inappropriate for the situation. Where attempts to provide supportive protection services in the home environment are not viable the Department of Health and Social Services may enter into a Voluntary Agreement for Temporary Custody, with the intention of preparing the family for the child's return. The agreement temporarily transfers custody, but not guardianship, of the child to the Director of Child Welfare for a period of up to six months. Provisions are included for two additional six month terms for children under 13 years; for those over 13, the term may be renewed indefinitely until the child reaches 18 years of age.

A Voluntary Agreement for Temporary Guardianship transfers the legal guardianship and custody of the child to the Director for a period of up to six months with the same provisions for extension as in a Voluntary Agreement for Temporary Custody. Under this agreement, the Director has full authority to make major decisions in the child's best interest, including decisions regarding who shall have actual custody, but does not have the right to place the child for adoption.

In determining whether a voluntary agreement is appropriate in a situation of abuse or neglect, consideration is given to such factors as the seriousness of the abuse or neglect, the willingness and ability of the family to contract for services and also, the length of previous departmental involvement with and knowledge of the family, if any. A voluntary agreement is the preferred option when a child is in need of protection due to a physical, mental or emotional handicap for which the parent is unable to provide.

Court-Ordered Protection

Upon apprehension of an abused or neglected child, or in the event that previous voluntary agreements have not met with success, a protection hearing is held in the Supreme Court of PEI to determine the most appropriate intervention. Where the judge finds that the child is in need of protection, one of the following orders is issued: a Supervision Order, a Temporary Order for Custody and Guardianship, or a Permanent Guardianship Order.

Under a Supervision Order, the child is returned to the parents under the supervision of the Director for a specified period not to exceed six months. The Director has the authority to request a review of the Supervision Order which may result in a further extension of the order for up to six months more, or request the implementation of either a Temporary Order for Custody and Guardianship or a Permanent Guardianship Order.

A Temporary Order commits the child to the temporary custody and guardianship of the Director for a period of up to six months. At any time during the period of this order, the Director may also apply for a review hearing and have the order renewed for another six month term. However, in no case shall an extension be made which results in the child being in continuous care for a period exceeding 18 months.

The effect of a Permanent Guardianship Order is that the Director becomes the sole guardian of the child until the child attains the age of majority (18 years), marries, is adopted, or the order is terminated by a judge. The Director may extend services to age 21 to a child who is a permanent ward who reaches the age of majority and is a full-time student or is mentally/physically incapacitated.

Sub-section 50(4) of the *Family and Child Services Act* states that a restraining order may be issued by a judge, upon application by the Director of Child Welfare, to prevent an individual from "harassing, visiting, communicating with or otherwise interfering with any child who is the subject of an agreement or order under this Act".

Child Abuse Register

Prince Edward Island does not have a child abuse register.

Child Abuse and Neglect Protocols

The Prince Edward Island Child Welfare Association has prepared the "Child Sexual Abuse Protocol: Guidelines and Procedures for a Co-ordinated Response to Child Sexual Abuse in Prince Edward Island" in an effort to promote consistency and collaboration between the departments of Health and Social Services, Justice, Education, and the police when investigating allegations of child sexual abuse. It should be noted that while referred to as a protocol, it has never been approved as such; rather, it presently serves only as an operational guideline. The document presents practical and cooperative instructions for the initial investigation and for subsequent intervention by relevant professionals, such as educators, medical health and mental health personnel, and examines the availability of treatment for victims of child sexual abuse in PEI. The report includes a working definition of child sexual abuse and a statement of principles designed to provide a comprehensive framework for investigations. Also incorporated in the report are specific guidelines for: reporting the abuse; follow-up; accessing the child in intra-familial and extra-familial abuse cases; interviewing the child, alleged offender and other family members; support for the child; immediate protection for the child; medical examinations; assessment; and case management.

Statistics

Data presented in this section are from the management information system (MIS) of the Department of Health and Social Services and are shown for March 1991 and 1992.

Children in care refers to those children who are in need of protection under the *Family and Child Services Act* where there has been a transfer of custody and/or guardianship. Children in care fall under the following legal statuses: voluntary care agreement (includes Voluntary Agreement for Temporary Guardianship, Voluntary Agreement for Temporary Custody and Permanent Guardianship Agreement [voluntary relinquishment for adoption purposes]), apprehended, permanent ward (Permanent Guardianship Order), and temporary ward (Temporary Order for Custody and Guardianship). In addition, a child in care may be a ward of another province, in an adoption home pending finalization or may have been in care, have returned home and be receiving post-care services ("follow-up to child in care").

The data include all native children in care.

Due to the limitations noted in Chapter 1, Introduction, these data should not be compared with data for other jurisdictions.

Table 3.1   Children in Care[1] by Legal Status and Age Group as at March 31, 1992

Legal Status	0-11 years	12 years and older	Total	Percentage
Apprehended	26	6	32	15.5
Temporary ward[2]	3	7	10	4.9
Permanent ward[3]	15	64	79	38.3
Voluntary care agreement[4]	24	38	62	30.1
Wards of another province	1	-	1	0.5
Adoption placements[5]	6	3	9	4.4
Follow-up to child in care[6]	3	6	9	4.4
Unknown	2	2	4	1.9
Total	**80**	**126**	**206**	
Percentage	**38.8**	**61.2**	**100.0**	**100.0**

1. Data represent the number of children in care under the legal statuses shown
2. Includes children in care under a Temporary Order for Custody and Guardianship.
3. Includes children in care under a Permanent Guardianship Order.
4. Includes children in care under a Voluntary Agreement for Temporary Guardianship, Voluntary Agreement for Temporary Custody, or Permanent Guardianship Agreement (voluntary relinquishment for adoption purposes).
5. Permanent wards who have been placed in an adoption home pending finalization.
6. Includes children who have been in care, have returned home and are receiving post-care services.

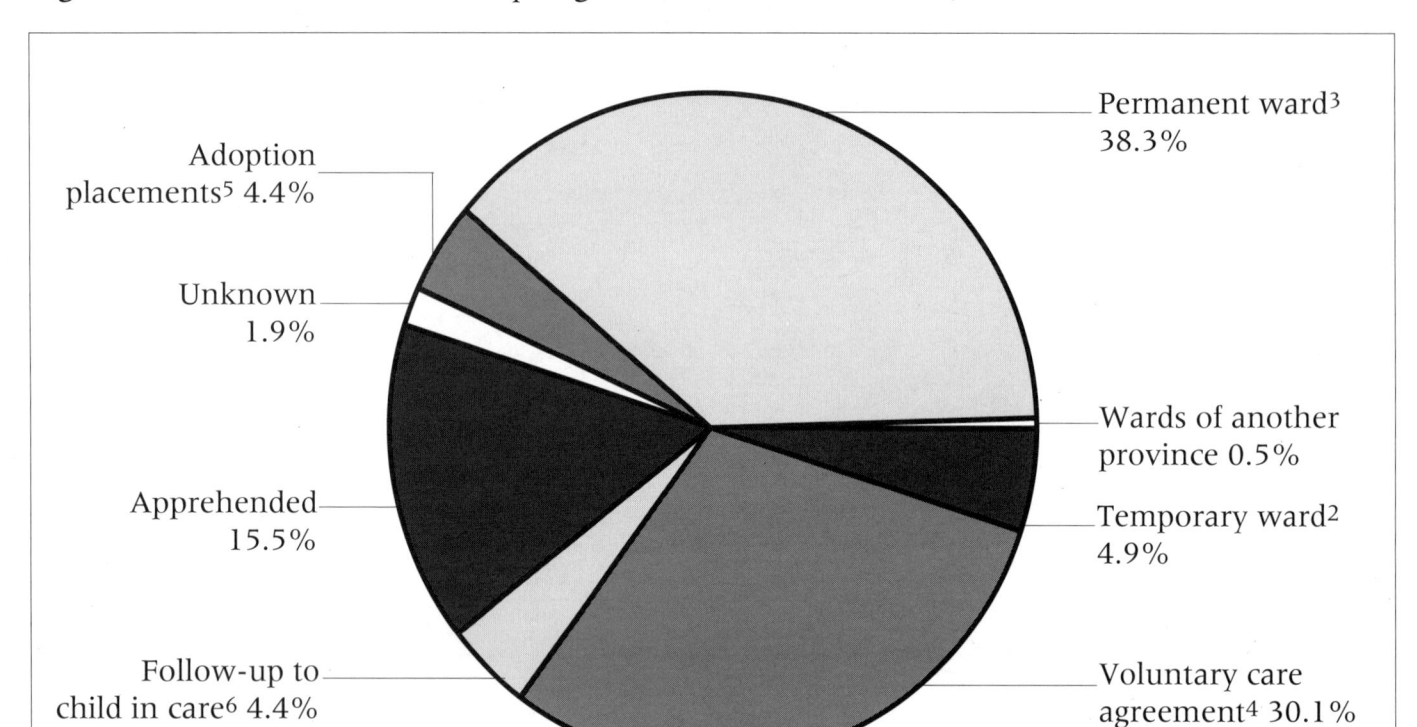

Figure 3.1   Children in Care[1] by Legal Status as at March 31, 1992

- Permanent ward[3] 38.3%
- Adoption placements[5] 4.4%
- Unknown 1.9%
- Apprehended 15.5%
- Follow-up to child in care[6] 4.4%
- Wards of another province 0.5%
- Temporary ward[2] 4.9%
- Voluntary care agreement[4] 30.1%

Children in care: 206

1. Data represent the number of children in care under the legal statuses shown.
2. Includes children in care under a Temporary Order for Custody and Guardianship.
3. Includes children in care under a Permanent Guardianship Order.
4. Includes children in care under a Voluntary Agreement for Temporary Guardianship, Voluntary Agreement for Temporary Custody, or Permanent Guardianship Agreement (voluntary relinquishment for adoption purposes).
5. Permanent wards who have been placed in an adoption home pending finalization.
6. Includes children who have been in care, have returned home and are receiving post-care services.

Chapter 3 - Prince Edward Island

Figure 3.2   Children in Care[1] by Placement Type as at March 31, 1991[2]

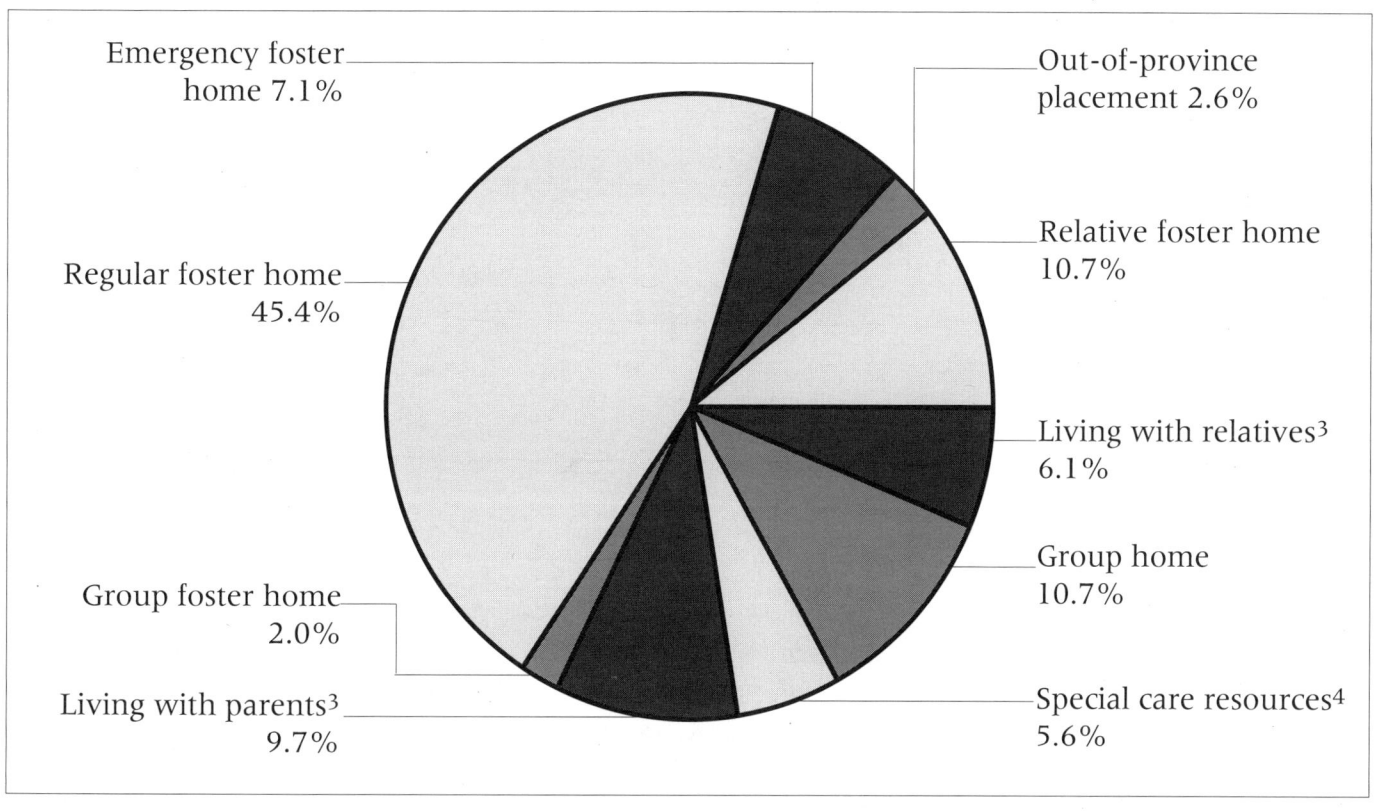

Children in care: 196[2]

1. Data represent the number of children in care under the following legal statuses: voluntary care agreement (includes Voluntary Agreement for Temporary Guardianship, Voluntary Agreement for Temporary Custody and Permanent Guardianship Agreement [voluntary relinquishment for adoption purposes]), apprehended, permanent ward (Permanent Guardianship Order), and temporary ward (Temporary Order for Custody and Guardianship). In addition, a child in care may be a ward of another province, in an adoption home pending finalization or may have been in care, have returned home and be receiving post-care services ("follow-up to child in care").
2. Placement type data are not available for March 1992.
3. Includes children placed with parents or relatives pending a hearing, permanent wards returned home where an order has not yet been rescinded, or children returned to one parent with the exclusion of the other.
4. Includes the Adolescent Treatment Unit at Hillsborough Hospital.

Resource Material

Legislative Material

Family and Child Services Act. Revised Statutes of Prince Edward Island 1988, F-2.01.

Adoption Act. Revised Statutes of Prince Edward Island 1988, A-4.

Reports

Kopachevsky, J., Lawlor, B., Mazer, D., McInnis, K. *Child Sexual Abuse; Needs Assessment and Intervention Model.* Prince Edward Island, 1991.

McQuaid, Charles R. *Inquiry into Police and Department of Justice Policies and Procedures in Cases of Inter-Spousal and Intra-Family Violence.* Prince Edward Island, 1991.

Prince Edward Island, Department of Health and Social Services. *Annual Report 1990-91.*

_____. *Partners for Prevention; Islanders Talk About Family Violence, Volumes I and II.* Charlottetown, 1991.

Other Material

Prince Edward Island, Department of Health and Social Services. "Child Protection Services Policy Manual", Charlottetown.

Prince Edward Island Child Welfare Association. "Child Sexual Abuse Protocol: Guidelines and Procedures for a Co-ordinated Response to Child Sexual Abuse in Prince Edward Island", March 1986.

Pamphlets, Department of Health and Social Services

"Victim Services – helping victims of crime"

Chapter 4 – Nova Scotia

Administration and Service Delivery

Under the *Children and Family Services Act*[1], the Minister of Community Services in Nova Scotia is the person primarily responsible for investigating all reports that a child may be in need of protective services. These reports include allegations of child abuse and neglect. The Act also provides for the delegation of this responsibility to Directors within the Department of Community Services and to agencies[2] providing child and family services.

Within the Department, the Family and Children's Services Division, located in Halifax, is responsible for the administration of child protection services. Specifically, the Division has the mandate for policy development in the area of family and children's services; for the child protection budget; and for funding of foster homes, children's residential facilities, transition houses, adoption services, preventive services and agency/office evaluations. The Division also coordinates initiatives in the area of family violence.

Child protection and family support services are provided by workers in five district offices and 14 private non-profit family and children's services agencies. District offices and agencies report, on program matters, to the Director of Family and Children Services at headquarters. Child protection services to Indians on reserves are provided by MicMac Family and Children's Services, which has an office on mainland Nova Scotia and one on Cape Breton Island. A judge may order that Indians not living on reserve may receive services from MicMac Family and Children's Services rather than from the local office or agency.

As part of the provincial Family Violence Prevention Initiative, the province has established a Committee on Procedures for a Coordinated Response for Victims of Family Violence. The Committee will develop a protocol to ensure that a coordinated response for victims of family violence occurs.

Definitions

The *Children and Family Services Act* provides the legislative basis for the provision of services to children in need of protective services. A **child** is defined under Section 3, for both protection and adoption purposes, to be a person under sixteen years of age. Under Sub-section 48(1), the permanent care and custody of a child may be extended until the child reaches 21 years of age.

Under Sub-section 22(2), a child is defined to be **in need of protective services** where:

---

1. Except Sections 54 to 60 and Section 73 which have not yet been proclaimed.
2. Agencies include Children's Aid Societies and Family and Children's Services Agencies.

"(a) the child has suffered physical harm, inflicted by a parent or guardian of the child or caused by the failure of a parent or guardian to supervise and protect the child adequately;

(b) there is a substantial risk that the child will suffer physical harm inflicted or caused as described in clause (a);

(c) the child has been sexually abused by a parent or guardian of the child, or by another person where a parent or guardian of the child knows or should know of the possibility of sexual abuse and fails to protect the child;

(d) there is substantial risk that the child will be sexually abused as described in clause (c);

(e) a child requires medical treatment to cure, prevent or alleviate physical harm or suffering, and the child's parent or guardian does not provide, or refuses or is unavailable or is unable to consent to, the treatment;

(f) the child has suffered emotional harm, demonstrated by severe anxiety, depression, withdrawal, or self-destructive or aggressive behaviour and the child's parent or guardian does not provide, or refuses or is unavailable or unable to consent to, services or treatment to remedy or alleviate the harm;

(g) there is a substantial risk that the child will suffer emotional harm of the kind described in clause (f), and the parent or guardian does not provide, or refuses or is unavailable or unable to consent to, services or treatment to remedy or alleviate the harm;

(h) the child suffers from a mental, emotional or developmental condition that, if not remedied, could seriously impair the child's development and the child's parent or guardian does not provide, or refuses or is unavailable or unable to consent to, services or treatment to remedy or alleviate the condition;

(i) the child has suffered physical or emotional harm caused by being exposed to repeated domestic violence by or towards a parent or guardian of the child, and the child's parent or guardian fails or refuses to obtain services or treatment to remedy or alleviate the violence;

(j) the child has suffered physical harm caused by chronic and serious neglect by a parent or guardian of the child, and the parent or guardian does not provide, or refuses or is unavailable or unable to consent to, services or treatment to remedy or alleviate the harm;

(k) the child has been abandoned, the child's only parent or guardian has died or is unavailable to exercise custodial rights over the child and has not made adequate provisions for the child's care and custody, or the child is in the care of an agency or another person and the parent or guardian of the child refuses or is unable or unwilling to resume the child's care and custody;

(l) the child is under twelve years of age and has killed or seriously injured another person or caused serious damage to another person's property, and services or treatment are necessary to prevent a recurrence and a parent or guardian of the child does not provide, or refuses or is unavailable or unable to consent to, the necessary services or treatment;

(m) the child is under twelve years of age and has on more than one occasion injured another person or caused loss or damage to another person's property, with the encouragement of a parent or guardian of the child or because of the parent or guardian's failure or inability to supervise the child adequately."

Under Sub-section 24(1), a child **suffers abuse** by a parent or guardian when the child is in need of protective services within the meaning of clauses (a),(c),(e),(f),(h),(i), or (j) of the definition of a child in need of protective services.

Abuse by someone other than a parent or guardian, including a stranger, is defined under Sub-section 25(1). The definition is similar to the definition of abuse for the Child Abuse Register which is provided below.

For the purposes of the Child Abuse Register, Section 62 defines **abuse of a child** to mean that the child:

"(a) has suffered physical harm, inflicted by the person or caused by the person's failure to supervise and protect the child adequately;

(b) has been sexually abused by the person or by another person where the person, having the care of the child, knows or should know of the possibility of sexual abuse and fails to protect the child; or

(c) has suffered serious emotional harm, demonstrated by severe anxiety, depression, withdrawal, or self-destructive or aggressive behaviour, caused by the intentional conduct of the person."

This definition is quite broad and is considered to be an attempt to protect all children in the community from abuse and neglect, not just children abused by their parent or guardian.

The Act also stipulates certain legislated rights for children which include the right for any child 12 years of age or older to receive notice of a protection hearing and the right to be made a party to the hearing and have counsel, if the court orders it is in the child's best interests; the right for any child 16 or older to be a party to a hearing unless the court orders otherwise; and the right to counsel on request. Where a parent consents to an order, a child 12 years of age or older is entitled to understand the nature and consequences of the consent, must consent to the order, and is entitled to independent counsel in this matter.

Mandatory Reporting of a Child in Need of Protective Services

Under Section 23 of the *Children and Family Services Act*, anyone having information, confidential or not, indicating that a child may be in need of protective services, or information of potential child abuse by a stranger, must report the situation to a local family and children's services agency or district office. Failure to report will, upon conviction, result in a fine of not more than $2,000, imprisonment not exceeding six months, or both. Furthermore, under Sub-section 24(2), anyone who performs professional or official duties with respect to a child, excluding a lawyer, and who has reasonable grounds to suspect that a child is or may be suffering or may have suffered abuse must report the suspicion to an agency. This section applies whether the information reported is confidential or privileged and results in higher penalties for failing to report (a fine of up to $5,000, imprisonment for up to one year, or both). Any person who makes a false or malicious report is guilty of an offence and upon conviction may be fined up to $2,000, imprisoned up to six months, or both.

Investigation of an Allegation of Child Abuse or Neglect

After an allegation has been made, child protection workers in family and children's services agencies/district offices have the legal mandate to investigate all reports that are appropriate in terms of the definition of a child in need of protective services. The worker must determine the validity of the allegation and ascertain if there is a need for child protective intervention and/or service. Life threatening situations must be investigated within one hour; dangerous but not life threatening within the same working day; damaging but not life threatening within two working days; low risk situations within ten working days; and no risk situations within 21 working days. The police are generally notified of all reports that have been received. With respect to cases of abuse or neglect by someone other than a parent or guardian, family and children's services staff is only involved in the initial investigation to determine if the child is in need of protective services. These cases are monitored by the workers, however, concerning potential entry in the Child Abuse Register.

To assist child protection workers in effectively carrying out their responsibilities, the Department provides a mandatory two week training course. This Core Program is modeled after the Core Training Program developed by the Institute for the Prevention of Child Abuse in Toronto. The course provides training in the area of child protection and includes training specific to child abuse. The Department also offers a joint training program for child protection staff and police to foster and encourage a coordinated response to sexual abuse.

A worker may make an application to court to determine whether a child is in need of protective services or may, without a warrant, take a child into care where there are reasonable and probable grounds to believe the child is in need of protection. Where it is believed that the child is in immediate danger and access is refused, the worker may seek a warrant from a Judge authorizing the worker to conduct a search of the premises using force if necessary, conduct a physical exam of the child, interview the child, search the premises for evidence, and, where necessary, take the child into care.

For investigations of suspected child sexual abuse, agencies and district offices are encouraged to have a formal protocol in place to ensure an arrangement of mutual reporting and full disclosure of all pertinent information between the police and the designated social worker or protection worker with the Department or agency throughout the investigation. A medical examination of the child is conducted immediately in emergency situations, at a local hospital or by a designated physician. When interviewing the child, the protocol entitled "The Step-Wise Interview: A protocol for interviewing children" (see section on Child Abuse and Neglect Protocols) is followed. The protection worker may contact the Child Abuse Register at this time to determine whether or not the alleged perpetrator has been recorded for past abuse.

The evaluation of all evidence gathered in the investigative process is conducted and documented by the child protection worker. The evaluation process, including the decision to proceed with or suspend an investigation, is then completed in consultation with the supervisor and includes the holding of a case conference. This is a formal meeting, attended by as many members of the family and children's services staff involved in a particular case as possible, to review systematically the situation of the child and the family and to decide on future activities. The Washington State Risk Factor Matrix, a risk management tool, is now used to assist workers in determining whether or not a child is in need of protective services, in making informed decisions about the choice of placement and services for a child, and in justifying and documenting decisions.

Under Sub-section 30(2) of the Act, an agency may apply to the Trial Division of the Supreme Court for a Protective Intervention Order. This orders that a specified person cease to reside with a child or not contact or associate in any way with a child. This type of order is often used if violence is directed towards a spouse or a child and may result in the child being in need of protection as defined under the Act. The order may be made for a period of up to six months and may be renewed for periods of six months each.

Protection workers are also required to receive and investigate reports from people who report alleged abuse of a child by a person who is not related to the child in any way. The agency must investigate the report to determine if the parent is responsible in some way for causing or allowing the child to be in a position where he/she was abused. The agency/district office must also determine if the parent is willing to accept responsibility for ensuring that the child will continue to be protected, including making use of available community resources to assist the child's recovery from the assault. If the agency is not convinced that the parent is acting to protect the child or to make use of available community resources, it may determine that the child is in need of protective services.

Investigations of reports of a native child being in need of protection follow the same procedures.

Voluntary Agreements

If services cannot be provided to the child and family while the child remains in the home, a parent may agree to have the child temporarily placed outside the home by entering into a Temporary Care Agreement with an agency/district office. The care and supervision of the child are transferred to the agency for up to six months while the parent retains guardianship of the child; with a renewal, the maximum term of the agreement is 12 months. This agreement is meant to be temporary with the intention being that the child will return to the parent. This type of agreement is generally used in cases of child neglect but not in cases of abuse.

A parent or guardian who is unable to provide the services required by a child with special needs may enter into an agreement with an agency/district office for the care and custody of the child or provision of services to meet the child's needs. A special need is defined as "a need that is related to, or caused by, a behavioral, emotional, physical, mental or other handicap or disorder." This includes special needs related to or caused by social, psychological and environmental circumstances. A Special Needs Agreement may be made for a period of up to one year and may be renewed with the approval of the Minister for further periods of up to one year each.

Court-Ordered Protection

When an abused or neglected child is believed to be in need of protective services, is apprehended, or when the voluntary service options are not feasible, have expired or have been breached, application is made to the Family Court for an order regarding care of the child. When the court determines that the child is in need of protective services, it may make one of several orders – a Supervision Order, a Temporary Care and Custody Order or a Permanent Care and Custody Order. A Supervision Order stipulates that a child remain in the care and custody of a person other than a parent or guardian, under supervision of the agency, or be returned to the family under supervision of the agency, for up to one year. Under a Temporary Care and Custody Order, a child is placed in the care of an agency for up to six months from the date the child was taken into care or one year from the date the child was found to be in need of protection. The parent is still the child's legal guardian when the child is under a Supervision Order or a Temporary Care and

Custody Order. Under a Permanent Care and Custody Order, the agency becomes the child's legal guardian. The term of a Permanent Care and Custody Order with respect to an unmarried child may be extended until the child turns 19 years of age and may be further extended to age 21 if the child is disabled or still in school.

In some situations, instead of removing the child, the worker may petition the Family Court to remove the perpetrator. The court issues a No Contact Order which orders a parent, guardian or any other person not to reside with, to contact, or associate with the child until the Family Court makes an order to the contrary. It must be made within thirty days of the matter coming before the court and can last until the protection hearing, which must be held within ninety days of the matter being brought before the court. No contact provisions may also be specified under a Supervision Order.

Child Abuse Register

Nova Scotia is one of three provinces with a child abuse register. The Child Abuse Register, which was established within the Department of Community Services in 1976, was completely revamped in 1991 by the *Children and Family Services Act* to include perpetrators who are not parents or guardians of the abused child and to make the Register available for screening purposes.

In an effort to respect the privacy and confidentiality of a child victim and his/her family, data contained in the Register is restricted to information respecting the perpetrator of the abuse. Information concerning victims is maintained separately and may only be released for research purposes with the consent of the Minister or his/her delegate.

Purpose

The Register has three purposes:

1. To assist in the protection of children (primary purpose):

(a) where a children's services agency or district office is conducting an investigation to determine whether a child is in need of protective services;

(b) for the screening of prospective foster parents, adoptive parents or persons caring for or working with children, including volunteers.

2. To assist in identifying persons who may pose a risk for future harm to children.

3. For the purposes of research in the areas of:

(a) children in need of protection;

(b) children who are subjected to abuse;

(c) the families of children described above; and

(d) the nature and extent of child abuse.

Anyone may request information on child victims for research purposes; however, the research must be approved by the Minister or his/her delegate. Only non-identifying information is made available for research purposes. Information for screening purposes can only be released with the permission of the person being screened.

Basis for Entering Names

Cases of physical, sexual and/or emotional abuse perpetrated by any person, including a parent, guardian, caregiver or a stranger, towards a child under the age of sixteen years are recorded in the Register in one of three processes. Information concerning a case must be provided by the Clerk of the Court when the Family Court finds that a child is in need of protective services because of abuse or when a person is convicted of an offence against a child under the *Criminal Code of Canada* in a Criminal Court. Also, information may be provided to the Register by family and children's services agency staff if the Family Court has granted an order that, based on the child protection worker's evidence, states that an individual poses a risk of harming children.

In addition, the names of certain persons whose names appeared in the former Child Abuse Register have been added to the current Register. Registration in the current Register occurred if the person was convicted of an offence against a child under the *Criminal Code* or if a finding that a child was in need of protective services on the basis of abuse was made in Family Court.

Rights of the Registered Person

A person whose name is entered in the Child Abuse Register must be notified of the entry by registered mail in order to protect the confidential nature of the information. The registered person has the right to inspect the information relating to himself/herself that has been entered in the Register, including the report filed by the Clerk of the Court who made the finding. The registered person has 30 days in which to appeal to the Appeal Division of the Supreme Court the decision that, on the balance of probabilities, he/she has abused a child. The registered person may apply to the Family Court at any time to have his/her name removed from the Register. The person's name must be automatically removed from the Register where official notification has been received from a court that the finding that was the basis of the registration was quashed or reversed or there was a successful appeal of the registration.

When family and children's services agency staff apply to the Family Court to enter a name on the Register when there has been no court finding or conviction, the alleged abuser must be notified. The alleged abuser has 30 days to object to the application, and has the right to be present when the Court considers the application.

Access to Information for Screening Purposes

One of the purposes of the Register is to provide information to assist in the screening of persons applying to be adoptive parents, foster parents, caregivers or volunteers working with children. Before any information is released, a request in writing must be made and the written consent of the registered person must be obtained. As outlined in the Regulations under the *Children and Family Services Act*, information may be disclosed to the following:

(a) any Federal, Provincial or Municipal government department, board or agency that provides services to children;

(b) any corporation, society, agency or business that provides services to children;

(c) any agency, child care service, child caring facility, or child placing agency operating under the *Children and Family Services Act* and regulations;

(d) a person who remunerates another person for the care of his or her children in a private home on a regular basis; and

(e) such other persons, groups or organizations as may be designated by the Minister.

Access to Information for Child Protection and Research Purposes

Agency workers who are conducting a child abuse or neglect investigation may contact the Child Abuse Register by phone or may ask their Executive Director/District Supervisor to search the on-line computer system in their agency to determine whether or not an alleged perpetrator has been recorded for past abuse. Non-identifying information contained in the Child Abuse Register may be utilized for research purposes if the request has been approved by the Minister of Community Services.

Child Abuse and Neglect Protocols

To ensure an arrangement of mutual reporting and full disclosure of all pertinent information during an investigation of suspected child abuse, the Department of Community Services has established several protocols and guidelines to be followed by those involved. The Department has established a "Child Sexual Abuse Protocol", which is to be used by each investigative team, consisting of a police officer and a child protection worker. It is a recommended practice in the protocol that individuals who have received specialized training be assigned to conduct such investigations. The protocol includes recommended procedures to be followed by agencies and district offices with respect to interventions and guidelines for interviewing children. For example, one section of the Protocol outlines "The Step-Wise Interview: A protocol for interviewing children" that is the recommended protocol to be followed when interviewing alleged victims of abuse. In addition, as part of their responsibilities, children's services agencies are to develop an emergency response procedure with local hospitals or designated physicians. The emergency physician is to work in consultation with the investigative team. Another recommended procedure is the video or audio taping of the interview with the child.

The Department of Community Services also has "Guidelines – Child Abuse in Facilities for the Care of Children" for responding to allegations of abuse in residential facilities and "A Protocol for Investigations of Abuse in Foster Care". A "Domestic Violence Protocol" has been drafted for use by family and children's services agencies and transition houses. This protocol includes guidelines on risk management, case conference procedures and the handling of disclosure of sexual abuse in transition houses. "A Handbook for Early Childhood Educators" has been written by the Department of Community Services and published by the Association for Early Childhood Education. This handbook outlines possible indicators of child abuse, legal responsibilities, and reporting policies and procedures.

The Department is currently drafting a protocol in collaboration with the departments of Health, Education, the Solicitor General's Office and the Attorney General's Office that will assist professionals in responding to allegations of child abuse. Local areas are encouraged to develop protocols that will address their own needs.

The Committee on Procedures for a Coordinated Response for Victims of Family Violence is developing a protocol to ensure that a coordinated response for victims of family violence occurs. The standards developed will be incorporated into various protocols pertaining to family violence.

Statistics

The following tables and graphs are based on available data from the Department of Community Services. Data on the Department's Child Abuse Register are for the period September 3, 1991 to August 31, 1992. Data on protection and children in care were extracted from the Case Management System and are for the period April 1 to March 31, 1992 and as at March 31, 1992.

In Nova Scotia, protection services include services to all families/children considered to be at risk or in need of protection. Children in care refers to any child who has had a transfer of custody and/or guardianship through a Temporary Care Agreement, a Special Needs Agreement, apprehension, a Temporary Care and Custody Order (includes status during adjournments in child protection hearing), a Permanent Care and Custody Order, or voluntary relinquishment for adoption purposes. Data on natives are included in the statistics.

Not all abused or neglected children are taken into care; many may receive services from the Department of Community Services voluntarily or under the terms of a Supervision Order.

Due to the limitations noted in Chapter 1, Introduction, these data should not be compared with data for other jurisdictions.

Table 4.1 Child Abuse Register: Recorded Cases[1] by Type, September 3, 1991 to August 31, 1992

Type	Number	Percentage
Physical abuse	52	26.0
Sexual abuse	148	74.0
Total	**200**	**100.0**

1. 191 cases were recorded on the Child Abuse Register as a result of a criminal conviction. In addition, 8 cases were recorded as a result of Section 22(a) or (c) (child is found in need of protective services by Family Court) and 1 case was recorded as a result of Section 63(3) (Family Court decision that a person has abused a child).

Table 4.2 Child Abuse Register: Sex of Abusers, September 3, 1991 to August 31, 1992

Sex	Number	Percentage
Male	185	92.5
Female	15	7.5
Total	**200**	**100.0**

Figure 4.1   Child Abuse Register: Abusers by Relationship to Victim, September 3, 1991 to August 31, 1992

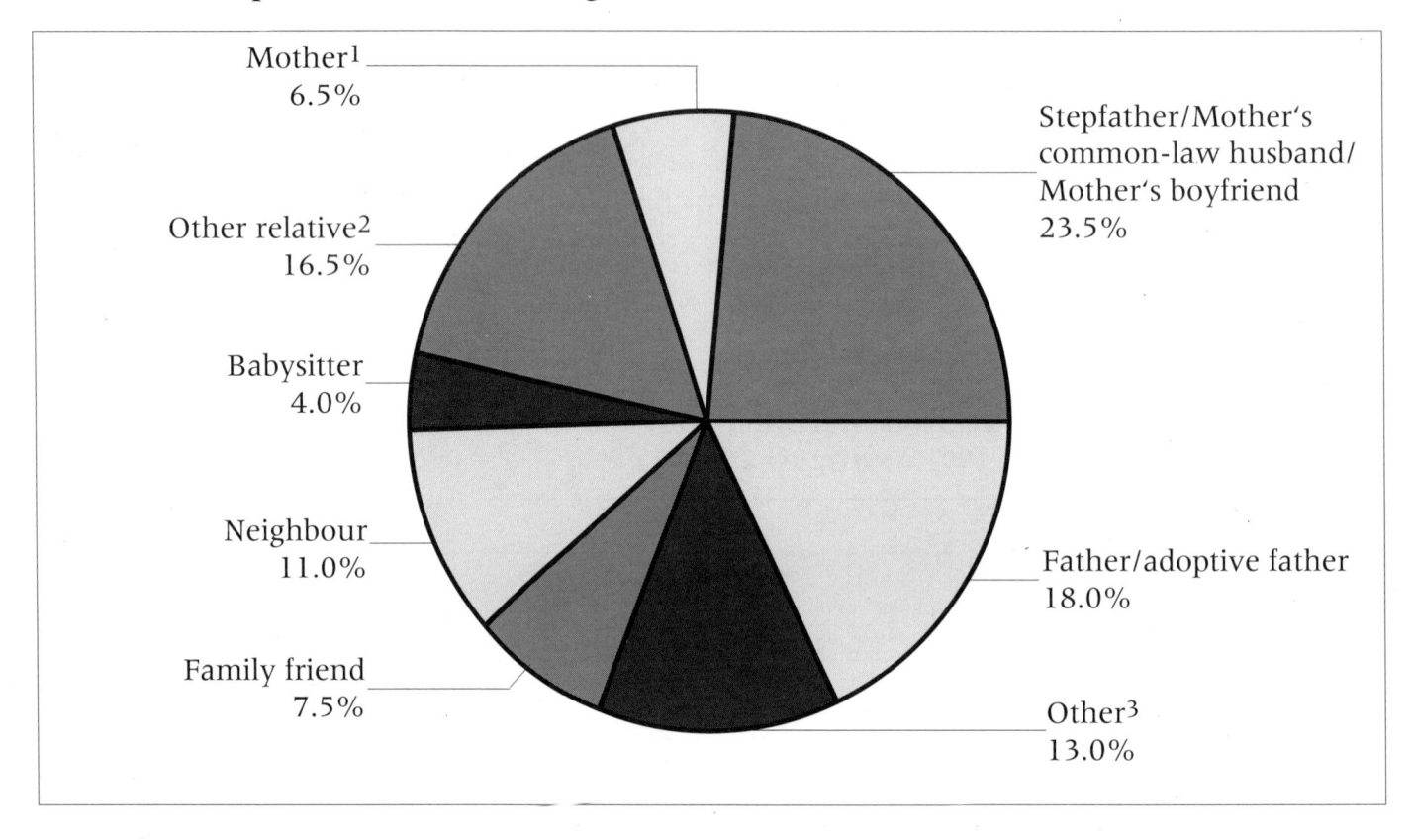

- Mother[1] 6.5%
- Stepfather/Mother's common-law husband/Mother's boyfriend 23.5%
- Other relative[2] 16.5%
- Babysitter 4.0%
- Neighbour 11.0%
- Family friend 7.5%
- Father/adoptive father 18.0%
- Other[3] 13.0%

Number of abusers: 200

1. Includes mother, adoptive mother and step-mother.
2. Includes uncle, cousin, brother, and grandfather.
3. Includes school employee, fellow student/tutor, clergy, stranger, foster father, child's boyfriend and other.

Table 4.3 Protection[1] Cases[2] from April 1, 1991 to March 31, 1992 and as at March 31, 1992

	Number	Percentage
Children provided protection in own home[3] (April 1, 1991 – March 31, 1992)	7,066	100.0
Protection cases (as at March 31, 1992)		
Abuse[4] and neglect	1,563	69.4
Family Support[5]	690	30.6
Total	**2,253**	**100.0**

1. Includes families receiving protective services as defined in the *Children and Family Services Act*.
2. Cases refer to number of families.
3. Includes children receiving protective services in their own home.
4. Includes cases of abuse as defined in the *Children and Family Services Act*.
5. Includes the provision of intensive services to families in crisis on a short-term basis, where children are assessed as being at high risk and would likely come into care in the near future (50-60 days) if services were not provided.

Table 4.4 Children in Care[1] by Legal Status, April 1, 1991 to March 31, 1992 and as at March 31, 1992

	Number	Percentage
Children brought into care[1] (April 1, 1991 – March 31, 1992)		
Voluntary Agreements (Temporary)[2]	844	68.0
Voluntary Agreements (Permanent)[3]	25	2.0
Taken into Care[4]	267	21.5
Care and Custody[5]	105	8.5
Total	**1,241**	**100.0**
Total number of children in care[1] (as at March 31, 1992)	1,561	100.0
Children in care and custody[5]	904	57.9

1. Includes children where there has been a change of custody and/or guardianship under the legal statuses shown.
2. Includes children under a Temporary Care Agreement or a Special Needs Agreement.
3. Children voluntarily given up for adoption under Section 68 of the *Children and Family Services Act*.
4. Includes children who have been apprehended and children who are the subjects of a Temporary Care and Custody Order (includes status during court adjournment).
5. Represents children who are the subjects of a Permanent Care and Custody Order (permanent wards).

Chapter 4 - Nova Scotia

Figure 4.2   Children in Care and Custody[1] by Placement Type as at March 31, 1992

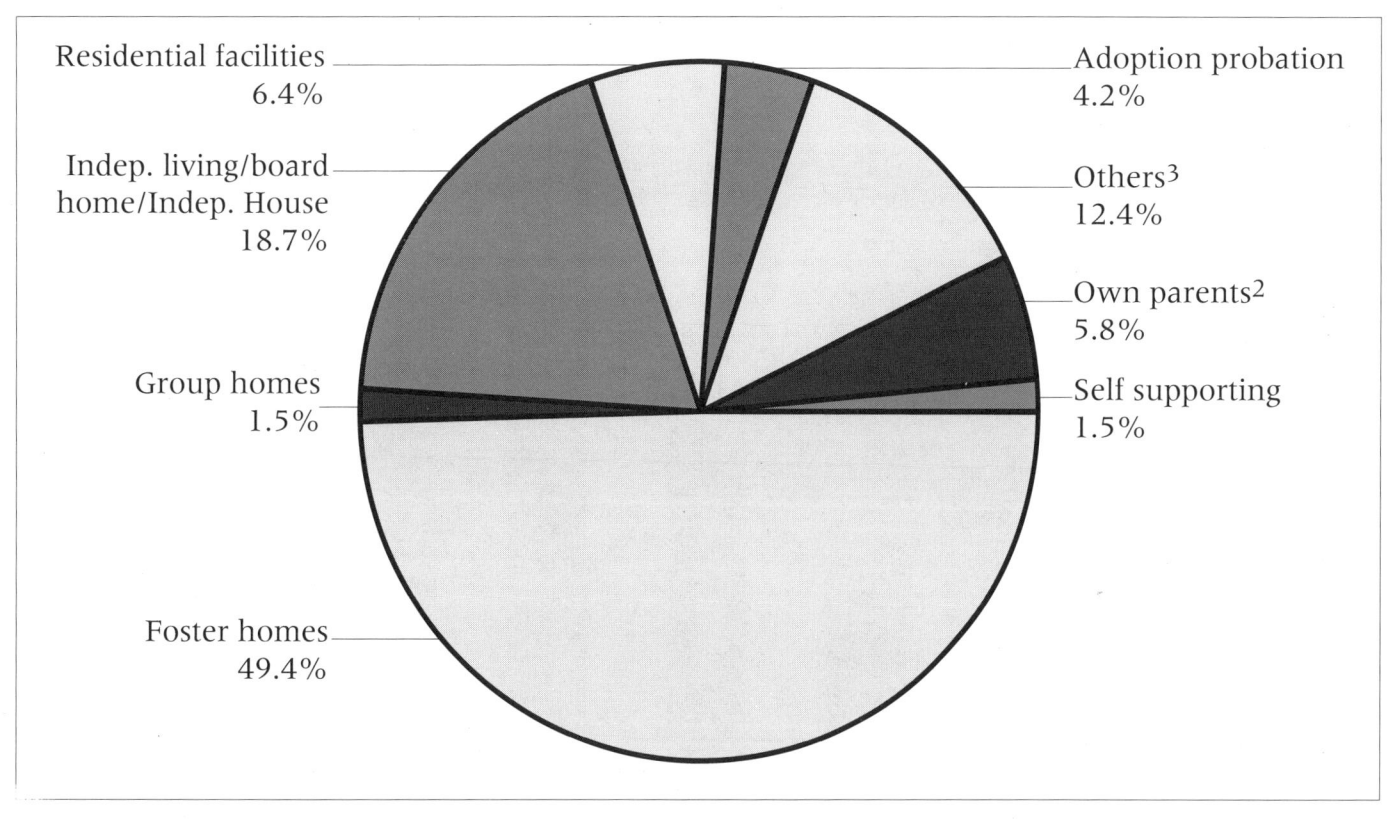

Residential facilities
6.4%

Indep. living/board home/Indep. House
18.7%

Group homes
1.5%

Foster homes
49.4%

Adoption probation
4.2%

Others[3]
12.4%

Own parents[2]
5.8%

Self supporting
1.5%

Children in care and custody: 904[1]

1. This is a subset of all children in care and only includes children who are the subjects of a Permanent Care and Custody Order (permanent wards).
2. Children who were made permanent wards of the Department and later in adolescence chose to return to live with a parent.
3. This category includes S.O.S. Village, the Young Offenders Act Community Facility, Free Homes and other placements.

Figure 4.3 Children in Care and Custody[1] by Age Group as at March 31, 1992

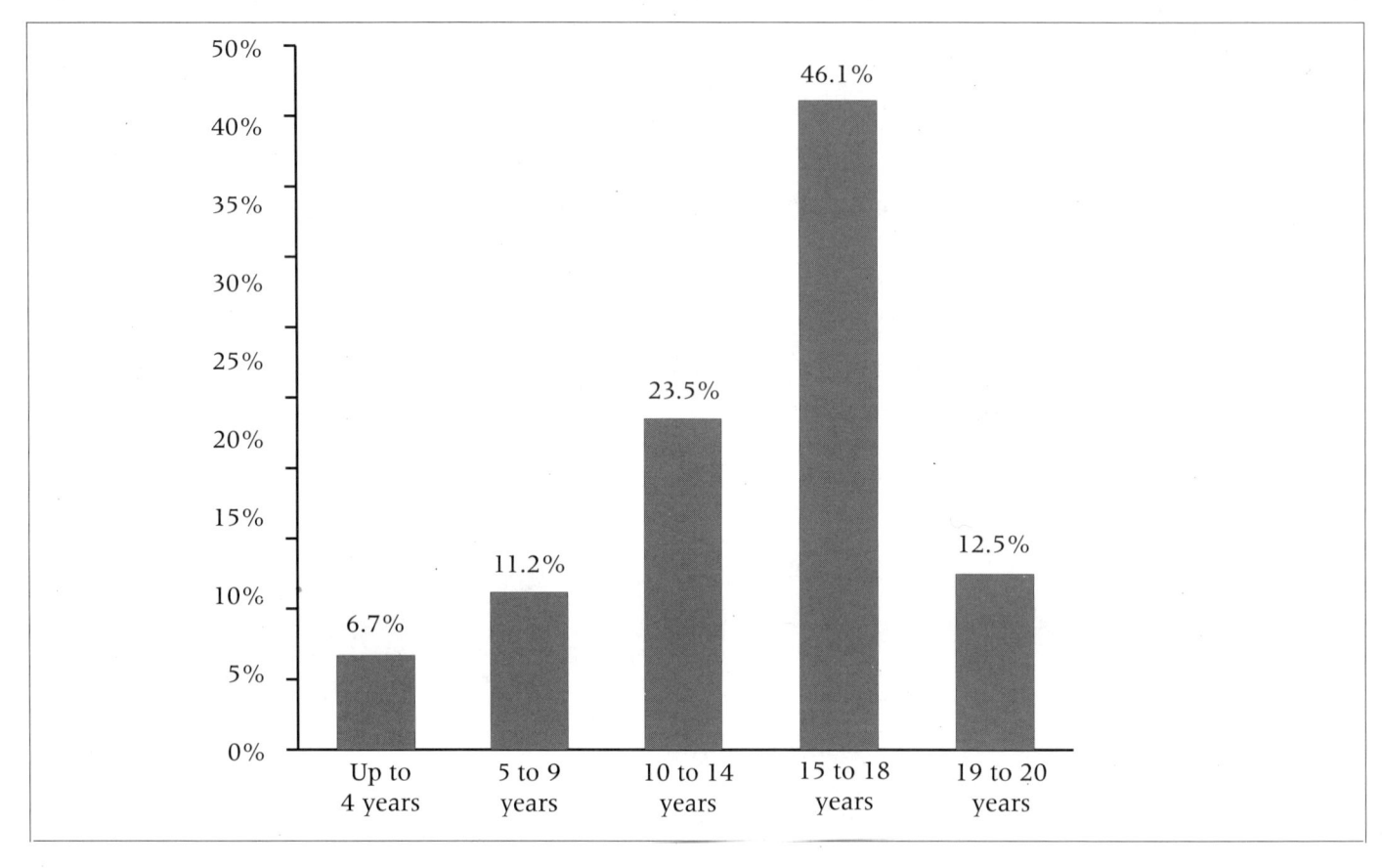

Age Group	Percentage
Up to 4 years	6.7%
5 to 9 years	11.2%
10 to 14 years	23.5%
15 to 18 years	46.1%
19 to 20 years	12.5%

Children in care and custody: 904[1]

1. This is a subset of all children in care and only includes children who are the subjects of a Permanent Care and Custody Order (permanent wards).

Resource Material

Legislative Material

Children and Family Services Act, Statutes of Nova Scotia. 1990, c. 5.

Reports

Nova Scotia, Department of Community Services. *Annual Report*. 1991.

Other Material

Nova Scotia, Department of Community Services. "Child Protection Manual", Halifax, 1991.

_____. *Child Abuse: A Handbook for Early Childhood Educators*, 1990.

_____. *Child Sexual Abuse Protocol*, 1991.

_____. *Domestic Violence Protocol*, 1992.

_____. *Guidelines: Child Abuse in Facilities Responsible for the Care of Children*, 1990.

_____. *Protocol for Investigations of Abuse in Foster Care*.

Chapter 5 – New Brunswick

Administration and Service Delivery

The Minister of the Department of Health and Community Services, under the authority of the *Family Services Act,* is responsible for investigating all reports of suspected cases of child abuse and neglect in the province. This responsibility is carried out by authorized employees of the Minister, who are referred to as child protection workers or child protection investigators.

The Family and Community Social Services Division manages and delivers all child and family services mandated under the *Family Services Act*. The Division is coordinated and directed by the Department's head office, located in Fredericton, with most services delivered by the 12 regional offices located throughout the province. Some services are also provided through contracts with private agencies and individuals. All regional offices report to one of two Executive Directors in the Division. The Family Services Unit of the Division is responsible for policy, interpretation of legislation and program revision in the following areas of children's services: child protection (known as Child Protection Services); one parent services; community-based services to special needs children; support services to education; adoption; child care; and child placement facilities. The Family and Community Social Services Division also chairs an Interdepartmental Committee on Family Violence whose mandate is to monitor, recommend and/or coordinate governmental initiatives related to family violence issues.

Ten of the province's fifteen Indian Nations have signed agreements that establish social service agencies within individual native communities to deliver their own child and family services. The five reserves that do not have agencies, as well as all off-reserve Indians, receive services from the regional office in their area.

Definitions

In the *Family Services Act*, which includes adoption and child protection provisions, a **child** is defined under Section 1 as "any person who is, or who appears to be, under the age of majority" (i.e., under 19 years). However, regulations stipulate that for child protection purposes a **child** means a person actually or apparently under the age of 16 and includes a disabled person actually or apparently under the age of 19. Under Sub-section 49(5) services may be extended, in certain situations, beyond the age of 19 to children who were in the permanent care and custody of the Department of Health and Community Services.

Furthermore, under Section 1 of the Act, a **child** includes: "an unborn child; a stillborn child; a child whose parents are not married to one another; a child to whom a person stands in loco parentis, if that person's spouse is a parent of the child; when used in reference to the relationship between an adopted person and his birth mother or birth father, a person who has attained the age of majority".

Under Section 31, **a child's security or development may be considered to be in danger** (i.e., a child in need of protection) when:

"(a)   the child is without adequate care, supervision or control;

(b)   the child is living in unfit or improper circumstances;

(c)   the child is in the care of a person who is unable or unwilling to provide adequate care, supervision or control of the child;

(d)   the child is in the care of a person whose conduct endangers the life, health or emotional well-being of the child;

(e)   the child is physically or sexually abused, physically or emotionally neglected, sexually exploited or in danger of such treatment;

(f)   the child is living in a situation where there is severe domestic violence;

(g)   the child is in the care of a person who neglects or refuses to provide or obtain proper medical, surgical or other remedial care or treatment necessary for the health or well-being of the child or refuses to permit such care or treatment to be supplied to the child;

(h)   the child is beyond the control of the person caring for him;

(i)   the child by his behaviour, condition, environment or association, is likely to injure himself or others;

(j)   the child is in the care of a person who does not have a right to custody of the child, without the consent of a person having such right;

(k)   the child is in the care of a person who neglects or refuses to ensure that the child attends school; or

(l)   the child has committed an offence or, if the child is under the age of twelve years, has committed an act or omission that would constitute an offence for which the child could be convicted if the child were twelve years of age or older."

Although formal definitions of **abuse and neglect** are not stipulated under the *Family Services Act*, the inter-departmental "Guidelines for Protecting Child Victims of Abuse and Neglect" (see section on Child Abuse and Neglect Protocols) provide the following working definitions:

"(a)   **Physical Abuse**
Physical abuse refers to all actions resulting in non-accidental physical injury, from bruises and cuts to burns, fractures and internal injuries. Such abuse is distinguished from acceptable or reasonable use of force by its severity, its inappropriateness for the age of the child, and its lack of a healthy corrective purpose regarding the child's behaviour.

(b)   **Sexual Abuse**
Sexual abuse refers to any sexual acts involving a child and a parent/caretaker, any person in a position of trust, and any other adult. Sexual abuse can range from a parent/caretaker permitting or exposing a child to sexual acts, to actual molestation of the child by an adult. Molestation includes acts of exposure, fondling or masturbation, and intercourse, including incest. Sexual involvement may or may not be accompanied by physical abuse. Inappropriate sex play among children may serve as a strong indicator that a child has been sexually abused by an adult, or by an older child.

(c) **Physical Neglect**
Physical neglect covers acts of omission on the part of the parent/caretaker. Failure to provide for a child's basic needs and appropriate level of care with respect to food, clothing, shelter, health hygiene and safety, as determined by the community's minimum level of care standards. This includes the failure to provide adequate supervision, anticipatory prevention of injury, medical attention and the opportunity to receive an adequate education.

(d) **Emotional Maltreatment**
Emotional maltreatment is the most difficult form of abuse and neglect to define and identify. Emotional abuse includes overt rejection, criticism and excessive demands of performance for a child's age and ability. Emotional abuse refers to the failure of the parent/caretaker to provide adequate psychological nurturance necessary for a child's growth and development."

The above definitions provide a framework for the mandatory intervention by responsible agencies and individuals in situations of child abuse. Since the primary responsibility for the care and development of children is entrusted to parents/caretakers, the definitions focus on the behaviours of these people.

Mandatory Reporting of a Child Whose Security or Development is in Danger

Under Sub-section 30(1) of the *Family Services Act*, anyone who has information causing them to suspect that a child has been abandoned, deserted, physically or emotionally neglected, physically or sexually ill-treated or otherwise abused must report that information directly to child protection authorities. A person who reports suspected child abuse or neglect to other authorities (i.e., health personnel, police) is advised to also notify child protection authorities. Mandatory reporting in suspected child abuse and neglect situations is limited to children under the age of 16 and to disabled children under the age of 19.

All persons are required to report, including professionals who encounter abuse and neglect in carrying out their duties or within a confidential relationship. Solicitor-client privilege is the only confidential relationship excepted from this duty. For those who do report, no legal action can be taken against them when they act in good faith. Under Sub-section 30(2), any professional who receives such information in a professional capacity may be charged with an offence under the Act for failing to report. In addition, under Sub-section 30(4), the Minister of the Department of Health and Community Services may require any professional society, association or other organization authorized under the laws of the province to regulate the professional activities of the person and cause an investigation to be made into the matter.

Investigation of an Allegation of Child Abuse or Neglect

Each regional office has a mechanism to screen all reports of children whose security or development may be in danger. Screening involves not only the acceptance of referrals but also redirecting inappropriate ones to the appropriate community resource. Reports of alleged sexual abuse, physical abuse or threats to physical safety must be investigated immediately. All other reports or referrals must be investigated with a home visit within four working days. The worker must determine the validity of the allegation and ascertain if there is a need for child protection intervention and/or service. The worker's assessment will include consideration of the definition, in the *Family Services Act*, of whether the child's security or development may be considered to be in danger.

The worker must advise the police of all reports of sexual abuse, serious physical abuse or serious neglect that are being investigated. An initial joint investigation by Child Protection Services and the police is conducted. The police determine if a criminal offence has been committed as defined by the *Criminal Code*. After seeing the child, the worker arranges a medical examination if there appears to be an inadequately explained injury or one that appears to have been inflicted by the parent or someone acting in the parent's place. The worker shall also arrange a medical examination where there are other indications of possible abuse, even though visual injuries are not apparent, i.e., suspected sexual abuse, serious symptoms of malnourishment or "failure to thrive".

If the child is not found to be in need of protection, the worker may offer to continue working with the family or refer the family to other services as appropriate. Where a child's security or development is believed to be in danger and in-home services or an agreement (see section on Voluntary Agreements) are inappropriate, a worker is authorized under the *Family Services Act* to seek a warrant to enter or search any premises or area to apprehend the child. Where the child is believed to be in immediate danger, the Act also permits the worker to enter any premises without a warrant to search for and remove the child. This provision is used only where the physical safety of the child is threatened and any delay in removing the child could result in injury. In any apprehension, the worker may request police assistance.

The Department of Health and Community Services provides a training program for workers that is entitled Child Protective Services. The program includes modules on intake and investigations, ongoing services and the Court. Also available for consultation is the Court Procedures Manual, which was developed jointly by the departments of Justice, Income Assistance and Health and Community Services. In addition, certain staff who have received special training or have significant experience in dealing with victims and/or perpetrators of child abuse, provide direct client service in either individual or group counselling.

Referrals of extra-familial child abuse (involving persons other than parents, caretakers or other persons residing in the household of the child) are assessed and investigated by the Department of Health and Community Services as well. The role of Child Protection Services is to assure that the victim, and other children, will be protected from further harm from the alleged perpetrator. The worker must also determine whether parental neglect or lack of appropriate supervision was a factor in the abuse and must assure that the victim has access to and receives appropriate treatment and support services to overcome the effects of the abuse.

Investigations of reports of a native child being in need of protection follow the same procedures.

Voluntary Agreements

If the provision of services in the home is unsuccessful in protecting the child, the worker must take steps to remove the child. The goal of a temporary alternate placement is to protect the child while efforts are made to enable the child's early return to his family. The Department of Health and Community Services may enter into a Custody Agreement with a parent to accept a voluntary transfer of custody, care and control of a child for up to one year, with extensions only made in exceptional cases. Guardianship rights are retained by the parent for the duration of the agreement. Although Custody Agreements can be used in cases of child abuse and neglect, if it is suspected that long term involvement is needed to keep the child in care, a court order is usually obtained. Custody Agreements may also be used to provide specialized services to a child with special needs.

Court-Ordered Protection

Where voluntary measures are not suitable or a child has been apprehended, the worker must apply for a court hearing. When the Court of Queen's Bench determines that the child is in need of protection, it may make one of the following orders regarding the child's care. A Supervisory Order authorizes the Department of Health and Community Services to exercise supervision of the child and the child's family in the family home for up to six months, with the parent retaining custody and guardianship of the child. The order may be extended for further periods of six months each. A Custody Order allows removal of the child from the home for up to six months, and may be extended for additional six month periods to a maximum of 24 months. Custody, care and control of the child are transferred to the Department for the duration of the Custody Order. A Guardianship Order stipulates that the child be removed from the home and that the care, custody, and control of the child and all parental rights and responsibilities with respect to the child be permanently transferred to the Department.

A child who was under a Guardianship Order at the age of 19 may have services extended beyond 19 under a Post Guardianship Services Agreement if the child is enrolled in an educational program or is not self-sufficient by reason of a physical, mental, or emotional disability. There is no upper age limit if services are provided to a child for educational purposes if that child has been enrolled in that program continuously since the age of 19 until graduation or withdrawal. An upper age limit of 24 applies to disabled persons who are receiving services.

In addition, the *Family Services Act* provides for a Protective Intervention Order which prohibits a person from residing in the same premises as the child, or contacting or associating with the child for up to six months if it is in the opinion of the court that the person is a source of danger to the child's security or development.

Child Abuse Register

There is no formal Child Abuse Register in New Brunswick. The Department does, however, maintain an on-line computerized system of information on all families served in the province.

Child Abuse and Neglect Protocols

To operationalize the province's commitment to work cooperatively in addressing the problem of child abuse and neglect, a series of protocols has been developed by representatives from four departments – Health and Community Services, Justice (including Solicitor General), Education, and Income Assistance. These "Guidelines for Protecting Child Victims of Abuse and Neglect" provide direction to those organizations and professionals who have a responsibility for children and an obligation to protect them from abuse and neglect. The series comprises seven booklets that were produced to assist different individuals and organizations that deal with victims of child abuse and neglect. All the booklets include the following: an outline of the law in New Brunswick covering child abuse; a definition of child abuse; guidelines for recognizing child abuse; and guidelines for managing child abuse.

In addition, each report includes specific guidelines for identifying, reporting and investigating child abuse and neglect that are specifically applicable to various individuals and organizations. These individuals and organizations include:

1. Health and Community Services (Public Health, Mental Health and Hospitals)
2. Physicians
3. Foster Homes, Group Homes and Other Child Care Facilities
4. Early Childhood Development Facilities
5. Justice (Police, Crown Prosecutor, Probation Services)
6. Education (Schools and Student Services Personnel)
7. Department of Income Assistance

An eighth booklet was also produced which provides resource material including: guidelines for interviewing children; guidelines for testifying in Court; indicators of child abuse and neglect; prevention of child abuse and neglect; the multi-disciplinary team (social, legal, psychological and medical personnel) and child abuse; treatment of child abuse and neglect; relevant sections under the *Family Services Act*; provisions under the *Criminal Code* relating to child abuse and neglect; and social institutions and child abuse and neglect – a description of roles and responsibilities.

Statistics

The following tables and graphs are based on data provided by the Department of Health and Community Services through their Management Information System known as RPSS.

In New Brunswick, protection data refer to families receiving child protection services from the Department, regardless of whether or not the child is in the custody of the Department. Children in care refer to any child where there has been a transfer of custody and/or guardianship and the child is under one of the following legal statuses: Protective Care, Custody Agreement, Supervisory Order, Custody Order, Guardianship Order or Agreement (voluntary relinquishment for adoption) (includes Post Guardianship Services Agreements) and wards from other jurisdictions. With the exception of New Brunswick and the Northwest Territories, all other jurisdictions exclude Supervisory Orders from their legal statuses for children in care.

Data on natives on reserves are excluded from the following statistics.

Due to the limitations noted in Chapter 1, Introduction, these data should not be compared with data for other jurisdictions.

Table 5.1   Reports[1,2] by Type, April 1, 1991 to March 31, 1992

Type	Number	Percentage
Child abuse		
Physical	1,521	20.0
Sexual	1,478	19.4
Sub-Total	**2,999**	**39.4**
Spousal abuse occurring within family	476	6.2
Neglect	2,865	37.6
Child beyond control	1,280	16.8
Total	**7,620**	**100.0**

1. All reports received by the Department of a child being in need of protection are investigated. Only primary presenting problem based on caller's allegation has been recorded.
2. Reports relate to number of families and include all referrals or requests for services under child protection programs. More than one report was received concerning some families; however, the presenting problem may be different.

Figure 5.1   Reports[1] by Referral Source, April 1, 1991 to March 31, 1992

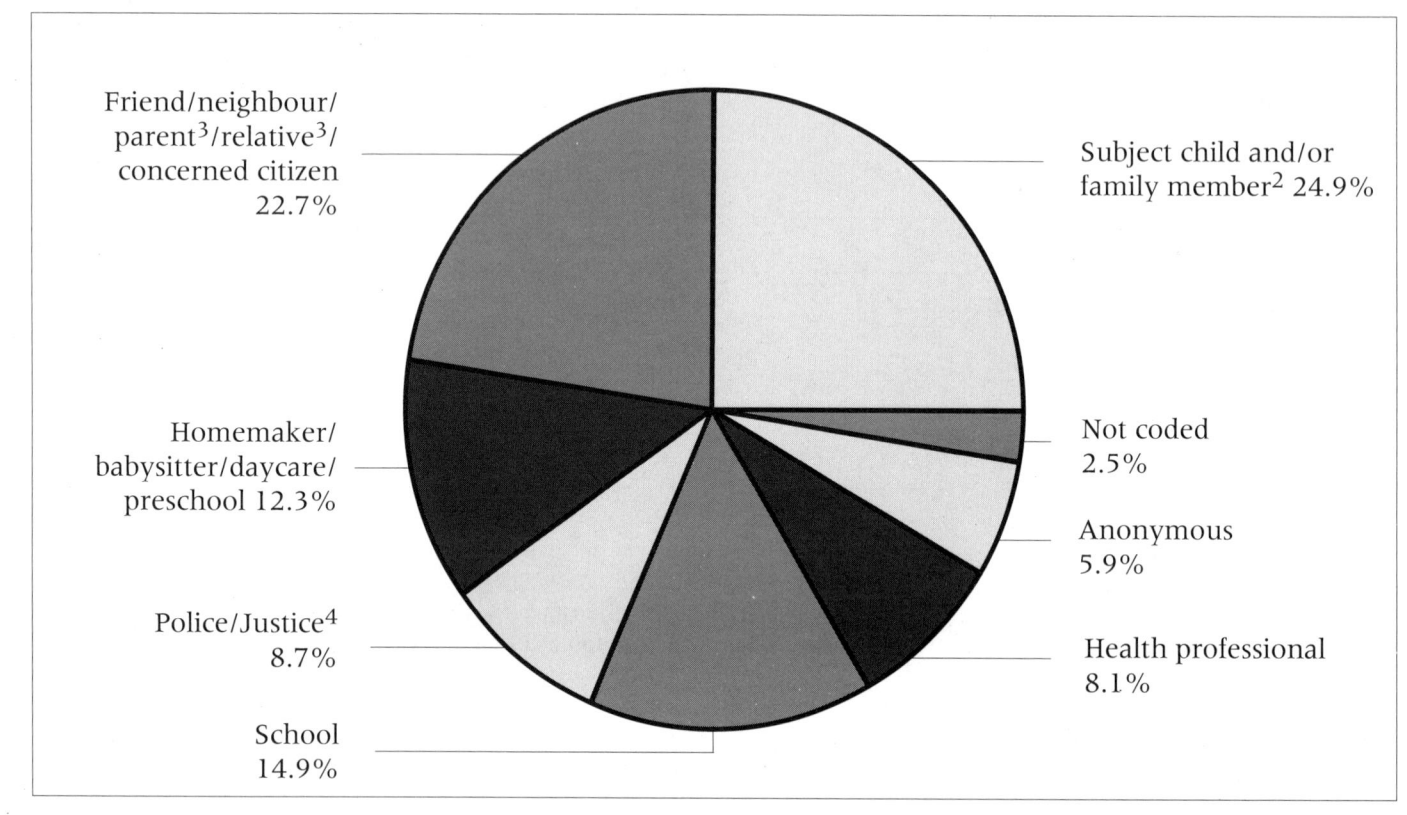

- Friend/neighbour/parent[3]/relative[3]/concerned citizen 22.7%
- Subject child and/or family member[2] 24.9%
- Not coded 2.5%
- Anonymous 5.9%
- Health professional 8.1%
- Homemaker/babysitter/daycare/preschool 12.3%
- Police/Justice[4] 8.7%
- School 14.9%

Total Reports: 7,620

1. Reports relate to number of families and include all referrals or requests for services under child protection programs. All reports received are investigated. More than one report was received concerning some families.
2. Includes only those cases where the family has requested services.
3. Refers to persons residing outside the family household.
4. Includes courts, lawyers, probations officers and other legal professionals.

Table 5.2   Outcome of Investigation of Reports[1] Received during March 1992

Outcome	Number	Percentage
Report rejected[2]	49	7.0
Refer to another district office or to community services	45	6.5
Provide family support/ refer for child protection[3]	157	22.5
Admit child to care	53	7.6
No service indicated	7	1.0
Not coded	35	5.0
Serviced at intake[4]	94	13.5
Being investigated	257	36.9
Total	**697**	**100.0**

1. Refers to number of families. All reports are investigated. More than one report was received concerning some families.
2. Includes known malicious reports or unfounded or inappropriate referrals.
3. Family has requested service. Includes family intervention situations without removing the child from the home.
4. Includes families in crisis provided emergency counselling or who have been referred to mental health services or private agencies for service.

Table 5.3   Protection Cases[1] by Reason for Intervention[2] during March 1992

Reason	Number	Percentage
Physical abuse	168	8.6
Sexual abuse/incest	221	11.3
Emotional abuse/physical neglect	476	24.4
Multiple problems	917	47.1
Other[3]	166	8.5
Total	**1,948**	**100.0**

1. Cases refer to number of families receiving child protection services from the Department of Health and Community Services where the child(ren) involved may or may not be in the custody of the Department. Services include voluntary and mandatory support services to children and families in their own homes and to children in care.
2. Reason for intervention is determined following the worker's investigation and assessment.
3. Includes problems of school/social/legal difficulties, drug and alcohol problems, child beyond control, parent-child relationship difficulties.

Table 5.4   Children in Care[1] by Legal Status during March 1992

Legal Status	Number	Percentage
Protective Care[2,3]	22	1.9
Custody Agreement[3]	185	15.6
Supervisory Order[3]	80	6.7
Custody Order[3]	138	11.6
Guardianship (includes post-guardianship)[4]	738	62.1
Wards from other jurisdictions	26	2.2
Total	**1,189**	**100.0**

1. Children who are in need of protection under the *Family Services Act* and are in care under the legal statuses shown. With the exception of New Brunswick and the Northwest Territories, all other jurisdictions exclude Supervisory Orders from their legal statuses for children in care.
2. Protective care is a service which provides an immediate safeguard for a child's security and development.
3. These categories include temporary statuses (i.e., child not in permanent care and custody of the Department) totalling 425. Note that 25 children had a change of status within the temporary statuses category.
4. Includes Guardianship Agreements (voluntary relinquishment for adoption) and Orders (726 children) and Post Guardianship Services, where services are extended to youths beyond age 19 at the termination of guardianship status provided they are in school or have special needs for a pre-defined period (12 children).

Figure 5.2   Children in Care[1] by Legal Status during March 1992

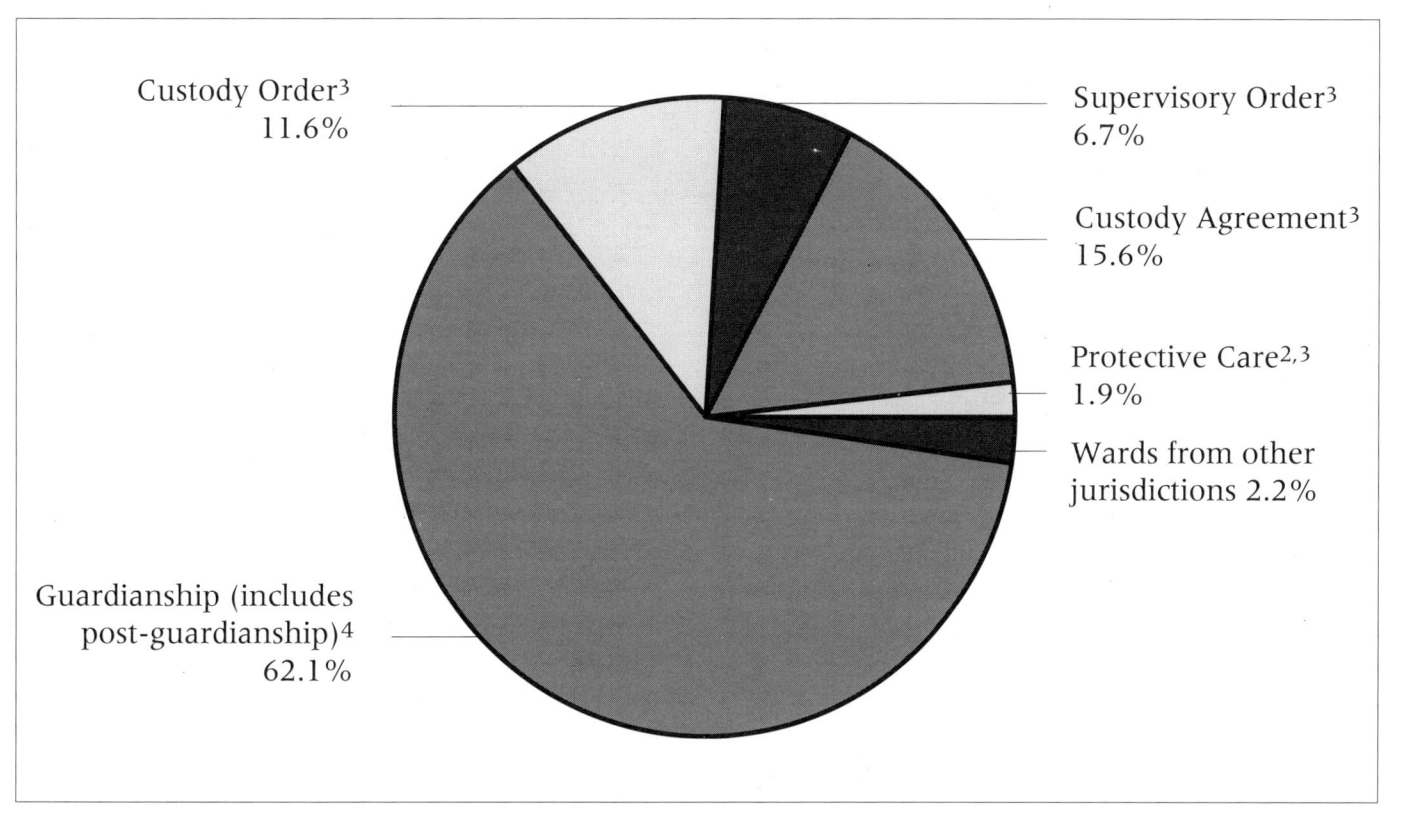

Custody Order[3]
11.6%

Supervisory Order[3]
6.7%

Custody Agreement[3]
15.6%

Protective Care[2,3]
1.9%

Wards from other jurisdictions 2.2%

Guardianship (includes post-guardianship)[4]
62.1%

Children in care: 1,189

1. Children who are in need of protection under the *Family Services Act* and are in care under the legal statuses shown. With the exception of New Brunswick and the Northwest Territories, all other jurisdictions exclude Supervisory Orders from their legal statuses for children in care.
2. Protective care is a service which provides an immediate safeguard for a child's security and development.
3. These categories include temporary statuses (i.e., child not in permanent care and custody of the Department) totalling 425. Note that 25 children had a change of status within the temporary statuses category.
4. Includes Guardianship Agreements (voluntary relinquishment for adoption) and Orders (726 children) and Post Guardianship Services, where services are extended to youths beyond age 19 at the termination of guardianship status provided they are in school or have special needs for a pre-defined period (12 children).

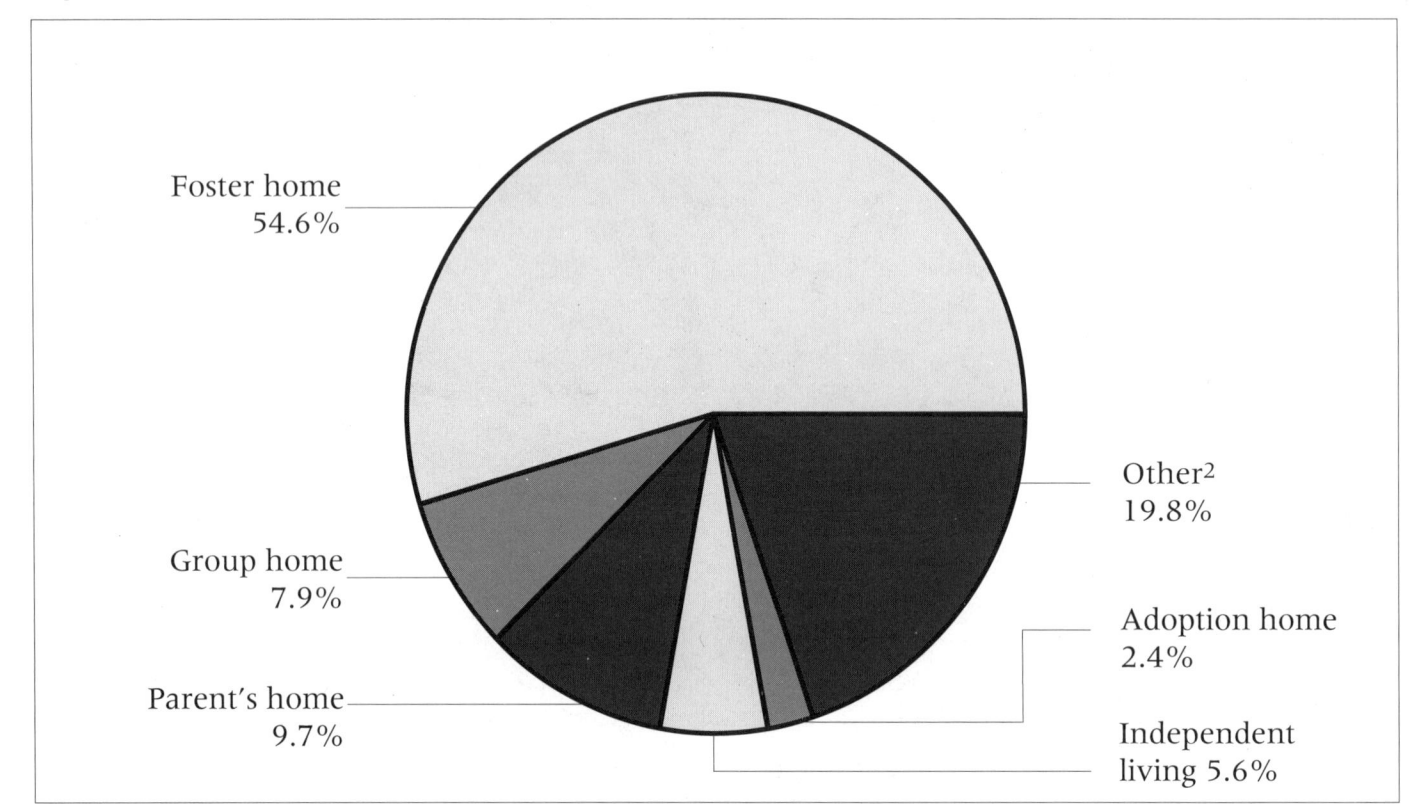

Figure 5.3 Children in Care[1] by Placement Type during March 1992

Foster home 54.6%
Other[2] 19.8%
Group home 7.9%
Adoption home 2.4%
Parent's home 9.7%
Independent living 5.6%

Children in care: 1,189

1. Children who are in need of protection under the *Family Services Act* and are in care under the following legal statuses: Protective Care, Custody Agreement, Supervisory Order, Custody Order, Guardianship Agreement or Guardianship Order (includes Post Guardianship Services) and wards from other jurisdictions. With the exception of New Brunswick and the Northwest Territories, all other jurisdictions exclude Supervisory Orders from their legal statuses for children in care.
2. Includes emergency shelter, CBS children home, therapeutic homes, institutions, special needs home, YOA and unknown.

Chapter 5 - New Brunswick

Table 5.5 Children in Permanent Care[1] by Reason[2] during March 1992

Reason	Number	Percentage
Physical abuse	6	0.8
Sexual abuse	61	8.4
Neglect	19	2.6
Multiple problems	219	30.2
No problem identified[2]	43	5.9
Other[3]	378	52.1
Total	**726**	**100.0**

1. Refers to children in the care of the Department under a Guardianship Order or Guardianship Agreement only.
2. Cases are recorded according to the current presenting problem. This problem will change the longer a child has been in care as they are no longer recorded according to the initial reason they were brought into care. Children who have adapted well to foster care may have no problem currently identified.
3. Includes problems of school/social/legal difficulties, drug and alcohol problems, child beyond control, parent-child relationship difficulties.

Table 5.6 Children in Permanent Care[1,2] by Reason[3], Age and Sex during March 1992

Reason	0-5 years M	0-5 years F	6-12 years M	6-12 years F	13-19 years M	13-19 years F	M	F	Total	Total %
Child abuse										
Physical	0	0	1	0	3	2	4	2	6	0.9
Sexual	0	0	5	8	16	32	21	40	61	8.9
	0	0	6	8	19	34	25	42	67	9.8
Multiple problems	1	2	24	13	95	84	120	99	219	32.1
Neglect	1	0	3	4	7	4	11	8	19	2.8
Other[4]	38	28	42	37	114	119	194	184	378	55.3
Total	40	30	75	62	235	241	350	333	683[1,2]	
Percentage	5.9	4.4	11.0	9.1	34.4	35.3	51.2	48.8	100.0	100.0

1. Refers to children in the care of the Department under a Guardianship Order or Guardianship Agreement only.
2. Excludes 43 children in permanent care where there was no problem identified.
3. Cases are recorded according to the current presenting problem. This problem will change the longer a child has been in care as they are no longer coded according to the initial reason they were brought into care.
4. Includes problems of school/social/legal difficulties, drug and alcohol problems, child beyond control, parent-child relationship difficulties.

Figure 5.4   Children in Permanent Care[1,2] by Age Group during March 1992

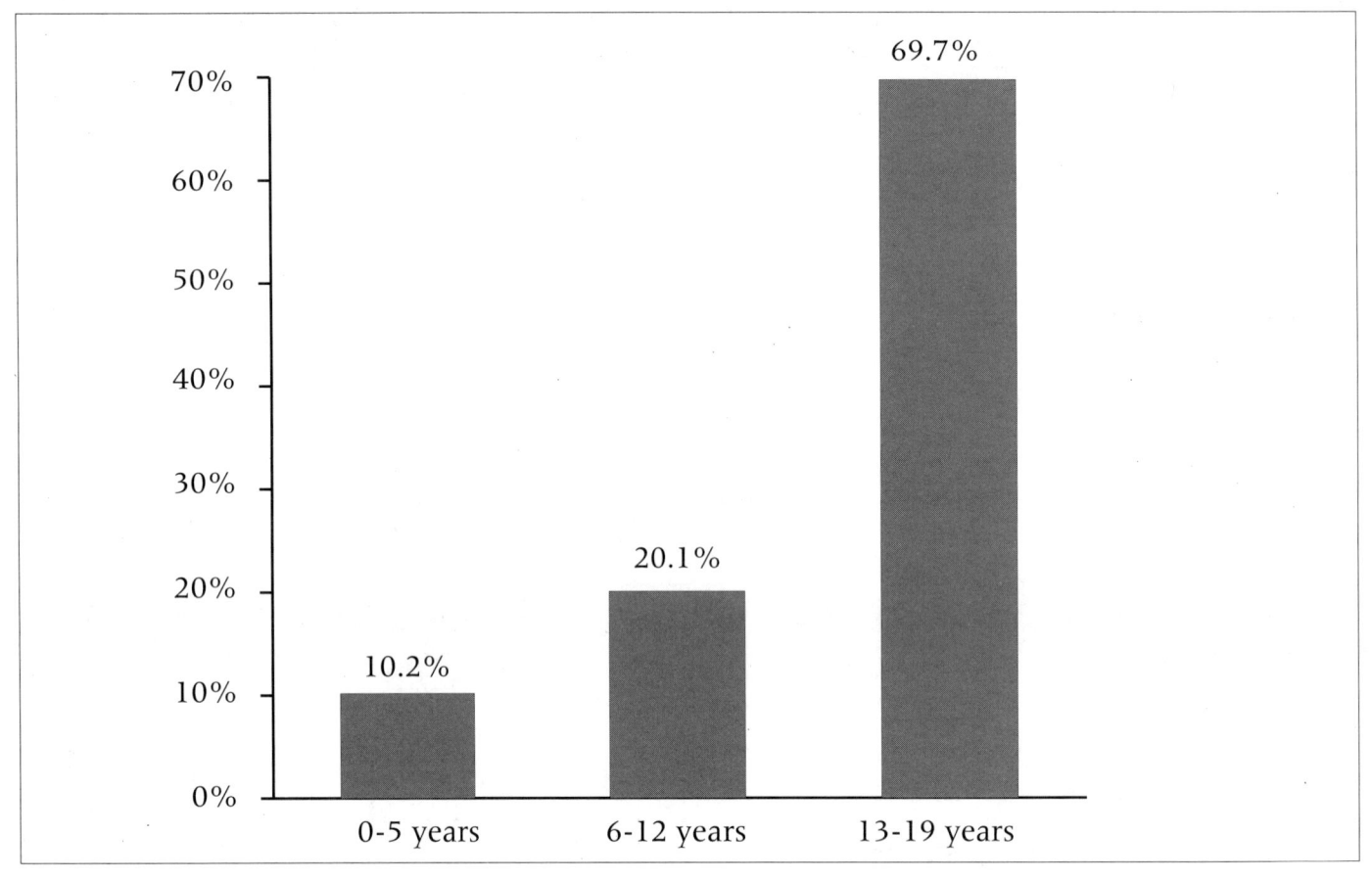

Age Group	Percentage
0-5 years	10.2%
6-12 years	20.1%
13-19 years	69.7%

Children in permanent care: 683[1,2]

1. Refers to children in the care of the Department under a Guardianship Order of Guardianship Agreement only.
2. Excludes 43 children in permanent care where there was no problem identified.

Resource Material

Legislative Material

Family Services Act, Statutes of New Brunswick 1980, C.F.-2.2, as amended.

Reports

New Brunswick, Department of Health and Community Services. *Annual Report*. 1990-91.

Other Material

New Brunswick, Department of Health and Community Services, Department of Justice, Department of Education, Department of Solicitor General and Department of Income Assistance. *Guidelines for Protecting Child Victims of Abuse and Neglect*, 1989.

New Brunswick, Department of Health and Community Services, Department of Justice. *Guidelines for Interviewing Victims of Child Abuse by Videotape*, 1989.

New Brunswick, Department of Health and Community Services, Department of Income Assistance and Department of Justice. *Court Procedures Manual, The Family Services Act*, 1988.

New Brunswick, Department of Health and Community Services. "Child Protection Services Standards Manual", Fredericton.

Chapter 6 – Quebec

Administration and Service Delivery

In Quebec, the *Quebec Charter of Human Rights and Freedoms* and the *Civil Code of Quebec* provide the basic framework for the legal system; together they set out the fundamental principles concerning the rights and interests of children as well as parental authority. The *Youth Protection Act*[1] is the legislative authority concerning services to families and children in need of protection. The Act falls primarily under the jurisdiction of the *ministère de la Santé et des Services sociaux* (Ministry of Health and Social Services).

The *Service des programmes aux jeunes et à leur famille* (Child and Family Services Division) of the *Direction générale des programmes* (Programs Branch) in the Ministry of Health and Social Services is responsible for the design, development and promotion of programs for children and their families in the areas of community prevention and intervention for newborns, infants and school age children. The Division is also involved in the design, development and promotion of adoption and post-adoption services, family mediation and the provision of psycho-social expertise to the Quebec Superior Court. The Division participates in the development of government action in the areas of family violence and family policy. In addition, the Division provides the framework for the development and implementation of regional organizational plans and encourages the harmonization of interministerial initiatives concerning youth.

Health and social services are delivered by an extensive network of establishments throughout the 18 health and social service regions in Quebec. These establishments are governed by the *Act Respecting Health Services and Social Services*. Within each region there is a *Centre de protection de l'enfance et de la jeunesse* (Child and Youth Protection Centre) which is responsible for the coordination of child protection services. There is a *Directeur de protection de la jeunesse* (Director of Youth Protection) in each Child and Youth Protection Centre who is responsible for intervening in cases where a child's security or development is or may be considered to be in danger. Child protection services may be delivered by designated institutions, agencies or individuals licensed by the Ministry of Health and Social Services.

The *Youth Protection Act* does not permit delegation of authority to the Council or Chief of an Indian band to provide child protection services to the native community; this remains the responsibility of the Child and Youth Protection Centre in each region. The administration of the Act in the aboriginal community is the responsibility of a team, often headed by a native person with social work training, which is located either in the Child and Youth Protection Centre or in an

---

1. The *Youth Protection Act* is currently being revised. The amended Act should be proclaimed in the Spring of 1994.

Indian agency, depending on the region. There are exceptions to this rule for the Cree, the Naskapi and the Inuit; they are already integrated into the health and social services network via the *Convention de la Baie James et du Nord québécois* (1975) (James Bay Agreement) and the *Convention du Nord-Est québécois* (1978) (North-East Quebec Agreement). In the regions covered by these agreements, statutory social services are organized and delivered independently (but in conformity with the Act) by a regional health and social services council over which an aboriginal nation has majority control.

The *Youth Protection Act* established the *Commission de la protection des droits de la jeunesse* (Youth Rights Protection Commission). The Commission, which reports directly to the *ministère de la Justice* (Ministry of Justice), is primarily a monitoring body with respect to children's rights. Section 41 of the Act specifies that the Director of Youth Protection must notify the Commission of each case of a child who is the victim of sexual or physical abuse.

Within the Ministry of Health and Social Services, a working group consisting of representatives from several divisions is responsible for the development of ministerial initiatives in the area of family violence. In addition, an interministerial committee on spousal and family violence has been mandated to develop a government strategy on spousal violence. The new policy should be released by December 1994.

Definitions

Under Sub-section 1(c) of the *Youth Protection Act*, a **child** is defined as a person under eighteen years of age. This definition conforms to the *Civil Code of Quebec* definition of the age of majority. Section 64 of the *Youth Protection Act* further states that a child in compulsory foster care may, by order of the Court, continue to receive care and services until age 21.

Sections 38 and 38.1 of the Act define when the security or development of a child is or may be considered to be in danger.

Section 38 states that "for the purposes of this Act, **the security or development of a child is considered to be in danger where:**

a) his parents are dead, no longer take care of him or seek to be rid of him;

b) his mental or affective development is threatened by the lack of appropriate care or by the isolation in which he is maintained or by serious and continuous emotional rejection by his parents;

c) his physical health is threatened by the lack of appropriate care;

d) he is deprived of the material conditions of life appropriate to his needs and to the resources of his parents or of the persons having custody of him;

e) he is in the custody of a person whose behaviour or way of life creates a risk of moral or physical danger for the child;

f) he is forced or induced to beg, to do work disproportionate to his capacity or to perform for the public in a manner that is unacceptable for his age;

g) he is the victim of sexual abuse or he is subject to physical ill-treatment through violence or neglect;

h) he has serious behavioural disturbances and his parents fail to take the measures necessary to remedy the situation or the remedial measures taken by them fail."

Section 38.1 states that "**the security or development of a child may be considered to be in danger where:**

a) he leaves his own home, a foster family, a reception centre or a hospital centre without authorization while his situation is not under the responsibility of the director of youth protection;

b) he is of school age and does not attend school, or is frequently absent without reason;

c) his parents do not carry out their obligations to provide him with care, maintenance and education or do not exercise stable supervision over him, while he has been entrusted to the care of an establishment or foster family for two years."

Unlike other jurisdictions, Quebec's child protection legislation does not include provisions concerning a child with special needs (i.e., physically or mentally handicapped). Such children receive services under the *Act Respecting Health Services and Social Services*. A child with special needs may be found to be in need of protection if he is in a situation where his security or development is or may be in danger as defined in Sections 38 and 38.1 of the Act.

Sexual abuse and physical ill-treatment are the result of an action or failure to act which leads to trauma or physical injury, or which involves exploitation of the child for sexual purposes. The following definitions are paraphrased from the «*Manuel de référence sur la Loi sur la protection de la jeunesse*» (Reference Manual on the Youth Protection Act) and elaborate on Sub-section 38(g) of the *Youth Protection Act*.

Sexual abuse means actions involving sexual stimulation or attempted sexual stimulation, which may or may not lead to injury or trauma. Some of these actions are defined in the *Criminal Code* and include incest, sexual contact, inducement to sexual contact, etc.

Physical ill-treatment includes any act committed in such a way as to provoke physical injury or trauma. These actions are unreasonable and excessive in nature and have serious consequences on the child's health, development or survival. They go beyond the limitations of parental corporal punishment as defined in Section 651 of the *Civil Code of Quebec*. Blows causing bodily harm and intoxication of the child through medication, drugs or alcoholic beverages are examples of excessive physical force.

The notion of negligence in Sub-section 38(g) of the *Youth Protection Act* refers to situations in which the parent or guardian does not take the necessary steps to prevent sexual or physical ill-treatment. An example would be where the child has been physically or sexually abused by other persons (strangers, relatives, daycare or school personnel etc.) and the parent does not take the necessary steps to protect him.

The legal definition of **neglect** corresponds to Sub-sections 38(b) to 38(f) of the *Youth Protection Act*. It is primarily any act of omission on the part of the parent in meeting the basic needs of a child or in sparing a child from suffering. Neglect also includes active and deliberate behaviour to deprive a child of care.

The *Youth Protection Act* recognizes the following children's rights: the right to adequate services taking into account the organization and resources of the establishments or bodies in the education field providing such services; the right to give or refuse consent; the right to be informed; the right to be heard and consulted; the right to consult and be represented by a lawyer; the right to communicate in all confidentiality; and the right to be kept in appropriate premises. Many of these rights are also recognized in the *Act Respecting Health Services and Social Services*. In addition, Section 39 of the *Quebec Charter of Human Rights and Freedoms* stipulates that all children are entitled to the protection, security and attention of their parents or other persons in a parental role.

Decisions made under the *Youth Protection Act* must be in the best interests of the child and respect the child's rights.

Mandatory Reporting where the Security or Development of a Child is or may be in Danger

Section 39 of the *Youth Protection Act* summarizes the mandatory reporting requirements for cases of children whose security or development is suspected or alleged to be in danger. Any person is required to report a situation where a child is being sexually abused or physically ill-treated [Sub-section 38(g)] to the Director of Youth Protection. Only professionals in the discharge of their duties are required to report all other situations where a child's security or development is or may be in danger [Sub-sections 38(a), (b), (c), (d), (e), (f) and (h) and Section 38.1]; other persons may report but are not obliged to. However, lawyers who, in the discharge of their duties, are aware of any situation as described in Section 38 or 38.1 are exempted from the requirement to report. Each Child and Youth Protection Centre operates a 24 hour emergency line for receiving reports. This obligation to report reinforces society's collective responsibility for child protection.

No recourse may be taken against any person making a report in good faith. As well, the identity of the informant may not be disclosed without his consent.

Section 134 of the Act states that any person who has reasonable grounds to believe that a child's security or development is or may be considered to be in danger, and who is required to do so but fails to advise the Director, is guilty of an offence and liable to a fine of $250 to $650.

Evaluation (Investigation of an Allegation of Child Abuse or Neglect)

The *Youth Protection Act* defines the following stages in situations where a child's security or development may be in danger: receipt and processing of a report, evaluation (i.e., investigation of the situation), directing the child (i.e, determining the most appropriate type of intervention [voluntary or court-ordered measures]) and review of the situation.

Before proceeding with an investigation, all reports are received and processed. This is a fairly rapid process, which consists of ensuring that the child is under the age of 18, checking whether the child's security or development may be in danger as defined in the Act, and verifying the credibility of the informant and the information provided. Generally, the decision on whether to investigate a report must be taken within three days of its receipt.

If the Director determines that the report should be investigated, he must also determine whether urgent measures are required. These apply in the most serious cases where the child's security appears to be in grave and immediate danger, and may involve removing the child from the home. Where possible, the child and parent should be consulted to obtain their consent. If the parent or child disagree with the decision, the Director may nonetheless apply urgent measures. When a child is removed from the home, the Director may authorize medical services or care without parental consent. Urgent measures only apply for 24 hours, but may be extended for up to five days with a Court order.

Once a report is accepted, the Director of Youth Protection must decide how quickly to respond to the allegation. Reports are ranked according to their apparent severity: where a child is considered to be at real and immediate risk (code 1) the response is immediate; where a child is considered to be at risk in the near future (code 2) the response must be within 24 hours; in all other situations the response must be within four working days. The Director must then determine whether the security or development of a child is in danger. This is done by assessing the child's situation and living conditions, focusing on the exact nature of the facts, their impact on the child, the parent's capacity to protect the child and the child's environment.

In any investigation of an abuse allegation, the Director must interview the child before the parent. At this time the Director may decide to impose urgent measures. In situations of alleged abuse in a school or health and social services establishment, the child is jointly interviewed by the Director and the police according to existing protocols (see section on Child Abuse and Neglect Protocols). In these situations, all parties involved (Director, police, school or establishment and Attorney General) meet within 24 hours of accepting the report to formulate a joint plan. During the evaluation stage, medical experts may be consulted to assist in substantiating or refuting the allegation. All relevant information is gathered from the child, the parent, the reporting party, and any other person able to contribute to establishing the facts. The Director's assessment must be completed within 11 working days of the initial receipt of the report.

The Ministry is involved in the investigation of allegations of intra-familial abuse and in situations where the alleged abuse occurred in a school or health and social services establishment. Allegations of extra-familial abuse are referred to the police for investigation; however, the Ministry may become involved if the child's parent is unwilling or unable to protect the child. In all situations, the Director's primary responsibility is to ensure the security of the child. Where the Ministry is involved in a child protection situation where there may be grounds for criminal prosecution, the Director is not required to notify the police. The Director may, however, request police assistance during the course of an investigation.

In all child protection situations, it is the exclusive responsibility of the Director and delegated staff to determine whether the security or development of a child is in danger. Where the investigation determines that a child's security or development is in danger, the Director takes charge of the situation, **not** of the child, and must "direct the child" to determine the most appropriate type of intervention. Under the *Youth Protection Act*, the primary responsibility for the child still rests with the parent. The decision on the most appropriate type of intervention for a child is the exclusive responsibility of the Director or delegated staff. Options include the use of voluntary measures (agreements) or the referral of the matter to the Court.

In some situations, the Director may have determined that the child's situation can be quickly remedied. The «*intervention terminale*» (immediate intervention), while not provided for in the *Youth Protection Act* or formal process, is generally used if there is a strong likelihood that a problem can be resolved by the young person himself or his family. This occurs in cases where there is little risk of danger or where the parent is experiencing temporary difficulties. This option is not generally used in cases of child abuse or neglect.

Although there are no guidelines specific to the investigation of alleged abuse of native children not covered under existing provincial agreements, it is common practice to consult the child's band.

The Ministry of Health and Social Services is not responsible for setting training standards for social workers involved in child protection, including child abuse and neglect cases. Workers' qualifications (e.g., university or college training) are determined by the individual establishments.

Voluntary Measures (Agreements)

Where the Director feels that voluntary measures will correct the situation, a meeting is scheduled with the parent and the child for the purpose of reaching an agreement on the most appropriate measure(s) to be taken. An agreement must include an acknowledgement of the situation which must be corrected and the measures which will be undertaken. Any of the following voluntary measures, which are stipulated in Section 54 of the *Youth Protection Act*, may be recommended:

"a) that the child remain in his family environment and that his parents present a report periodically on the measures they apply in their own or in the child's regard to correct a previous situation;

a.1) that the parents commit themselves to participating actively in applying the measures intended to correct the situation;

b) that certain persons refrain from coming into contact with the child;

b.1) that the child commit himself not to come into contact with certain persons;

c) that the child be entrusted to other persons;

d) that a person working for an establishment or body provide aid, counsel or assistance to the child and his family;

e) refer the child to a hospital centre, a local community service centre or to a body in order that he may receive the care and assistance he may need;

f) that the child or his parents report in person, at regular intervals, to the director and inform him on the progress of the situation;

g) that the child receive certain health services;

h) that the child be entrusted for a fixed period to a reception centre or foster family chosen by the social service centre;

i) (subparagraph repealed)

j) that the child follow a course of training but not at school."

Alternative measures other than those proposed by the Director may also be negotiated with the parent and child. With all agreements, the parent and child, if 14 years of age or older, must provide their consent and the terms of the agreement must be recorded in writing.

A child (if aged 14 or over) and parent must be informed of their right to refuse any proposed measures. If no agreement is reached within twenty days, the Director must attempt to come to an agreement on new measures or refer the matter to the Court for a decision.

In recommending the use of voluntary measures, the Director must, as far as possible, call upon persons or organizations in the child's natural environment. Where it is recommended that the child be entrusted to a reception centre or hospital centre, it must be specified whether or not foster care is required.

An agreement cannot exceed more than one year, although the Director may extend the term of voluntary foster care of a child in a foster family or reception centre for consecutive periods of not more than six months at a time. Where a child's security or development is still considered to be in danger when the agreement terminates, the Director must either renegotiate the agreement or refer the matter to the Court.

Court-Ordered Measures

A matter may be referred to the Youth Court if the parent or child (14 years or older) and Director are unable to negotiate a voluntary agreement, if the Director decides to refer the case directly to the Court, or if a voluntary agreement is withdrawn and the Director feels the child is still at risk.

The Court may impose any of the voluntary measures previously described. In addition, it may order a person to ensure that the child and parent comply with the conditions imposed upon them and report periodically to the Director; withdraw the exercise of certain rights of parental authority from the parent; recommend that measures be taken to have a guardian appointed for the child; or make any other recommendation it considers to be in the best interests of the child.

During the investigation or the hearing, the Youth Court may issue an Order of Provisional Compulsory Foster Care. This temporarily places the child with a foster family or in a reception centre if, after assessing the situation, the Court considers that leaving or returning the child to his parent's home or place of residence is likely to cause serious harm. Such a measure may not exceed 30 days, although there may be one extension of up to 30 additional days.

The Director of Youth Protection may request that the Superior Court issue a Permanent Guardianship Order. This results in the Director being appointed as the child's permanent guardian. This may occur where the child has been the subject of a decision or a Court order under the *Youth Protection Act* and there is no possibility of allowing the child to return to his parent without danger; or where the child is abandoned, ignored, orphaned; or where the parent does not fulfil his/her obligations of care, maintenance and education of the child while the child is in foster care under the terms of the Act.

A child entrusted to the guardianship of the Director or another person is completely in the charge and under the responsibility of the Director (or the other person) until the child is adopted or reaches the age of majority. A child who is in compulsory foster care may, by Court order, remain there until age 21. When the Superior Court declares the father and mother **totally** deprived of parental authority, the Director becomes guardian *ex officio* of the child if the child does not have a guardian appointed under the *Civil Code of Quebec*. When the Superior Court declares the father and mother **partially** deprived of parental authority, it may appoint the Director as guardian if the child does not have one appointed under the *Civil Code of Quebec*. The guardianship ceases *pleno jure* once the Director is advised of a judgment appointing a guardian for the child.

Child Abuse Register

The province of Quebec does not operate a child abuse register. Section 41 of the *Youth Protection Act* does, however, stipulate that the Director must report any cases of child abuse to the Youth Rights Protection Commission. The Commission functions primarily as a monitoring body with respect to children's rights.

Child Abuse and Neglect Protocols

Over the years, a number of protocols have been developed by the Ministry of Health and Social Services and its partners with a view to improving the approach to various aspects of child protection.

The «*Protocoles réception et traitement des signalements, évaluation et orientation*» (Protocols for Receipt and Processing of Reports, Evaluation and Directing the Child) were developed in 1988 subsequent to the Harvey report, which analyzed procedures relating to the receipt and processing of reports, evaluation and directing the child in child protection cases. Their purpose is to provide workers with guidelines in their interventions and ensure that the child can be tracked throughout the child protection process. Specifically, the protocols aim to set specific objectives and limitations for each step; to link the legal objectives, proposed clinical objectives and the activities involved; to provide clear and workable definitions of the basic concepts; and to separate the stages of evaluation and intervention, recognizing that they are distinct.

The «*Protocole relatif à l'application des mesures de protection de la jeunesse à l'intention de la personne autorisée*» (Protocol Concerning the Application of Youth Protection Measures for Authorized Personnel) is an extension of the Protocol for Receipt and Processing of Reports, Evaluation and Directing the Child. It acts as a link between the decision of appropriate intervention measures and their actual implementation. It focuses on how to connect the evaluation-intervention stage with the implementation stage, indicating who is involved and what activities are required within the implementation mandate.

The «*Protocole d'intervention intersectorielle dans les situations d'abus sexuels institutionnels*» (Multidisciplinary Intervention Protocol in Institutional Abuse Situations) was jointly developed by the ministries of Health and Social Services, Justice and the ministère de la Sécurité publique (Public Security). It is intended to clarify and harmonize the roles and responsibilities of the Director of Youth Protection, law enforcement officers and the representative of the Attorney General in situations of institutional sexual abuse.

The «*Entente relative à l'intervention intersectorielle à la suite d'allégations d'abus sexuels en milieu scolaire*» (Multidisciplinary Intervention Agreement on Responding to Allegations of Sexual Abuse in the School) was jointly developed by the ministries of Health and Social Services, Justice, Public Security and the ministère de l'Éducation (Education). This agreement outlines an integrated approach by all parties, stressing cooperation between the school, the school board, the Director of Youth Protection, the law enforcement agencies and the representative of the Attorney General. It applies in any situation where allegations of sexual abuse are made involving a school employee and a current or former pupil of that school.

The «*Protocole d'évaluation et d'intervention médico-sociale pour la protection des enfants maltraités*» (Medico-social Evaluation and Intervention Protocol for the Protection of Abused Children) was developed to improve cooperation between the medical and social communities concerning child abuse. It provides information and outlines the types of medical procedures which should be applied in a hospital or doctor's office, and the functional links to be established between hospital medical staff and social workers.

Statistics

The tables that follow have been developed from the «*Système d'information clientèle L.P.J.*» (Youth Protection Act Client Information System) of the Ministry of Health and Social Services. They either cover the period April 1, 1991 to March 31, 1992 or describe the situation as at March 31, 1992. These data cover activities relating to the protection of children and youth under the age of 18 whose security or development is in danger as defined in the *Youth Protection Act*.

The first three tables present the youth protection process – receipt and processing of a report, evaluation (i.e., investigation) and directing the child (i.e., protection measures undertaken). Data are also included on the number of child interventions under the *Youth Protection Act*. These represent the number of situations where a child's security or development is in danger as defined in the Act and where the Director of Youth Protection has taken charge of the situation. It should be noted that in the province of Quebec, the Director **does not assume responsibility for the child, but rather for the child's situation**. A child may receive services voluntarily or by court order, either in the family home or in an establishment licensed under the *Act Respecting Health Services and Social Services*. These data are much broader than the children in care data presented for other jurisdictions.

Data on natives are included in these tables.

Special needs children, who may receive services under child protection legislation in all other jurisdictions, are excluded from the following data. In Quebec, special needs children may be assisted under the provisions of the *Act Respecting Health Services and Social Services*.

Due to the limitations noted in Chapter 1, Introduction, these data should not be compared with data for other jurisdictions.

Table 6.1 Receipt and Processing of Reports[1], April 1, 1991 to March 31, 1992

	Number	Percentage
Reports accepted[2]	24,159	49.5
Reports rejected	24,619	50.5
Total	**48,778**	**100.0**

1. Represents the number of reports received of children whose security or development may be in danger as defined in the *Youth Protection Act*. There may be more than one report concerning a specific child.
2. To be accepted, a report must meet the following criteria: the child must be under 18 years of age; the situation reported must appear to correspond to the situations described in Section 38 or 38.1 of the *Youth Protection Act*; and the informant and the information reported must seem credible.

Table 6.2 Investigations[1] Carried Out by Nature of Decision, April 1, 1991 to March 31, 1992

Nature of Decision	Number	Percentage
Security or development at risk[2]	9,276	44.7
Security or development not at risk	10,021	48.3
File closed under the Act for other reasons	1,453	7.0
Total	**20,750**[1]	**100.0**

1. Does not correspond to the number of reports accepted (Table 6.1). Not all reports are investigated since (a) multiple reports may have been received concerning the same child; (b) an investigation may have already been conducted and a decision on the most appropriate type of intervention may be pending; or (c) the child may already be receiving services under the Act.
2. As defined in Section 38 or 38.1 of the *Youth Protection Act*.

Chapter 6 - Quebec

Table 6.3 Youth Protection Measures Undertaken by Type, April 1, 1991 to March 31, 1992

Measures	Number	Percentage
New voluntary agreements[1]	4,134	49.0
New Court orders[2]	2,653	31.4
Continuation of services[3]	466	5.5
Closure of file, after an «intervention terminale»[4]	661	7.8
Closure for other reasons[5]	527	6.2
Total	**8,441**	**100.0**

1. As described in the section on Voluntary Measures.
2. As described in the section on Court-Ordered Measures.
3. Continuation of services (with or without modifications to the existing case plan) under the *Youth Protection Act*, either voluntarily or by Court order.
4. «Intervention terminale» represents a short-term intervention by the Director of Youth Protection, on a voluntary basis.
5. Closure of the file for other reasons such as: court denial of request since it does not deem the child's security or development to be in danger as defined in the Act; inability to proceed; or transfer to another Child and Youth Protection Centre.

Table 6.4 Child Interventions[1] under the *Youth Protection Act* (via Court Order or Voluntary Measures) by Reason[2] as at March 31, 1992

Reason	Court Orders	Voluntary Measures	Total
Abandonment	1,054	436	1,490
Neglect	4,422	3,413	7,835
Physical ill-treatment	564	548	1,112
Sexual abuse	828	593	1,421
Behavioural problems	2,149	2,201	4,350
Total	**9,017**	**7,191**	**16,208**
Percentage	**55.6**	**44.4**	**100.0**

1. Where a child's security or development is in danger as defined in the *Youth Protection Act*, the Director of Youth Protection takes charge of the child's situation, **not** of the child. The Act stipulates that the child's parent has responsibility for the child.
2. Reasons correspond to those defined in Sections 38 and 38.1 of the Act.

Figure 6.1   Child Interventions[1] Under the *Youth Protection Act* by Reason[2] as at March 31, 1992

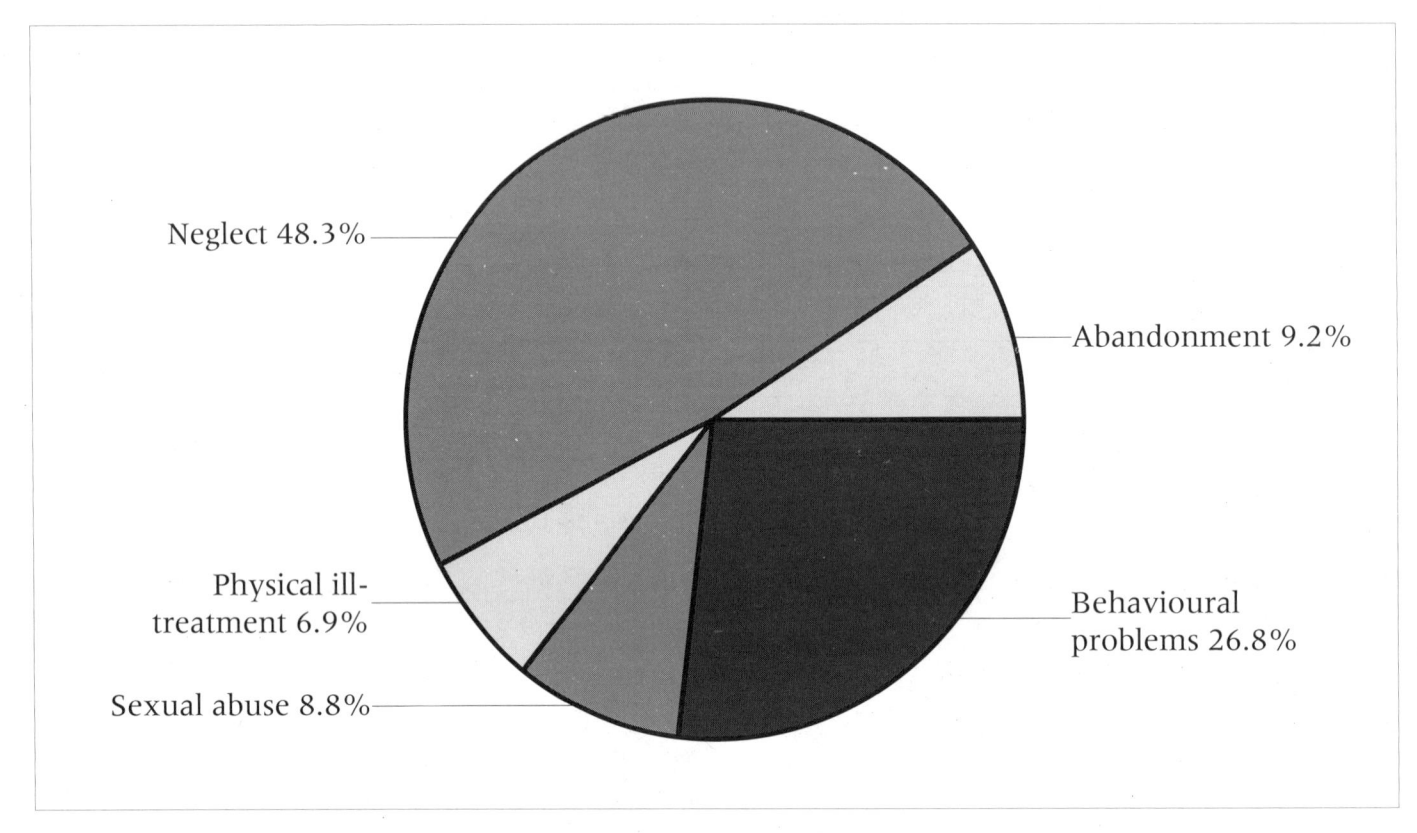

Neglect 48.3%

Abandonment 9.2%

Behavioural problems 26.8%

Sexual abuse 8.8%

Physical ill-treatment 6.9%

Total number of child interventions under the *Youth Protection Act* : 16 208

1. Where a child's security or development is in danger as defined in the *Youth Protection Act*, the Director of Youth Protection takes charge of the child's situation, **not** of the child. The Act stipulates that the child's parent has responsibility for the child.
2. Reasons correspond to those defined in Sections 38 and 38.1 of the Act.

Table 6.5 Child Interventions[1] under the *Youth Protection Act* by Type of Placement Resource as at March 31, 1992

Placement Resource	Number	Percentage
Intermediate[2]	5,703	35.2
Institutional[3]	2,621	16.2
Natural environment[4]	7,884	48.6
Total	**16,208**	**100.0**

1. Where a child's security or development is in danger as defined in the *Youth Protection Act*, the Director of Youth Protection takes charge of the child's situation, **not** of the child. The Act stipulates that the child's parent has responsibility for the child.
2. This refers to any substitute living arrangement falling under the jurisdiction of a Child and Youth Protection Centre, ranging from a foster family, a family type resource for a child referred by the Centre, or other intermediary resource.
3. A rehabilitation centre, for example.
4. Generally, the child's home.

Reference Material

Legislative Material

Gouvernement du Québec. *Loi sur la protection de la jeunesse/Youth Protection Act*, L.R.Q., chapitre P-34.1.

Reports

Québec, ministère de la Santé et des Services sociaux. *Rapport sur l'analyse des activités de réception et de traitement des signalements, et d'évaluation et d'orientation en protection de la jeunesse*, Annexes, 1988.

_____. *La protection sur mesure, un projet collectif*, 1991.

Québec, ministère de la Justice et ministère de la Santé et des Services sociaux. *La protection de la jeunesse... plus qu'une loi*, 1992.

Other Material

Québec, ministère de la Santé et des Services sociaux. *Manuel de référence sur la protection de la jeunesse/ Reference Manual on the Youth Protection Act*, 1989.

_____. *Protocole d'évaluation et d'intervention médico-sociale pour la protection des enfants maltraités*, 1988.

_____. *Protocoles réception et traitement des signalements, évaluation et orientation*, 1988.

_____. *Protocole relatif à l'application des mesures de protection de la jeunesse à l'intention de la personne autorisée*, 1991.

Québec, ministère de la Justice, ministère de la Santé et des Services sociaux et ministère de la Sécurité publique. *Protocole d'intervention intersectorielle dans les situations d'abus sexuels institutionnels*, 1989.

Québec, ministère de l'Éducation, ministère de la Justice, ministère de la Santé et des Services sociaux et ministère de la Sécurité publique. *Entente relative à l'intervention intersectorielle à la suite d'allégations d'abus sexuels en milieu scolaire*, 1992.

Chapter 7 – Ontario

Administration and Service Delivery

The *Child and Family Services Act* mandates that the Ministry of Community and Social Services (MCSS) is responsible for the provision of child and family services in Ontario. This responsibility is carried out by the province's 54 Children's Aid Societies (CAS's) and a wide range of private profit and non-profit groups and organizations.

The Children's Services Branch of the Ministry in Toronto develops policies and programs for children, including those designed to protect children from physical/sexual/emotional abuse, and neglect; those for children with a mental or psychiatric disorder; and those for children with a social, emotional and/or behavioural problem. Administration of programs for children (among other programs) is the responsibility of the Operations Division, which has its head office in Toronto but is decentralized into four regional offices and 13 area offices. The managers of the Ministry's area offices act as Directors under the *Child and Family Services Act* to advise, supervise and monitor the Children's Aid Societies.

The delivery of mandated child welfare services, including investigation, protection and adoption, is provided by the 54 autonomous Children's Aid Societies which are located throughout the province. Each Children's Aid Society is responsible to a community Board of Directors, which is the CAS's primary governing body. In addition, CAS's are monitoried by the Ministry's area offices.

Currently, three Indian Child and Family Service Agencies (ICFSA's) are designated as Children's Aid Societies and deliver mandated child welfare services to natives on and off reserve in the territory of each of the three. Several additional Indian agencies are working towards designation as CAS's. In areas where there is no designated ICFSA, one of the other 51 local CAS's provides services to natives. Other Indian Child and Family Service Agencies may provide any of a range of family, mental health or young offender services, but not child welfare services. When any of these ICFSA's provide service in the same geographic area as a CAS, the two organizations are to develop a joint understanding of their respective roles and responsibilities with respect to native clients.

The Ontario Association of Children's Aid Societies (OACAS) in Toronto is a service and advocacy organization for member Children's Aid Societies. OACAS provides support to CAS's through consultation services, training programs and information services; promotes public awareness of child welfare programs; and collects service data from the CAS's. The Association also liaises with the Ministry of Community and Social Services and other organizations on behalf of the CAS's on many issues related to the interests and needs of vulnerable children and their families.

The Office of Child and Family Service Advocacy in the Ministry of Community and Social Services is mandated by the *Child and Family Services Act* to act on behalf of children and families receiving services from the Ministry when normal complaint procedures are not effective. The Office also advises the Minister on matters concerning those children and families.

The Interministerial Committee on Services for Children and Youth includes representatives from the Ministry of Community and Social Services. Its mandate is to achieve more effective and efficient services for children, youth and their families by coordinating policies and programs across ministries.

Definitions

Section 3 of the *Child and Family Services Act* defines a **child** for both child protection and adoption purposes as a person under 18 years of age. Under Sub-section 37(1), child protection services, including the mandatory investigation of a report of child abuse or neglect, are to be provided to a child under the age of 16. Care by a Children's Aid Society can be extended to age 18 for a child who is the subject of a court order for protection when the child turns 16. Section 32 specifies that services may be provided by agreement to a youth until the youth reaches age 18. Care and maintenance may be provided to a Crown (permanent) ward after the age of 18, under Sub-section 71(2).

Under Sub-section 37(2), a child is **in need of protection** where:

"(a) the child has suffered physical harm, inflicted by the person having charge of the child or caused by that person's failure to care and provide for or supervise and protect the child adequately;

(b) there is substantial risk that the child will suffer physical harm inflicted or caused as described in clause (a);

(c) the child has been sexually molested or sexually exploited, by the person having charge of the child or by another person where the person having charge of the child knows or should know of the possibility of sexual molestation or sexual exploitation and fails to protect the child;

(d) there is a substantial risk that the child will be sexually molested or sexually exploited as described in clause (c);

(e) the child requires medical treatment to cure, prevent or alleviate physical harm or suffering and the child's parent or the person having charge of the child does not provide, or refuses or is unavailable or unable to consent to, the treatment;

(f) the child has suffered emotional harm, demonstrated by severe,

(i) anxiety,

(ii) depression,

(iii) withdrawal, or

(iv) self-destructive or aggressive behaviour,

and the child's parent or the person having charge of the child does not provide, or refuses or is unavailable or unable to consent to, services or treatment to remedy or alleviate the harm;

(g) there is substantial risk that the child will suffer emotional harm of the kind described in clause (f), and the child's parent or the person having charge of the child does not provide, or refuses or is unavailable or unable to consent to, services or treatment to prevent the harm;

(h) the child suffers from a mental, emotional or developmental condition that, if not remedied, could seriously impair the child's development and the child's parent or the person having charge of the child does not provide, or refuses or is unavailable or unable to consent to, treatment to remedy or alleviate the condition;

(i) the child has been abandoned, the child's parent has died or is unavailable to exercise his or her custodial rights over the child and has not made adequate provision for the child's care and custody, or the child is in a residential placement and the parent refuses or is unable or unwilling to resume the child's care and custody;

(j) the child is less than twelve years old and has killed or seriously injured another person or caused serious damage to another person's property, services or treatment are necessary to prevent a recurrence and the child's parent or the person having charge of the child does not provide, or refuses or is unavailable or unable to consent to, those services or treatment;

(k) the child is less than twelve years old and has on more than one occasion injured another person or caused loss or damage to another person's property, with the encouragement of the person having charge of the child or because of that person's failure or inability to supervise the child adequately; or

(l) the child's parent is unable to care for the child and the child is brought before the court with the parent's consent and, where the child is twelve years of age or older, with the child's consent, to be dealt with under this Part."

A child who suffers abuse is defined as being in need of protection within the meaning of clauses (a),(c),(e),(f) or (h) of the definition of a child in need of protection.

Part V of the *Child and Family Services Act* specifies the rights of children in care under the Act. These include, among others, the right to be protected from corporal punishment, to be informed regarding a placement, to have access to counsel, to have appropriate educational opportunities, to have a plan of care, to participate in significant decisions which affect them, and to be informed about review/complaint procedures.

Mandatory Reporting of a Child in Need of Protection

Section 72 of the *Child and Family Services Act* stipulates that anyone who has reasonable grounds to believe that a child may be in need of protection must report the situation to a Children's Aid Society. This is a requirement even if the person informs another agency such as the police or a school. The failure of a professional who performs professional or official duties with respect to a child to report a suspicion that a child has suffered, or may be suffering, abuse is an offence under the Act. Under Sub-section 85(1), on conviction, the professional may be liable to a fine of not more than $1,000 and/or one year in prison. Only information exchanged under solicitor – client privilege is exempt from this provision. No action may be taken against a person who makes a report unless it is made maliciously or without reasonable grounds.

Investigation of an Allegation of Child Abuse or Neglect

Provincial standards regarding investigations of allegations of child abuse are outlined in *Revised Standards for the Investigation and Management of Child Abuse Cases by the Children's Aid Societies under The Child and Family Services Act* (see section on Child Abuse and Neglect Protocols). All allegations of the abuse of a child under the age of 16 must be investigated by a child protection worker within 24 hours. Abuse of a 16 or 17 year old who is not in the care of a CAS, or a report of previous abuse of a youth over 16, is referred to the police. The police also are to be informed of any cases that may involve a *Criminal Code* offence (sexual abuse, serious physical abuse or serious neglect). The police are to refer to a CAS any case involving a child under the age of 16 who may be in need of protection. An initial screening by a child protection worker is carried out to determine if the child is in need of protection or in danger of becoming in need of protection; to clarify the urgency of the situation; and to determine whether or not the services of the CAS will be appropriate. This screening should include contact with the provincial Child Abuse Register to determine if the alleged offender has been previously registered.

A CAS must carry out a full investigation of alleged cases of abuse or neglect by a person in charge of a child. This includes cases of failure to provide help to a child or to protect a child. A person in charge of a child generally means a parent, a guardian, or someone else in a caregiver role, such as a babysitter, day care worker or teacher. It could include a neighbour, if a child is visiting to play with a friend. Any report of abuse or neglect by someone not in charge of a child is to be reported to the police for a criminal investigation. The CAS may remain involved to provide services if there are children in the alleged offender's family in order to ensure they are not at risk.

The investigation of a case is to be carried out in a manner that is sensitive to the child's special needs or cultural identity. In any case involving both the police and a Children's Aid Society, joint interviewing by a police officer and a CAS worker is recommended. Police or CAS videotaping facilities are to be used if possible. The investigation is to include a medical examination within 24 hours of seeing the child if the alleged abuse indicates the possibility of injury, the need for medical care or the need for medical documentation. It is preferable that the child's parent accompany the child and worker or provide written consent. If neither option is available, the child may be apprehended in order that the examination may proceed. When the investigation is complete and the case is being assessed, the local child abuse review team or other professionals may be consulted.

Several Children's Aid Societies are using some form of a risk management index to assist workers in evaluating cases of abuse and neglect. Some of these risk management tools are used at intake, some at other stages of the investigation or case planning processes. The Brant and Simcoe Children's Aid Societies are each using their own modified version of the Child Well-Being Scale developed for the Child Welfare League of America. The Ottawa-Carleton and Cornwall Children's Aid Societies are involved in the pilot project with Manitoba to test the Manitoba Risk Estimation System.

When a child's safety may be in jeopardy if the child is left at home and the worker, in consultation with the supervisor, concludes as a result of an investigation that the child is in need of protection, the child may be apprehended if it is not possible to bring the child into care voluntarily. The child may be apprehended by a child protection worker or a police officer. Although a warrant from a justice of the peace is usually required for an apprehension, if waiting for a warrant would create a substantial risk to the health or safety of the child, the apprehension may be carried out without one. A worker may request the assistance of a police officer in apprehending a child.

If, at the conclusion of the investigation, the abuse has been verified, a report is to be made to the Child Abuse Register.

When a child protection case comes to court, it is mandatory under the *Child and Family Services Act* that a representative of the child's Band or native community is a party to the proceedings. The Band or designated native community representative is to receive a copy of any assessment report with respect to the child before the report goes to court.

Under the *Child and Family Services Act*, every Children's Aid Society must establish a child abuse review team which must include one medical doctor plus other professionals qualified to provide medical, psychological, developmental, educational, or social assessments. The teams are mandated to review any cases of child abuse referred to them by a CAS and to make recommendations concerning the cases. Prior to closing an abuse case and returning a child to the parent, the CAS must refer the case to the local team for review if the case is not being brought back to court. The CAS also may refer any other abuse case for which another opinion would be useful. Recommendations of the team could include whether or not the team feels the abuse has been verified and how the child may best be protected (for example, under a voluntary agreement or court order).

To assist staff in dealing with their cases, specialized training is offered locally to child protection workers and supervisors by the Institute for the Prevention of Child Abuse (IPCA) in Toronto. Programs are available in child protection, child sexual abuse, and supervision. IPCA also provides training programs for native child protection workers and for child abuse review teams.

Voluntary Agreements

The *Child and Family Services Act* specifies that the least intrusive appropriate intervention should be used to support families and protect children. Voluntary provision of support services to a family in its own home may be used in cases of child abuse or neglect where the safety of the child can be assured. In some of these situations, a formal contract outlining responsibilities of the family and the CAS is signed by both parties.

Where it is necessary for the child to be removed from the home, there are two formal agreements specified in the *Child and Family Services Act* which may be used to allow the child to receive the services of a CAS voluntarily – a Temporary Care Agreement and a Special Needs Agreement. The parent retains guardianship under an agreement. These formal voluntary agreements end automatically when the child reaches age 18, if the term is not completed prior to that date.

A Temporary Care Agreement allows for the temporary transfer of custody of a child to a Children's Aid Society with the agreement of the parent and consent of a child over 12 years of age (except where the child does not have the capacity to consent because of a developmental handicap). Such an agreement may be used in certain cases of child abuse or neglect if the worker feels that a voluntary option is feasible. The initial agreement must be signed before the child's 16th birthday and may have a term of up to six months; it may be extended for up to a total term of 12 months.

A Special Needs Agreement is used when the special needs of a child are such that the parent is unable to provide the services required. The agreement may include services in the home or care and custody of the child by a Children's Aid Society or the Minister of Community and Social Services (services provided directly by the Ministry area office). A Special Needs Agreement is not normally used in the case of abuse or neglect.

Sixteen and seventeen year olds who require residential and/or other services of a CAS or other agency may also enter into a Special Needs Agreement with a CAS or the Minister. The youth may have been abused and left the home for self-protection, may have been abandoned or the parent may have refused to provide support. The agreement may have an initial term of up to one year, with a possible extension of up to another year.

Court-Ordered Protection

When a child has been apprehended, or voluntary arrangements to support the family have not been successful in protecting the child, an application is made for a protection hearing in Unified Family Court or Provincial Court (Family Division). If, as a result of the hearing, the judge decides that the child is in need of protection, one of several orders may be made. These orders must all be made before the child turns 16.

Under a Supervision Order, the child remains with or is returned to, the parent or a relative, neighbour or other member of the child's community under the supervision of a Children's Aid Society. The duration of the order is from three to 12 months. Indefinite extensions are possible. A Society Wardship Order places a child in the care and custody of a CAS for up to 12 months. The parent gives up guardianship to a Children's Aid Society for the term of the order. The term may be extended as long as the total period of time in temporary care, by order and/or agreement, does not exceed 24 months. A combination of a Society Wardship Order for a specified period, followed by a Supervision Order, may also be made but must not exceed a total term of 12 months. A child may be made a permanent ward of the Crown under a Crown Wardship Order when circumstances justifying the order are unlikely to change within 24 months. A Crown Wardship Order permanently transfers care, custody and control of the child to the Crown. Society and Crown wardship end automatically when the child reaches age 18 or marries. In some circumstances, care and maintenance services for former Crown wards may be extended to age 21 while the child completes his/her education or requires services because of special needs.

Although rarely used, if an alleged offender will not leave the home voluntarily, a restraining order prohibiting a person's access to, or contact with, a child may be made under the *Child and Family Services Act* instead of, or in addition to, one of the above orders. The CAS may not return the child to the person named in the order or to someone who may allow the person access to the child. The initial order must not exceed six months; an extension may be made by the court for an additional period or periods of six months.

Child Abuse Register

Purpose

Under Sub-section 75(5) of the *Child and Family Services Act*, the Ministry of Community and Social Services must maintain a child abuse register. For the purposes of the Register, abuse is defined to be physical, sexual, and emotional abuse and failure to provide for a child or to protect a child in abuse situations. These are covered by clauses (a),(c),(e),(f) and (h) of Sub-section 37(2) of the Act (defines a child in need of protection).

Information in the Register is used for monitoring and tracking cases (for example, checking for previous abuse) and for research. The Register is not used to screen employees or volunteers who may work with children. There is pressure, however, from schools, child care agencies and others for such a screening mechanism. An interministerial committee on screening mechanisms is currently reviewing the Register as well as other options with respect to their utility in screening employees and volunteers.

Basis for Entering Names
Workers at the Children's Aid Societies are legally required to report to the Register every case of verified child abuse by a person in charge of a child. The worker verifies the abuse in consultation with the supervisor on the basis of credible evidence which includes information such as that obtained through interviewing the victim and others, and reviewing medical and police reports. The report is to be made within 14 days of the verification and includes information concerning the victim and alleged abuser.

The Register includes the names of the child victim and the alleged abuser, certain demographic data regarding the victim and alleged abuser, information concerning the abuse incident and action taken on behalf of the child.

Rights of the Registered Person
An alleged abuser whose name is entered on the Register is informed of this and the right to inspect the information regarding himself/herself on the Register. The person may then apply to the Director of the Register to have the name removed. The request may be granted or an expunction hearing may be held on ten days notice to all parties, to determine whether to grant or refuse the request. It is the CAS's task at the hearing to support the report of abuse; audio or videotapes of the child's statements may be used to do this. The alleged abuser does not have to prove innocence. If the hearing officer determines, on the balance of probabilities, that the request is legitimate, the registrant's name will be removed from the Register and/or other necessary amendments made. The decision may be appealed to the Divisional Court.

Unless a name is removed, it remains on the Register for 25 years. The child victim's name remains on the Register for 25 years.

It should be noted that because federal criminal law and provincial child and family law operate on different premises and require different standards of proof (the Register being less strict), a person may be acquitted in criminal court but still legally be registered on the Child Abuse Register.

Access to Register Information
Generally, information in the Register is confidential. Identifying information concerning a specific child or registered person may be disclosed only to the following persons in the execution of their duties:

(a) a coroner, medical doctor, or police officer carrying out an investigation or inquest;

(b) the Official Guardian of the Province of Ontario;

(c) an employee of the Ministry of Community and Social Services, a Children's Aid Society, or a recognized child protection agency outside Ontario;

(d) a person providing counselling services to a registered person;

(e) a medical doctor with written approval of the Director of the Register; or

(f) a child or registered person regarding information pertaining to himself or herself.

Non-identifying information may be disclosed to researchers.

Limitations of the Child Abuse Register
Although legally required to report verified cases of child abuse to the Register, not all Children's Aid Societies do. For those that do, the level of substantiation of reports varies (from verified on the basis of credible evidence to court convictions) and the

definition of a person in charge of a child varies (from parents only to including others such as teachers). As a result of such inconsistencies in reporting, the Register data are not complete.

Child Abuse and Neglect Protocols

The *Revised Standards for the Investigation and Management of Child Abuse Cases by the Children's Aid Societies Under The Child and Family Services Act* were revised jointly in 1992 by the Ministry of Community and Social Services, the Ontario Association of Children's Aid Societies, and the Institute for the Prevention of Child Abuse. The standards are to come into force on January 1, 1993. A self-instruction training package on application of the standards was developed by OACAS and IPCA and is available to all child protection staff; a coach within each Children's Aid Society provides additional support to staff in the use of the standards. A self-monitoring compliance mechanism has been developed by the Ministry and OACAS.

These provincial standards establish the minimum level of performance required to provide service and are mandatory for all Children's Aid Societies. The standards include the legislated meaning of to suffer abuse, a definition of an alleged abuser, standards with respect to the investigation of a report of child abuse plus standards related to the management of cases. They are to be used with respect to all reports of abuse of children under the age of 16, including alleged abuse of those in the care of a CAS.

The provincial standards establish that primary responsibility for the protection of children is with the Children's Aid Society and primary responsibility for the enforcement of the law and the prosecution of offences is with the police. They specify that each Children's Aid Society must have a protocol with all local police forces which includes mutual sharing of information regarding reports of suspected child abuse and the course of each investigation. The protocol(s) must ensure that the police are involved in all investigations where there is a potential *Criminal Code* offence. Any protocol developed before the standards become effective must be reviewed and updated if necessary. An example of a protocol is the "Child Abuse Protocol – An Investigative Procedure to Coordinate Response in the Regional Municipality of Ottawa-Carleton" which was developed by the Ottawa-Carleton Police/CAS Liaison Subcommittee on the Child Abuse Protocol. Committee members included personnel from the CAS of Ottawa-Carleton, police, staff of several boards of education, and staff from the Children's Hospital of Eastern Ontario.

Protocols and guidelines have also been written by other organizations interested in the welfare of children. The Institute for the Prevention of Child Abuse has developed a special paper, "Preferred Practices for Investigating Allegations of Child Abuse in Residential Care Settings", which is used as a guide by many Children's Aid Societies. The Institute also has produced a general reference, "General Guidelines to Assist in the Identification of Child Maltreatment" which includes indicators of abuse and neglect.

Other examples include the "Child Sexual Abuse Protocol" which was developed by the Metropolitan Toronto Special Committee on Child Abuse and is used by several Children's Aid Societies. Protocols covering the identification and reporting of child abuse cases have been developed by professional groups and institutions including the Ontario Teachers' Federation, specific hospitals and school boards as well as some volunteer organizations.

Statistics

The data in the following tables were provided by the Ontario Association of Children's Aid Societies. They are based on the Association's semi-annual survey of all Children's Aid Societies and represent data from the majority of the 54 Children's Aid Societies for the period January 1, 1991 to December 31, 1991 (allegations only) or as at December 31, 1991. The number of CAS's reporting data for each table is identified in a footnote to the table. Data are not included from the three Indian Child and Family Service Agencies which are designated as Children's Aid Societies. Data from the Child Abuse Register are not presented because of the limitations previously outlined.

Except for the number of allegations, the data represent the number of children in need of protection under the *Child and Family Services Act* and in care under the following legal statuses: Temporary Care Agreement, Special Needs Agreement (special needs children and 16 and 17 year old youth), Temporary Care and Custody (apprehensions and during adjournments in child protection hearings), Society Ward (temporary), Crown Ward (permanent), Extended Care and Maintenance (to age 21 for former Crown wards while completing education or requiring services because of special needs), and Adoption Consent (voluntary surrender of a child for adoption).

Not all children deemed to be in need of protection are taken into care. Many receive services in the home of a parent or other adult either voluntarily or under a Supervision Order. These children are not included in the data provided in this section.

Due to the limitations noted in Chapter 1, Introduction, these data should not be compared with data for other jurisdictions.

Table 7.1 Allegations[1] by Type, January 1, 1991 to December 31, 1991

Type	Number	Percentage
Child Abuse		
Physical	9,449	50.1
Sexual	8,216	43.5
Emotional	497	2.6
Sub-Total	**18,162**	**96.3**
Other	705	3.7
Total	**18,867**	**100.0**

1. Number of allegations refers to those which required an investigation, whether or not they were open or new cases and whether or not they were confirmed. Represents data from 50 Children's Aid Societies (CAS's). Does not include data from the three Indian Child and Family Service Agencies designated as CAS's or the one CAS which did not provide a breakdown of allegations by type.

Table 7.2 Children in Care[1] by Legal Status as at December 31, 1991

Legal Status	Number	Percentage
Temporary Care Agreement	1,530	15.2
Special Needs Agreement[2]	385	3.8
Temporary Care and Custody[3]	1,290	12.8
Society Ward (temporary)	1,880	18.7
Crown Ward (permanent)	4,131	41.1
Extended Care and Maintenance[4]	715	7.1
Adoption Consent[5]	107	1.1
Not coded	2	--
Total	**10,040**	**100.0**

1. Children in the care of 51 Children's Aid Societies (CAS's). Does not include children in the care of three Indian Child and Family Service Agencies designated as CAS's. Data represent the number of children in need of protection under the *Child and Family Services Act* and in care under the legal statuses shown.
2. Special needs children and 16 and 17 year old youth.
3. Apprehensions and during adjournments in child protection hearings.
4. Extension of care and maintenance for former Crown wards to age 21 while completing education or requiring services because of special needs.
5. Voluntary surrender of a child for adoption.

Chapter 7 - Ontario

Figure 7.1 Children in Care[1] by Legal Status as at December 31, 1991

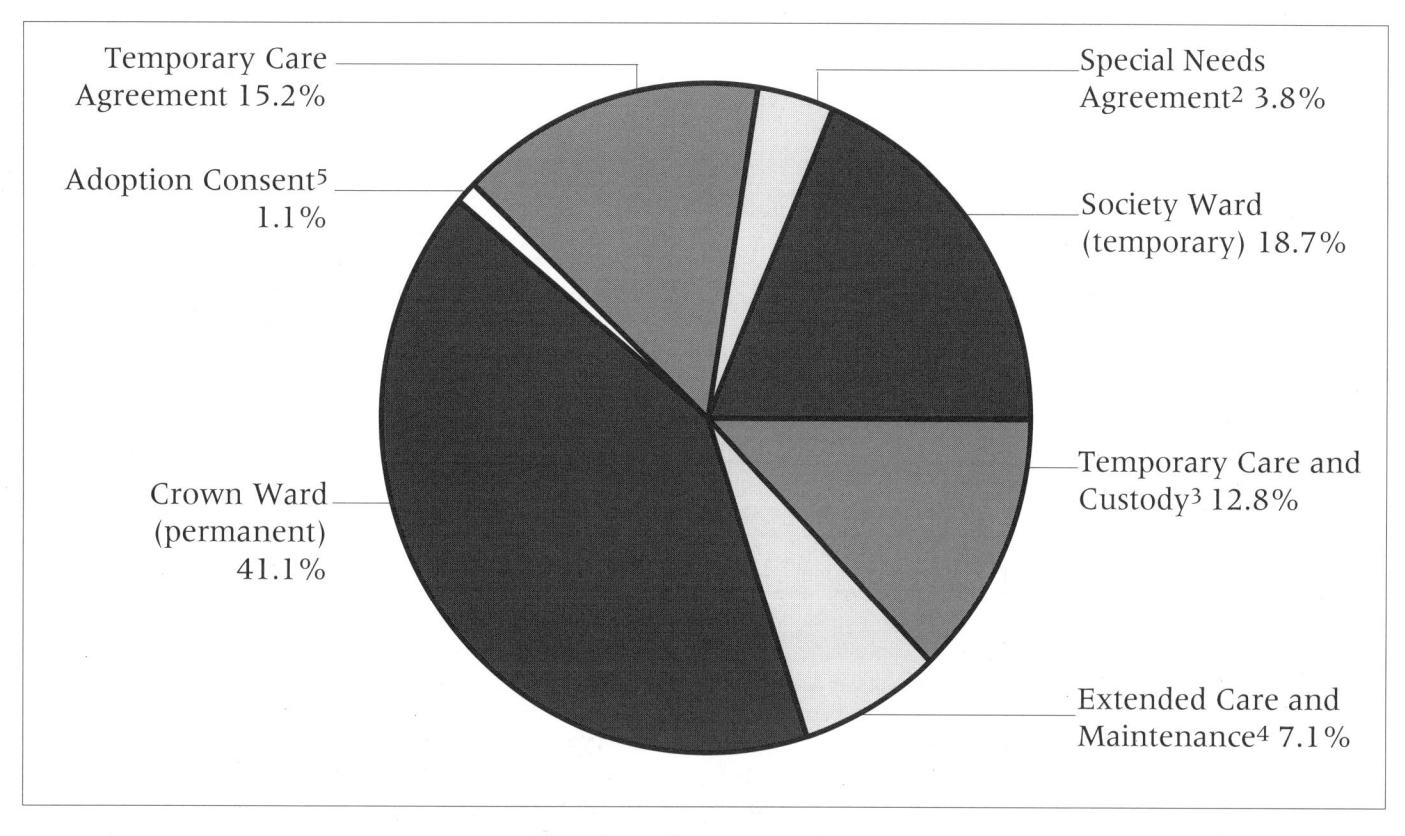

- Temporary Care Agreement 15.2%
- Adoption Consent[5] 1.1%
- Crown Ward (permanent) 41.1%
- Special Needs Agreement[2] 3.8%
- Society Ward (temporary) 18.7%
- Temporary Care and Custody[3] 12.8%
- Extended Care and Maintenance[4] 7.1%

Children in care: 10,040

1. Children in the care of 51 Children's Aid Societies (CAS's). Does not include children in the care of three Indian Child and Family Service Agencies designated as CAS's. Data represent the number of children in need of protection under the *Child and Family Services Act* and in care under the legal statuses shown.
2. Special needs children and 16 and 17 year old youth.
3. Apprehensions and during adjournments in child protection hearings.
4. Extension of care and maintenance for former Crown wards to age 21 while completing education or requiring services because of special needs.
5. Voluntary surrender of a child for adoption.

Table 7.3 Children in Care[1] by Placement Type and Age Group as at December 31, 1991

Placement Type	0-5 years	6-12 years	13-17 years	18-21 years	Total
Foster care	1,369	1,875	2,056	158	5,458
Group care	23	232	820	59	1,134
Institutional care	14	125	275	28	442
No cost group/institutions[2]	3	53	286	28	370
Adoption probation	370	112	13	1	496
Independent living	1	3	339	504	847
Elsewhere[3]	113	132	443	62	750
Total	**1,893**	**2,532**	**4,232**	**840**	**9,497**[1]
Percentage	**19.9**	**26.7**	**44.6**	**8.8**	**100.0**

1. Children in the care of 47 Children's Aid Societies (CAS's). Does not include children in the care of three Indian Child and Family Service Agencies designated as CAS's or four other CAS's unable to provide age breakdowns. Data represent the number of children in need of protection under the *Child and Family Services Act* and in care under the following legal statuses: Temporary Care Agreement, Special Needs Agreement (special needs children and 16 and 17 year old youth), Temporary Care and Custody (apprehensions and during adjournments in child protection hearings), Society Ward (temporary), Crown Ward (permanent), Extended Care and Maintenance (to age 21 for former Crown wards while completing education or requiring services because of special needs), and Adoption Consent (voluntary surrender of a child for adoption).
2. The CAS does not have to pay for the use of the residential facility.
3. Any other placement.

Chapter 7 - Ontario

Figure 7.2 Children in Care[1] by Placement Type as at December 31, 1991

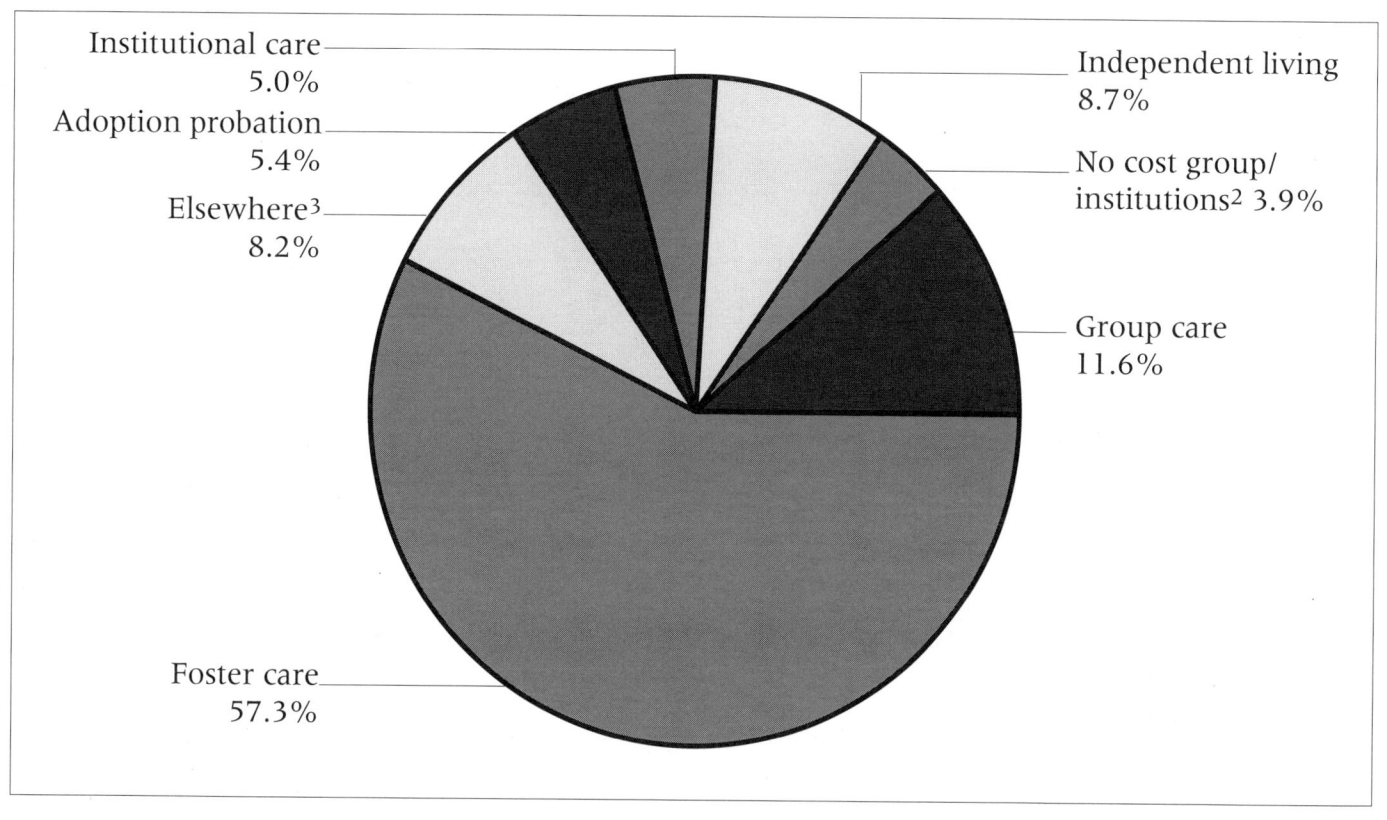

- Institutional care 5.0%
- Adoption probation 5.4%
- Elsewhere[3] 8.2%
- Foster care 57.3%
- Independent living 8.7%
- No cost group/institutions[2] 3.9%
- Group care 11.6%

Children in care: 10,040

1. Children in the care of 51 Children's Aid Societies (CAS's). Does not include children in the care of three Indian Child and Family Service Agencies designated as CAS's. Data represent the number of children in need of protection under the *Child and Family Services Act* and in care under the following legal statuses: Temporary Care Agreement, Special Needs Agreement (special needs children and 16 and 17 year old youth), Temporary Care and Custody (apprehensions and during adjournments in child protection hearings), Society Ward (temporary), Crown Ward (permanent), Extended Care and Maintenance (to age 21 for former Crown wards while completing education or requiring services because of special needs), and Adoption Consent (voluntary surrender of a child for adoption).
2. The CAS does not have to pay for the use of the residential facility.
3. Any other placement.

Figure 7.3   Children in Care[1] by Age Group as at December 31, 1991

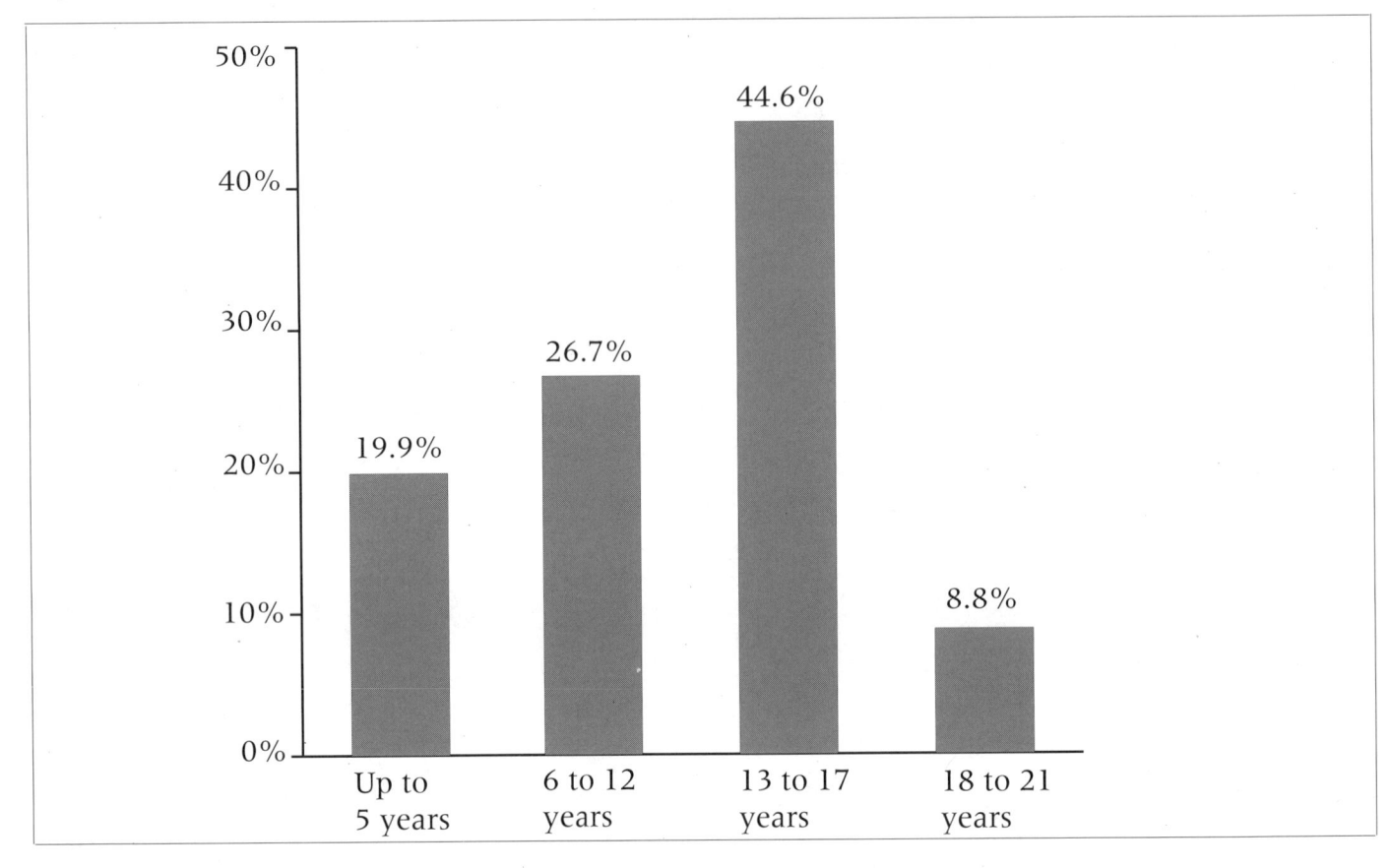

Age Group	Percentage
Up to 5 years	19.9%
6 to 12 years	26.7%
13 to 17 years	44.6%
18 to 21 years	8.8%

Children in care: 9,497[1]

1. Children in the care of 47 Children's Aid Societies (CAS's). Does not include children in the care of three Indian Child and Family Service Agencies designated as CAS's or four other CAS's unable to provide age breakdowns. Data represent the number of children in need of protection under the *Child and Family Services Act* and in care under the following legal statuses: Temporary Care Agreement, Special Needs Agreement (special needs children and 16 and 17 year old youth), Temporary Care and Custody (apprehensions and during adjournments in child protection hearings), Society Ward (temporary), Crown Ward (permanent), Extended Care and Maintenance (to age 21 for former Crown wards while completing education or requiring services because of special needs), and Adoption Consent (voluntary surrender of a child for adoption).

Resource Material

Legislative Material

Child and Family Services Act, Revised Statutes of Ontario 1990, c. C.11.

Reports

Bala, N.C. *Review of the Ontario Child Abuse Register*. Queen's University, Kingston, Ontario, September 1987.

Children First: Report of the Advisory Committee on Children's Services. Report to the Minister of Community and Social Services, November 1990.

Other Material (examples only)

Metropolitan Toronto Special Committee on Child Abuse. "Child Sexual Abuse Protocol", Toronto.

Ontario, Ministry of Community and Social Services. *Revised Standards for the Investigation and Management of Child Abuse Cases by the Children's Aid Societies Under The Child and Family Services Act*, 1992.

_____. "Children in Care Manual", Toronto, 1985.

_____. "Family Services Manual", Toronto, 1985.

_____. "Guidelines for Expunction Hearings: The Register", August 1987.

_____. "Guidelines for Reporting to the Register", August 1987.

Ottawa-Carleton Police/CAS Liaison Subcommittee on the Child Abuse Protocol. "Child Abuse Protocol – An Investigative Procedure to Coordinate Response in the Regional Municipality of Ottawa-Carleton", Ottawa, September 1989.

Sigurdson, Eric and Reid, Grant. *Child Abuse and Neglect – The Manitoba Risk Estimation System Reference Manual*, April 1990.

The Children's Aid Society of the County of Simcoe. "Intervention Spectrum", Midhurst, January 1992.

The Institute for the Prevention of Child Abuse. "Child Abuse Alert", Toronto.

_____. "Child Abuse Prevention", Toronto.

_____. "General Guidelines to Assist in the Identification of Child Maltreatment", Toronto.

_____. "Preferred Practices for Investigating Allegations of Child Abuse in Residential Care Settings", Toronto, December 1990.

Chapter 8 – Manitoba

Administration and Service Delivery

Under *The Child and Family Services Act*, the Director of Child and Family Services of the Department of Family Services is responsible for investigating allegations of child abuse or neglect. This responsibility is delegated to provincial child and family services agencies. The Child and Family Support Branch, located in Winnipeg, has program responsibility for child protection services as well as for adoption, residential care and family support. The Branch is responsible for planning a coordinated service system, policy and legislation, establishment of service standards, and the funding of such services.

Child protection services are delivered by 15 agencies (five native and five non-native agencies plus five of eight regional offices of the Department). The Income Security and Regional Operations Division, located in Winnipeg, is responsible for the administration of the regional offices. The link with the external and native child and family service agencies is through the Child and Family Support Branch. In addition, the Ma Mawi Wi Chi Itata Centre Inc., a non-mandated agency, provides a wide range of services to status and non-status Indians and Métis living in Winnipeg.

In June 1992, a bill received Royal Assent establishing a Children's Advocate. The bill becomes effective upon proclamation. The Advocate's role includes both case and systemic advocacy. Duties include advising the Minister, investigating complaints and representing children other than as legal counsel. The Advocate will ensure that children known to or in the care of Manitoba's child and family services system are protected and well-treated and that their rights, interests and preferences are respected when decisions affecting them are made.

Definitions

Under Section 1 of *The Child and Family Services Act*, a **child** is defined as "a person under the age of majority" (i.e., under 18 years of age) for both child protection and adoption purposes. Under Sub-section 50(2) an agency may, with written approval of the Director, extend care and maintenance of a child who is a permanent ward up to the child's 21st birthday.

Under Section 17, a **child is in need of protection** "where the life, health or emotional well-being of the child is endangered by the act or omission of a person". This may occur "where the child

(a) is without adequate care, supervision or control;

(b) is in the care, custody, control or charge of a person

(i) who is unable or unwilling to provide adequate care, supervision or control of the child, or

(ii) whose conduct endangers or might endanger the life, health or emotional well-being of the child, or

(iii) who neglects or refuses to provide or obtain proper medical or other remedial care or treatment necessary for the health or well-being of the child or who refuses to permit such care or treatment to be provided to the child when the care or treatment is recommended by a duly qualified medical practitioner;

(c) is abused or is in danger of being abused;

(d) is beyond the control of a person who has the care, custody, control or charge of the child;

(e) is likely to suffer harm or injury due to the behaviour, condition, domestic environment or associations of the child or of a person having care, custody, control or charge of the child;

(f) is subjected to aggression or sexual harassment that endangers the life, health or emotional well-being of the child;

(g) being under the age of 12 years, is left unattended and without reasonable provision being made for the supervision and safety of the child; or

(h) is the subject, or is about to become the subject, of an unlawful adoption under section 63 or of an unlawful sale under section 84 of the Act."

Under Section 1 **abuse** means "an act or omission of a parent or guardian of a child or of a person having care, custody, control or charge of a child, where the act or omission results in

(a) physical injury to the child,

(b) emotional disability of a permanent nature in the child or is likely to result in such a disability, or

(c) sexual exploitation of the child with or without the child's consent."

As abuse is defined in legislation, Manitoba does not have working definitions. Instead, Manitoba has published guidelines which explain the Act to professionals and lay persons. The "Manitoba Guidelines on Identifying and Reporting a Child in Need of Protection (Including Child Abuse)" include the following explanations:

"Legislative Intent
Abuse is limited to an act or omission by a person who has the "care, custody, control or charge of a child". The focus is on situations involving a parent, guardian, teacher, babysitter, day care worker, coach, group leader or anyone in a position of trust with a child."

"Identifying Child Abuse
The Act refers to three conditions or types of abuse – physical injury, emotional disability of a permanent nature and sexual exploitation with or without a child's consent. Where one or more of these conditions exists as a result of an act or omission of a parent, guardian or other care provider, the child ought to be considered as suffering abuse and the matter must be reported to an agency. Abuse involves both factors – the condition of the child and an act or omission of a care provider."

"Indicators of Abuse
Professionals and lay persons involved in working with or caring for children are encouraged to learn about the physical and behavioural indicators of abuse. These indicators are listed in the child abuse protocols published by the province in cooperation with medical practitioners, nurses, teachers and others. The protocols include indicators for physical, sexual and emotional abuse."

"Aggression and Sexual Harassment
Physical injury or sexual exploitation of a child caused by a person who does not have the care, custody, control or charge of the child is not abuse. Nevertheless, a child might be in need of protection as a result of the actions of a "third party". Reporting an incident to an agency is not necessary unless subsection 18 (1.1) of The Act applies (see Mandatory Reporting section). Where an agency is not notified, a parent or guardian must be informed where a person reasonably believes a child is in need of protection. The police may also be contacted where the reporting person believes an offence has been committed under the *Criminal Code*."

Under *The Child and Family Services Act,* a child 12 or older has the following rights: the right to be given notice of and be present at the protection hearing, unless a judge orders otherwise; the right to have and instruct a lawyer; and the right to be advised and to make his/her views known (this latter item also applies to children under 12 if a judge feels it is appropriate). In addition, all children have the right to be informed of their rights.

Mandatory Reporting of a Child in Need of Protection

Sub-section 18(1) of the Act states that in cases where a person has information that leads him reasonably to believe that a child is or might be in need of protection, he shall report the information to an agency or to a parent or guardian of the child. This requirement specifically applies where the person has acquired information through a professional or confidential relationship, except for a solicitor-client relationship. Sub-section 18(1.1) states that a person must report to an agency where the person:

"(a) does not know the identity of the parent or guardian of the child;

(b) has information that leads the person reasonably to believe that the parent or guardian

(i) is responsible for causing the child be in need of protection or,

(ii) is unable or unwilling to provide adequate protection to the child in the circumstances; or

(c) has information that leads the person reasonably to believe the child is or might be suffering abuse."

A person who fails to report a child in need of protection commits an offence punishable on summary conviction. *The Child and Family Services Act* does not stipulate the amount of the penalty, nor is a penalty defined under the Act for false or malicious allegations. The police and medical health professionals (i.e., medical abuse unit) are required by provincial guidelines and policy to notify and consult with an appropriate agency as soon as possible after receiving a referral or report.

Under Sub-section 18.2(1), where the Director has reasonable grounds to believe that a person has caused a child to be in need of protection or has failed to report suspected child abuse, the Director may report the person to the professional society or association or regulatory organization of which the person is a member or that governs the person's professional status. The professional society, association or regulatory organization will investigate the matter to determine whether the person's status should be reviewed or disciplinary proceedings commenced.

Investigation of an Allegation of Child Abuse or Neglect

The Child and Family Services Act requires an agency to investigate all reports that a child might be abused or neglected to determine if there is a need for further intervention. Each agency provides after-hour services and has local access numbers. All referrals are responded to by the end of the following working day. If the child is considered to be at serious risk or if there is insufficient information to determine if the child is at risk, the response is immediate. If an allegation of abuse is reported and serious physical injury or sexual abuse has occurred or appears to have occurred, a medical examination of the child is arranged immediately and the police are notified. The police, medical professionals, and other agencies or professionals involved in the investigation and treatment of the case share all relevant information. Suspected or alleged emotional abuse may require medical corroboration in some cases to establish a serious and persistent pattern of abuse likely to cause emotional disability of a permanent nature. The Provincial Child Abuse Registry is checked during each investigation to determine whether or not the alleged perpetrator or victim has been recorded for past abuse.

The Manitoba Risk Estimation System (MRES), designed by Grant Reid and Eric Sigurdson, is currently being implemented province-wide. MRES is a predictive assessment tool which is used after an agency's preliminary intervention to determine whether a child could be at risk of being in need of protection. It is not necessarily used to determine whether a child is in need of protection since this is decided on the basis of legislation.

Section 21 of the Act empowers an agency or the police to apprehend a child deemed to be in need of protection and take the child to a place of safety. A warrant to enter any premises to investigate a child protection situation is not required where there are reasonable and probable grounds to believe the child is in immediate danger or has been left alone and is unable to look after himself/herself. The police may be requested to assist in the entry into any premises and the apprehension of a child.

All agencies are required under the Act to establish child abuse committees to review cases of alleged child abuse. Committees include a child abuse coordinator, a qualified medical practitioner, a representative of the local police, a teacher or other representative of the local school division operating within the agency boundaries, and an agency board member or staff member other than the child abuse coordinator. The committee may not necessarily be involved in the actual investigation but is active throughout the investigation phase to review, monitor, facilitate involvement of other disciplines and provide recommendations to agencies. Where a committee is of the opinion that abuse has occurred, an agency is required to report to the Director the names of the victim(s) and perpetrator(s) which must be added to the Provincial Child Abuse Registry.

Agencies are also required to investigate referrals in situations of abuse involving persons other than a parent or guardian or of a person having care, custody, control or charge of the child (i.e., teacher, babysitter, day care worker, coach, group leader or anyone in a position of trust with the child). Although the primary focus is on child protection, the agency may also advocate for and offer services to the victim and the victim's family.

To assist them with investigation and intervention procedures, agency workers and supervisors are provided with orientation and training for child protection services through the written agency guidelines and regular training programs. Training for protection workers is primarily through the Directorate's series of eight training modules that are available to all staff; these are not mandatory. Agencies have also implemented their own training programs which are relevant to their particular jurisdiction, population served and cultural issues.

No special provisions exist in the Act for investigations regarding natives as the legislation applies to all children in the province, whether aboriginal or non-aboriginal. However, the five mandated Indian agencies ensure that any services provided under the Act are done so in accordance with local wishes and Indian traditions.

The Provincial Chief Medical Examiner's (CME) office is required under *The Fatality Inquiries Act* to complete an investigative review of all suspicious child deaths and also into the circumstances of every child who was in the care of an agency at the time of death or where an agency was actively involved during that period. The CME forwards the report to the Minister of Family Services with findings and recommendations for implementation by the specified agencies or departments. Implementation is facilitated by the Child and Family Support Branch.

A Child Death Review Committee, located in the office of the Provincial Chief Medical Examiner, was created in 1991 to review all child deaths that are suspicious and unnatural for the purposes of recommending whether an inquest should take place or whether other actions are required. Such a committee appears to be unique in Canada.

Voluntary Agreements

In Manitoba, services may be provided in the child's home under a voluntary agreement. A parent or guardian may enter into a Family Support Service Agreement with an agency regarding the placement of a homemaker or parent aide, to temporarily care for a child in the child's home where the parent or guardian is temporarily unable to care for a child or where a parent or guardian requires training in homemaking and child care. Family Support Service Agreements are valid for six months, but may be extended for an additional six month period.

Voluntary Placement Agreements may be used in cases where a parent or guardian is temporarily unable to make adequate provision for the care of a child. A family may also enter into a Voluntary Placement Agreement with an agency to assist them if they are having a temporary family crisis or if they have a child with special needs. Under the agreement, the agency assumes custody of the child for up to 12 months, but there is no surrender of guardianship. The agreement may be renewed for an additional 12 months where necessary. Voluntary Placement Agreements may be used for both child abuse and neglect cases and are often the preferred option in native communities.

Court-Ordered Protection

Where voluntary service options are not feasible and a child is believed to be in need of protection, the child is apprehended and an application may be made to Family Court for an order. Where a child is found to be in need of protection, the Court may order that (a) the child be returned to the parents or guardian under the supervision of an agency and subject to the conditions and for a period the judge considers necessary (Order of Supervision), (b) the child be placed with another person the judge considers best able to care for the child with or without a transfer of guardianship and subject to the conditions and for a period the judge considers necessary (Third Party Placement Order), (c) the agency be appointed guardian for up to a maximum of six to 24 months, depending on the age of the child (Temporary Order of Guardianship), or (d) the agency be appointed the permanent guardian of the child (Order of Permanent Guardianship).

For children less than 12 years of age, the maximum duration for renewals of temporary orders ranges from 15 to 24 months. For children 12 years of age and over, temporary orders may be renewed for 24 month periods up to age 18. Except for orders of permanent guardianship, Manitoba legislation provides for consent orders where all parties agree.

Where an Order of Permanent Guardianship expires as a result of a child reaching 18 years of age, an agency may, with the written approval of the Director, continue to provide care and maintenance until the former ward reaches 21 years of age. Continued service and financial support is provided if required by the child as part of transitional planning to adult life.

In addition, the Family Court may order an individual be removed from a child's home if it is believed that person has subjected or is likely to subject the child to abuse.

Child Abuse Registry

Purpose
There are two separate and distinct registries in Manitoba: a child victim registry and an abuser registry. The child victim registry is used primarily for tracking high risk children and families. The abuser registry is used primarily for screening potential employees who would be in positions of trust with children (i.e., agency employees, foster parents, teachers, day care providers, etc.). Both registries are also used for statistical purposes and for limited research.

Basis for entering names
There are three circumstances under which an agency must submit a name to the Registry:

1. Where there has been a conviction on the basis of abuse in a criminal proceeding.
2. Where there has been a finding in a court that a child is in need of protection on the basis of abuse (i.e., Family Court).
3. A child abuse committee is of the opinion that abuse occurred based on the opinion of a duly qualified medical practitioner or psychologist and other supporting evidence.

Under item 3, the Department must inform all persons involved that their names will be entered on the Registry unless an objection is filed within 60 days. Appeals are heard by the Registry Review Committee within 30 days. A written decision is provided by the Committee within 30 days of completing the hearing. Approximately 50 per cent of those being notified are objecting, and of these objections, about 50 per cent have successfully been upheld. It is estimated that approximately 10 to 20 per cent of all abuse cases investigated are entered in the Registry.

Removal of names
A child's name is removed when the child attains 18 years of age. An abuser's name is removed either when the child who was abused attains 18 years or after 10 years have elapsed since the last entry relating to the abuser, whichever is later.

Access
All names and information on the Child Abuse Registry are confidential and can only be accessed, by permission of the Director.

Mandated agencies, on application to the Director, are given access to both the victim and abuser registries where the Director is satisfied that the access is reasonably required to investigate whether a child may be in need of protection; assess foster parents, homemakers, adoptive parents, parent aides or persons applying for these positions; or assess applicants for employment with the agency.

Employers other than mandated agencies such as schools and day care centres have access to the abuser registry only. They are limited to information as to whether an abuser's name is on the registry where this information is reasonably required to assess an applicant for employment or assist in the care of a child.

Limitations

Information on the Registry deals primarily with abuse as defined in child protection legislation. The definition excludes cases where the offender did not have the care, custody, control or charge of the child at the time of the offence. Therefore there is no information on sexual aggression and harassment cases, since the police rather than the Department would likely be involved.

Child Abuse and Neglect Protocols

The "Manitoba Guidelines on Identifying and Reporting a Child in Need of Protection (Including Child Abuse)" were jointly issued by the departments of Family Services, Education and Training, Health and Justice. They contain detailed information on mandatory reporting, the investigative process and disclosure. The "General Protocol", prepared by the Department of Family Services, provides a general perspective to the public on the current legislation, the indicators of abuse and the legal requirements for reporting; this is currently being revised. In addition, the following professional protocols are in the process of revision: "The Physician's Protocols on Child Protection/Abuse"; "Child Abuse: A Handbook for Teachers"; and "Child Abuse: Nurses Protocol". The physician's protocol will be a handbook for physicians and will include guidelines on reporting requirements; the investigative process; medical, emotional, and behavioural management of abused and neglected children and their families; court process and confidentiality. New protocols for child (day) care workers and social workers have been developed and will be issued shortly.

Statistics

The following tables and graphs are based on data compiled by the Department of Family Services. Data on reports of alleged child abuse are based on information contained in the report entitled "Non-Identifying Statistical Information" submitted by each agency to the Department. These represent the number of reports of alleged child abuse received and subsequently followed up on by the source agency. Data are reported on both the alleged victim and abuser. Data on children in care are based on statistical information submitted by agencies on a regular basis to the Department. Information relating to all natives, both on and off reserve, is included in the data.

A child in care refers to a child in the care of an agency under *The Child and Family Services Act*. There are six legal statuses: apprehension (in or out of the home); Temporary Order of Guardianship; Permanent Order of Guardianship; Voluntary Surrender of Guardianship (usually for adoption purposes); Voluntary Placement Agreement; and, transfers from another jurisdiction. A child remains under apprehension until the agency withdraws the action or the courts dispose of the matter.

During the 1991-92 fiscal year, changes were made to the statistical reporting system. Certain data on reports of alleged child abuse which had been available for earlier years were not available; in these cases, the data have been presented for the 1990-91 fiscal year instead.

Not all abused or neglected children who are deemed to be in need of protection are taken into care; many receive services in the home of the parent or a designated third party either voluntarily or under a Supervision Order or a Third Party Placement Order. No data based on the Child Abuse Register are published at this time.

Due to the limitations noted in Chapter 1, Introduction, these data should not be compared with data for other jurisdictions.

Table 8.1   Reports[1] on Alleged Abused Children by Source[2], April 1, 1991 to March 31, 1992

Source	Number	Percentage
Child and Family Services Agencies	1,341	62.7
Native Agencies	269	12.6
Regional Offices	530	24.8
Total	**2,140**	**100.0**

1. Represents the number of reports of child abuse received under the mandatory reporting requirements of *The Child and Family Services Act* by agencies and regional offices. All reports received are investigated.
2. Refers to the agency or regional office which received the report.

Table 8.2   Reports[1] on Alleged Abused Children by Sex of Child, April 1, 1991 to March 31, 1992

Sex	Number	Percentage
Male	768	35.9
Female	1,372	64.1
Total	**2,140**	**100.0**

1. Represents the number of reports of child abuse received under the mandatory reporting requirements of *The Child and Family Services Act* by agencies and regional offices. All reports received are investigated.

Figure 8.1   Reports[1] on Alleged Abused Children by Age Group of Child, April 1, 1991 to March 31, 1992

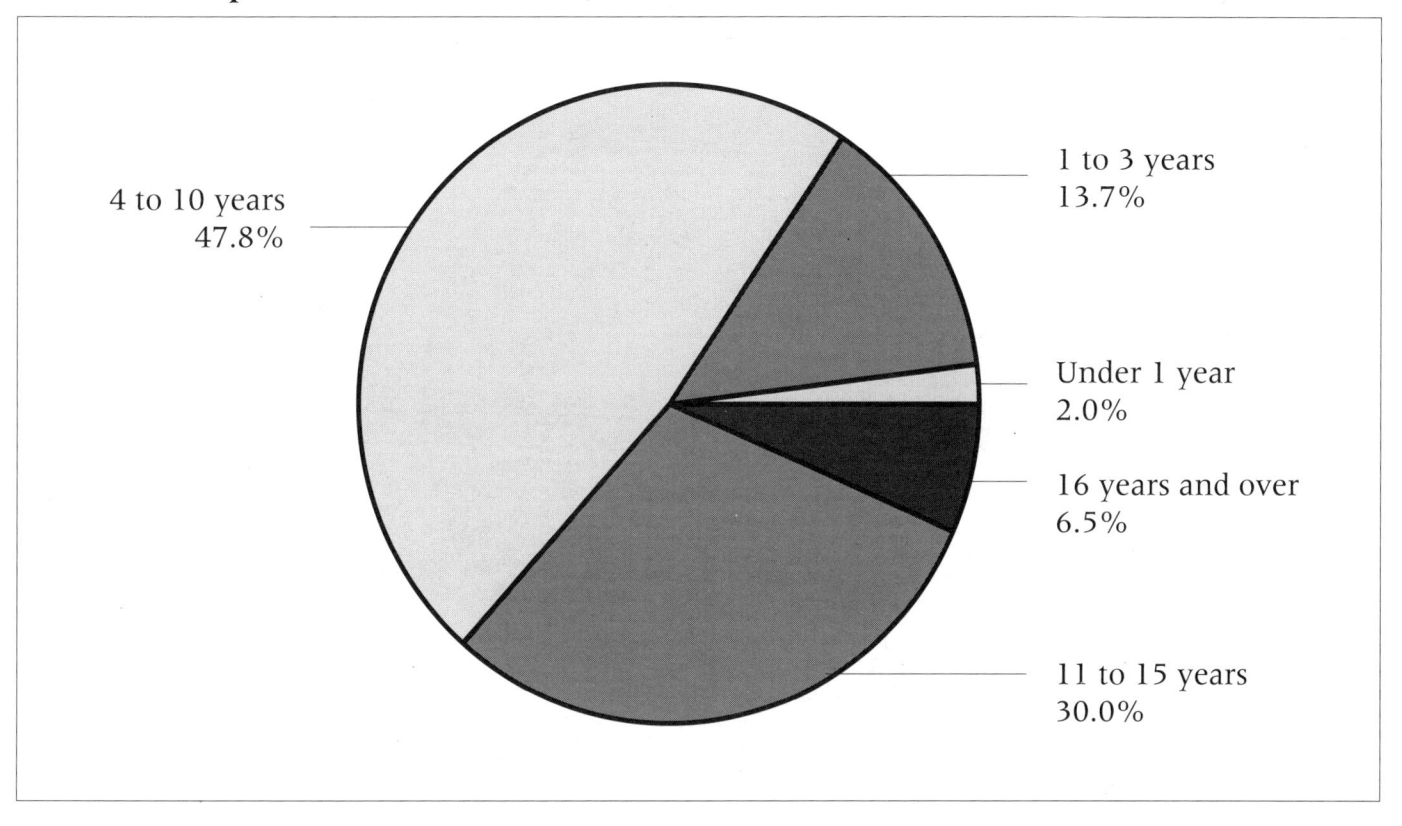

- 4 to 10 years 47.8%
- 1 to 3 years 13.7%
- Under 1 year 2.0%
- 16 years and over 6.5%
- 11 to 15 years 30.0%

Total number of reports: 2,140

1. Represents the number of reports of child abuse received under the mandatory reporting requirements of *The Child and Family Services Act* by agencies and regional offices. All reports received are investigated.

Figure 8.2 Reports[1] on Alleged Abused Children by Type of Trauma[2], April 1, 1990 to March 31, 1991[3]

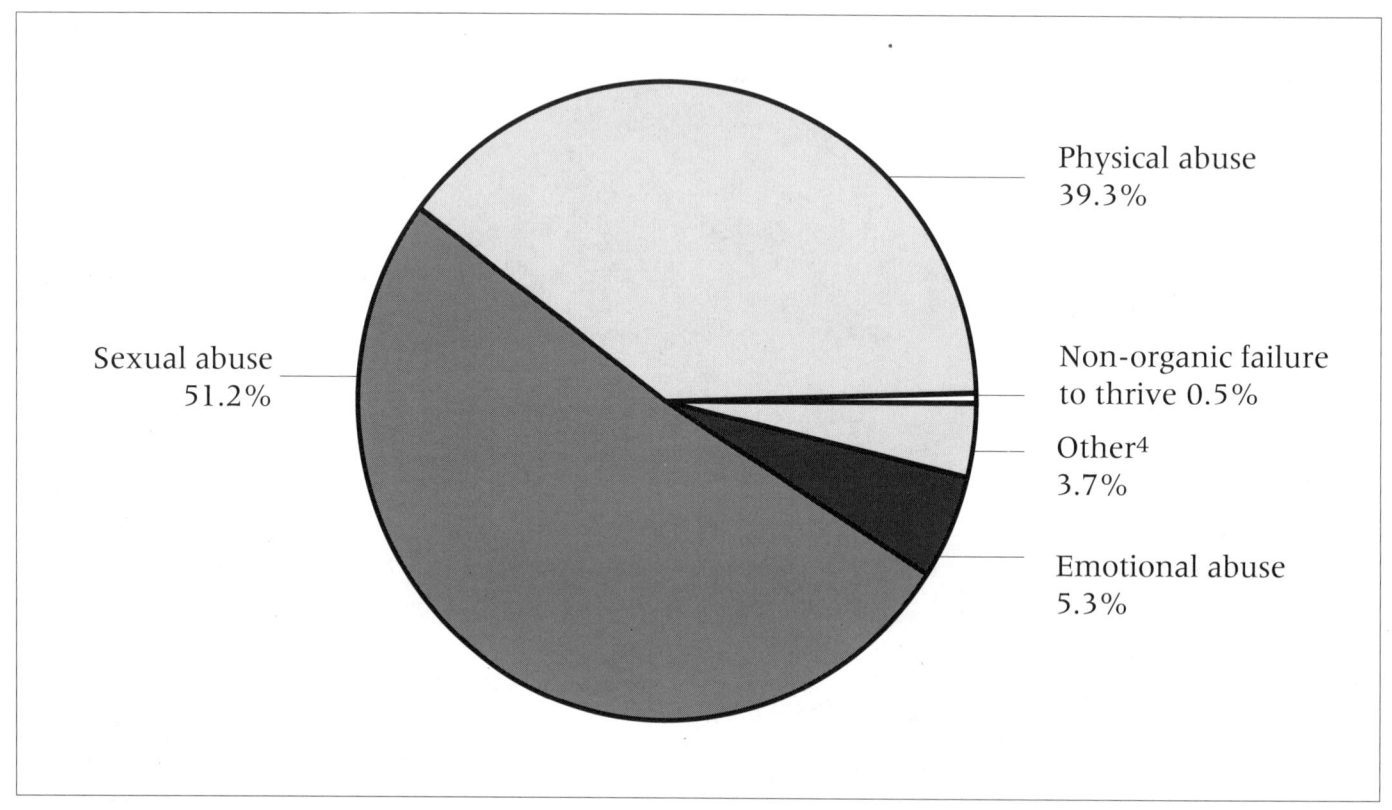

- Physical abuse 39.3%
- Non-organic failure to thrive 0.5%
- Other[4] 3.7%
- Emotional abuse 5.3%
- Sexual abuse 51.2%

Total types of trauma reported: 2,400[5]

1. Represents the number of reports of child abuse received under the mandatory reporting requirements of *The Child and Family Services Act* by agencies and regional offices. All reports received are investigated.
2. Based on the worker's assessment following the investigation.
3. Due to statistical reporting changes, these data are not available for the period April 1, 1991 to March 31, 1992. For the period April 1, 1990 to March 31, 1991, there were 2,237 abuse reports received.
4. Includes 2 deaths.
5. Exceeds the total number of reports received during the period (2,237) since more than one type of trauma was reported for some cases.

Chapter 8 - Manitoba

Figure 8.3   Reports[1] on Alleged Abused Children by Outcome[2], April 1, 1990 to March 31, 1991[3]

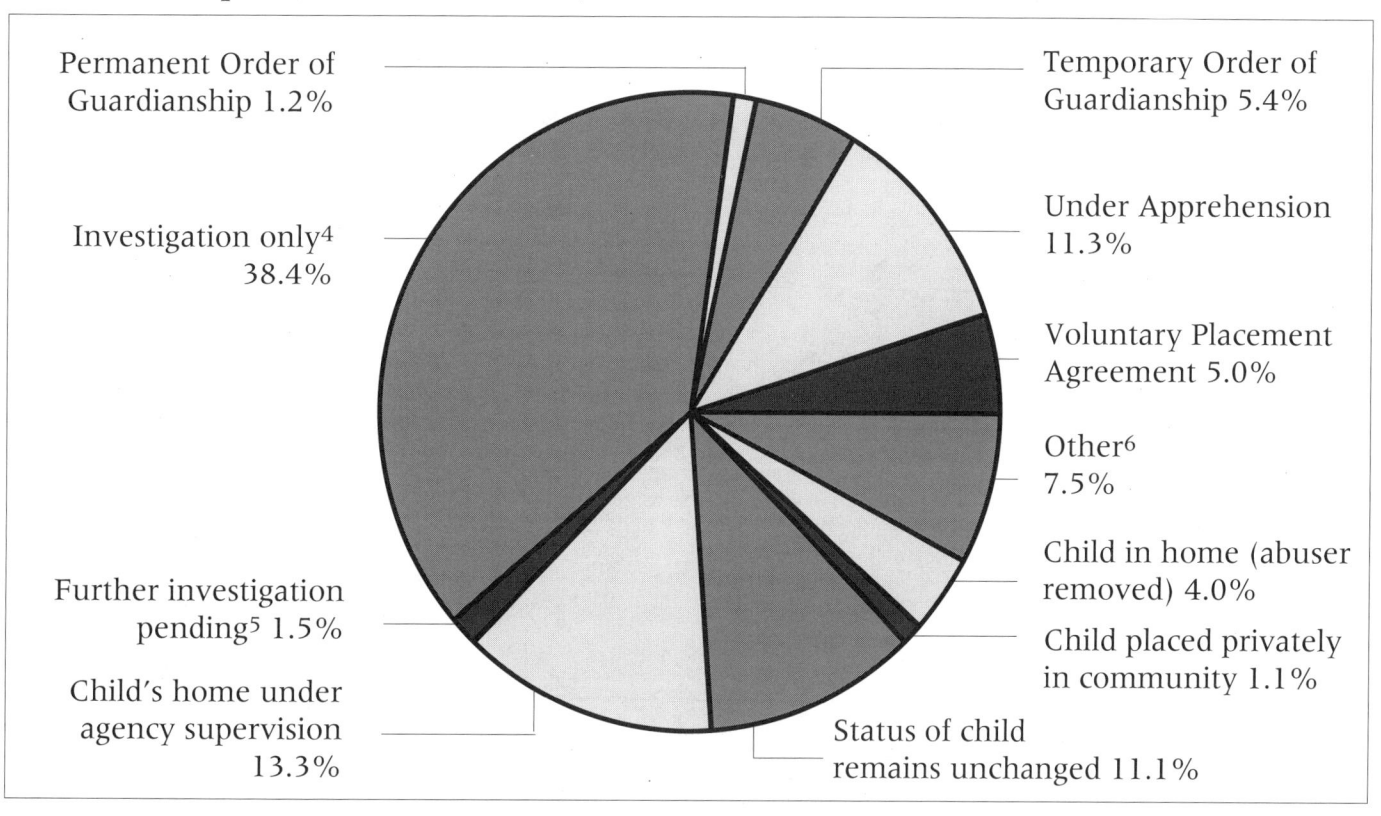

- Permanent Order of Guardianship 1.2%
- Investigation only[4] 38.4%
- Further investigation pending[5] 1.5%
- Child's home under agency supervision 13.3%
- Temporary Order of Guardianship 5.4%
- Under Apprehension 11.3%
- Voluntary Placement Agreement 5.0%
- Other[6] 7.5%
- Child in home (abuser removed) 4.0%
- Child placed privately in community 1.1%
- Status of child remains unchanged 11.1%

Total outcomes reported: 2,458[7]

1. Represents the number of reports of child abuse received under the mandatory reporting requirements of *The Child and Family Services Act* by agencies and regional offices. All reports received are investigated.
2. Represents the agency/regional office action taken to protect the child.
3. Due to statistical reporting changes, these data are not available for the period April 1, 1991 to March 31, 1992. For the period April 1, 1990 to March 31, 1991, there were 2,237 abuse reports received.
4. No further criminal action was taken following the investigation (e.g., due to inconclusive evidence).
5. Investigation ongoing as of March 31, 1991.
6. Includes 2 deaths.
7. Exceeds the total number of reports received during the period (2,237) since several agencies/regional offices reported more than one type of action per case.

Figure 8.4   Reports[1] on Alleged Abused Children by Relationship of Alleged Abuser, April 1, 1990 to March 31, 1991[2]

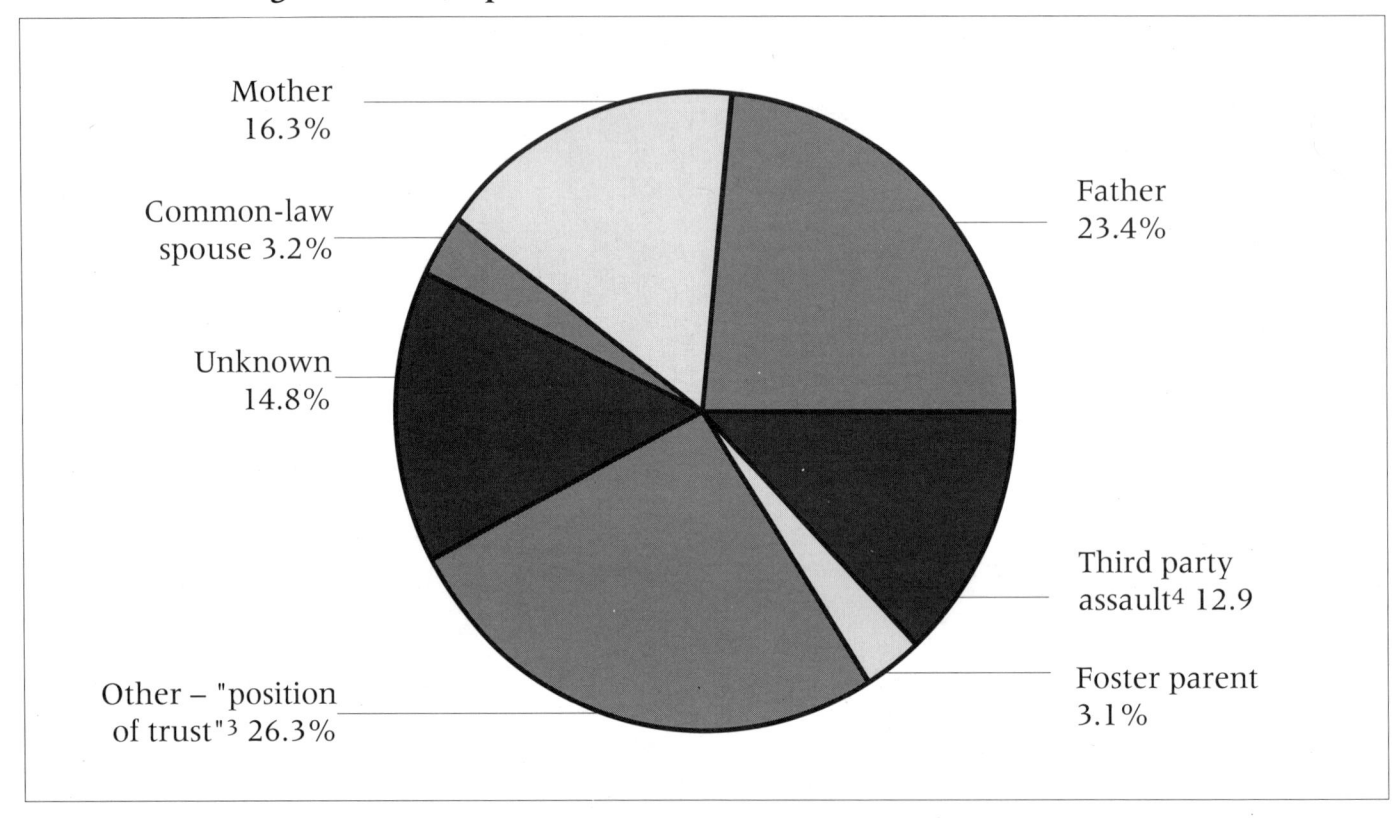

- Mother 16.3%
- Common-law spouse 3.2%
- Unknown 14.8%
- Other – "position of trust"[3] 26.3%
- Father 23.4%
- Third party assault[4] 12.9
- Foster parent 3.1%

Total number of abusers: 2,367[5]

1. Represents the number of reports of child abuse received under the mandatory reporting requirements of *The Child and Family Services Act* by agencies and regional offices. All reports received are investigated.
2. Due to statistical reporting changes, these data are not available for the period April 1, 1991 to March 31, 1992. For the period April 1, 1990 to March 31, 1991, there were 2,237 abuse reports received.
3. Any person other than the child's parent/guardian who had care, custody, control or charge of the child at the time the alleged abuse occurred.
4. Any person other than the child's parent/guardian or person in a position of trust.
5. Exceeds the total number of reports received during the period (2,237) since there was more than one abuser in certain cases.

Table 8.3 Reports[1] on Alleged Abused Children by Sex of Alleged Abuser, April 1, 1990 to March 31, 1991[2]

Sex	Number	Percentage
Male	1,559	65.9
Female	571	24.1
Unknown	237	10.0
Total	**2,367**[3]	**100.0**

1. Represents the number of reports of child abuse received under the mandatory reporting requirements of *The Child and Family Services Act* by agencies and regional offices. All reports received are investigated.
2. Due to statistical reporting changes, these data are not available for the period April 1, 1991 to March 31, 1992. For the period April 1, 1990 to March 31, 1991, there were 2,237 abuse reports received.
3. Exceeds the total number of reports received during the period (2,237) since there was more than one abuser in certain cases.

Figure 8.5 Reports[1] on Alleged Abused Children by Disposition of Alleged Abuser, April 1, 1990 to March 31, 1991[2]

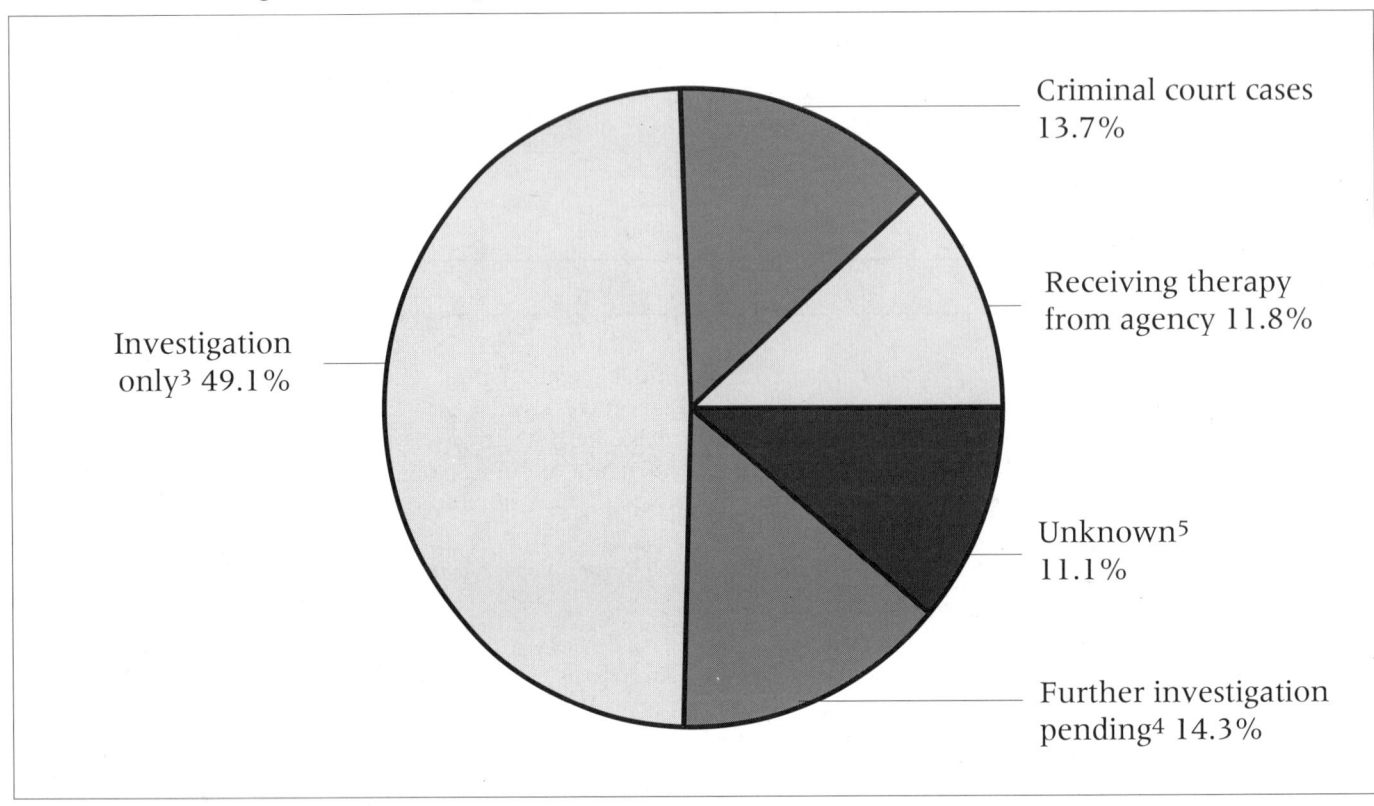

- Criminal court cases 13.7%
- Receiving therapy from agency 11.8%
- Unknown[5] 11.1%
- Further investigation pending[4] 14.3%
- Investigation only[3] 49.1%

Total number of dispositions: 2,440[6]

1. Represents the number of reports of child abuse received under the mandatory reporting requirements of *The Child and Family Services Act* by agencies and regional offices. All reports received are investigated.
2. Due to statistical reporting changes, these data are not available for the period April 1, 1991 to March 31, 1992. For the period April 1, 1990 to March 31, 1991, there were 2,237 abuse reports received.
3. No further criminal action was taken following the investigation (e.g., due to inconclusive evidence).
4. Investigation not concluded as at March 31, 1991.
5. Disposition of abuser not known as at March 31, 1991.
6. Exceeds the total number of reports received during the period (2,237) since there was more than one abuser in certain cases and several agencies/regional offices reported more than one disposition per abuser.

Chapter 8 - Manitoba   Page 113

Table 8.4   Children in Care[1] by Legal Status as at March 31, 1992

Legal Status	Number	Percentage
Wards[2]	3,656	67.6
Voluntary Placement Agreement	1,716	31.7
Other[3]	40	0.7
Total	**5,412**	**100.0**

1. Children in care represents children under the legal statuses shown.
2. Includes the following legal statuses: apprehension, Temporary Order of Guardianship, Permanent Order of Guardianship (including extension of service to age 21) and Voluntary Surrender of Guardianship Agreement (usually for adoption purposes).
3. Includes wards of other jurisdictions.

Figure 8.6   Children in Care[1] by Legal Status as at March 31, 1992

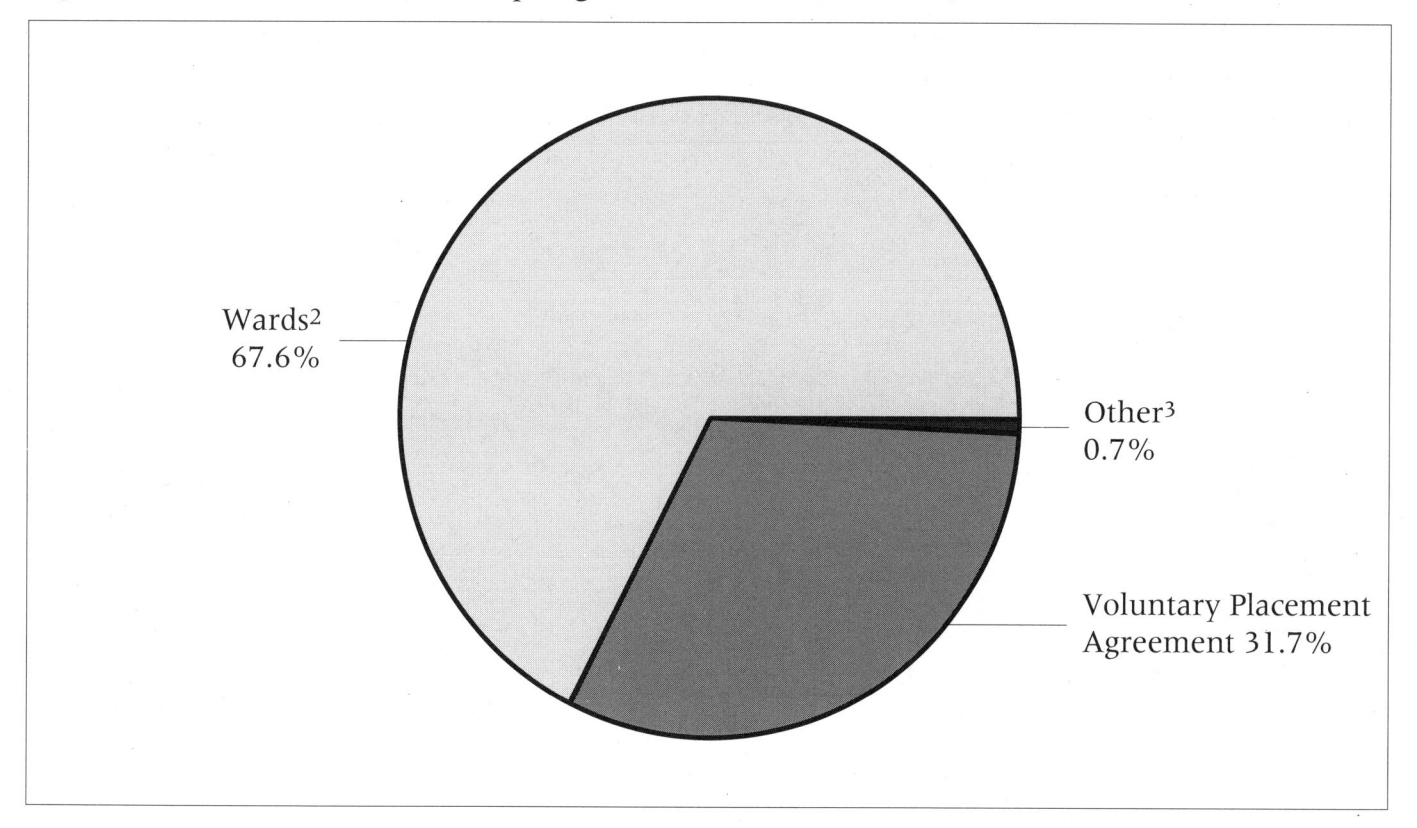

- Wards[2] 67.6%
- Other[3] 0.7%
- Voluntary Placement Agreement 31.7%

Total children in care: 5,412

1. Children in care represents children under the legal statuses shown.
2. Includes the following legal statuses: apprehension, Temporary Order of Guardianship, Permanent Order of Guardianship (including extension of service to age 21) and Voluntary Surrender of Guardianship Agreement (usually for adoption purposes).
3. Includes wards of other jurisdictions.

Figure 8.7 Children in Care[1] by Placement Type as at March 31, 1992

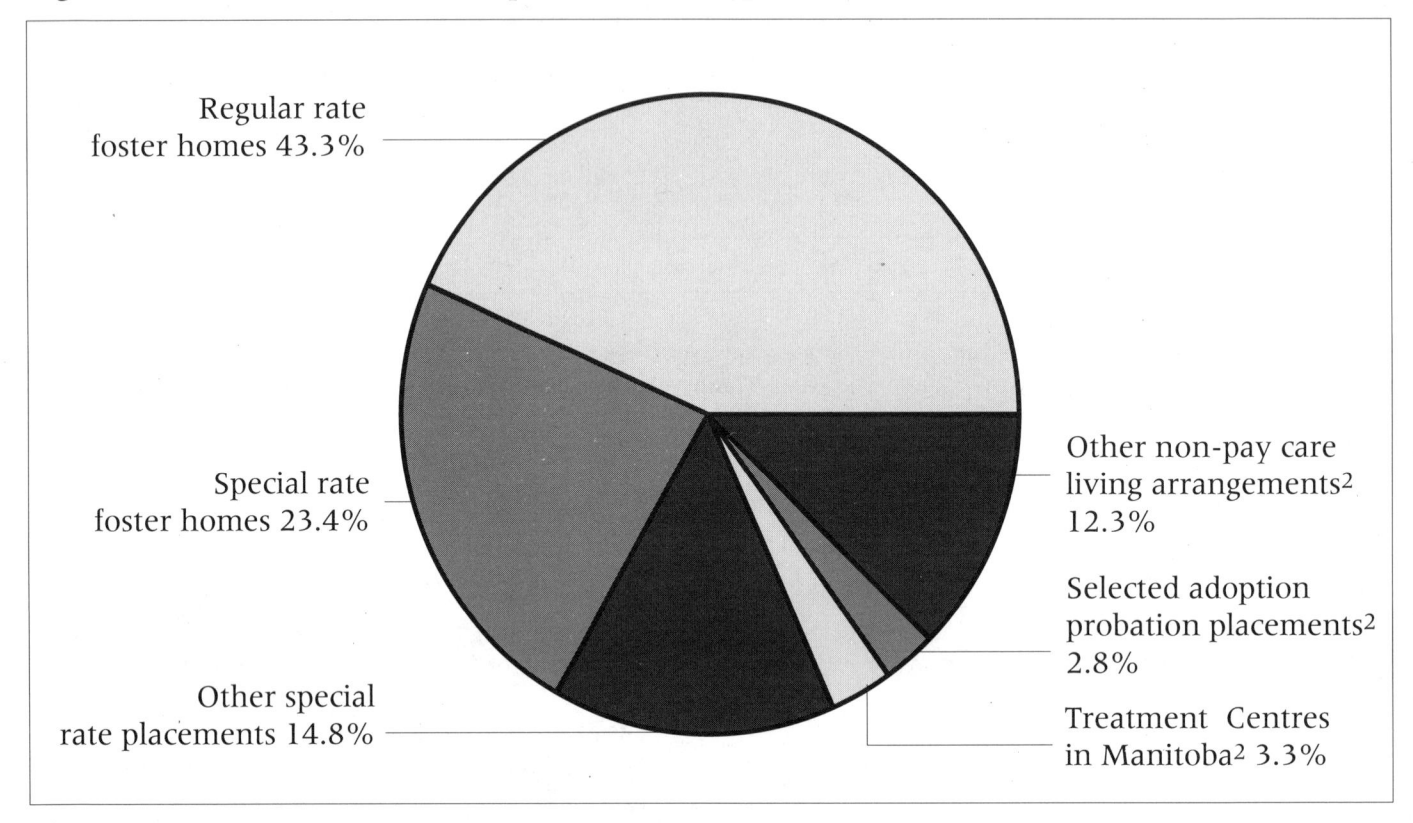

- Regular rate foster homes 43.3%
- Special rate foster homes 23.4%
- Other special rate placements 14.8%
- Other non-pay care living arrangements[2] 12.3%
- Selected adoption probation placements[2] 2.8%
- Treatment Centres in Manitoba[2] 3.3%

Total children in care: 5,412

1. Includes children under the following legal statuses: apprehension, Temporary Order of Guardianship, Permanent Order of Guardianship (including extension of service to age 21), Voluntary Surrender of Guardianship Agreement (usually for adoption purposes), Voluntary Placement Agreements and wards of other jurisdictions.
2. Placements where there is not a direct cost to the agency or region, but which may be funded through other sources.

Resource Material

Legislative Material

The Child and Family Services Act, Revised Statutes of Manitoba 1987, c. C80, as amended.

Reports

Manitoba, Department of Family Services. *Annual Reports*.

_____. *Government Response to the Independent Review on Reporting Procedures in Children's Residential Facilities*, 1992.

Suche, P. Colleen. *Independent Review of Reporting Procedures in Children's Residential Care Facilities*, 1992.

Sigurdson, Eric and Reid, Grant. *Child Abuse and Neglect – The Manitoba Risk Estimation System Reference Manual*, April 1990.

Other Material

Manitoba, Departments of Family Services, Education and Training, Health and Justice. *Manitoba Guidelines on Identifying and Reporting a Child in Need of Protection (including Child Abuse)*, 1989.

Manitoba, Department of Family Services. *Child Abuse: Nurses Protocol*, 1988.

_____. *General Protocol*, 1988.

_____. *The Physician's Protocols on Child Protection/Abuse*, 1992.

_____. "Program Standards Manual, Child and Family Services", Winnipeg.

Manitoba, Manitoba Teachers' Society, *Child Abuse: A Handbook for Manitoba Teachers*, 1988.

Chapter 9 – Saskatchewan

Administration and Service Delivery

The Department of Social Services in Saskatchewan is responsible for the development and delivery of child and family services. The Minister of Social Services administers *The Child and Family Services Act*, delegating responsibilities to a director in the Family and Youth Services Division and to child protection workers across the province.

Child abuse and neglect are child protection issues that fall under the authority of the Family and Youth Services Division. The Division is also responsible for the implementation of family violence programs, support services, young offender programs and adoption services. The central office, located in Regina, is responsible for program and policy development. The eleven regional offices reporting to the Associate Deputy Minister responsible for the Family and Youth Services Division and various district offices across the province deliver the actual services and programs.

Child protection workers from the regional and district offices provide protection services to children, often in cooperation with various individuals, non-governmental organizations and other departmental agencies. After hours emergency child protection services are provided by non-governmental mobile crisis units in Regina, Saskatoon and Prince Albert. In other regions, after hours emergencies are dealt with by departmental child protection workers.

As a member of the Provincial Interdepartmental Committee on Child Abuse, the Department is involved in the development and implementation of various initiatives aimed at prevention, treatment and public education with respect to all forms of family violence. The Committee, which also includes representatives from the departments of Health, Justice and Education, has been involved in the development and implementation of the "Provincial Child Abuse Investigation Protocol", the Five Year Child Sexual Abuse Strategy, the Integrated Family Treatment Project for Sexually Abused Children, and some offender treatment programs.

The Saskatoon Family Support Centre is an initiative undertaken by the Department of Social Services that provides programs and services aimed at educating parents on skills needed for effective parenting and the prevention of family violence. Other projects recently undertaken by the Department include The Family Builders Project, providing intensive in-home support to families with children at immediate risk of apprehension, and Regina's Integrated Family Treatment Project for Sexually Abused Children, which provides treatment to all members of the family to improve family functioning, prevent future abuse situations and provide emotional stability for the child.

The Child and Family Services Act authorizes the Minister of Social Services to enter agreements with native groups to deliver their own child welfare services. While the Department of Social Services currently has responsibility for the delivery of these services to native people, several Tribal Councils and Bands in Saskatchewan are planning the development of their own Indian Child and Family Services (ICFS) agencies. The Department is presently involved in consultations with the Meadow Lake, Battlefords, Yorkton and Saskatoon Tribal Councils, Touchwood, and the Peter Ballantyne Band regarding service protocols for ICFS agencies and possible delegation of authority under *The Child and Family Services Act*.

Definitions

Paragraph 2(1)(d) of *The Child and Family Services Act* defines a **child** as an unmarried person under 16 years of age. Section 18 provides for the apprehension of a 16 or 17 year old, in exceptional circumstances, who is in need of protection and is unable to protect himself/herself from a dangerous situation. Section 10 of the Act allows for residential and/or financial services agreements to be made with a 16 or 17 year old youth for whom no parent is willing to assume responsibility.

Section 56 authorizes the extension of services to age 21 to permanent/long-term care wards who are continuing their education.

For the purposes of adoption, under *The Adoption Act*, Paragraph 2(g) states that a **child** is a person who is under 18 years of age and has never been married.

Under Section 11 of *The Child and Family Services Act*, a **child is in need of protection** where:

"(a) as a result of action or omission by the child's parent:

i) the child has suffered or is likely to suffer physical harm;

ii) the child has suffered or is likely to suffer a serious impairment of mental or emotional functioning;

iii) the child has been or is likely to be exposed to harmful interaction for a sexual purpose, including conduct that may amount to an offence within the meaning of the *Criminal Code*;

iv) medical, surgical or other recognized remedial care or treatment that is considered essential by a duly qualified medical practitioner has not been or is not likely to be provided to the child;

v) the child's development is likely to be seriously impaired by failure to remedy a mental, emotional or developmental condition; or

vi) the child has been exposed to domestic violence or severe domestic disharmony that is likely to result in physical or emotional harm to the child;

(b) there is no adult person who is able and willing to provide for the child's needs, and physical or emotional harm to the child has occurred or is likely to occur; or

(c) the child is less than 12 years of age and:

i) there are reasonable and probable grounds to believe that: a) the child has committed an act that, if the child were 12 years of age or more, would constitute an offence under the *Criminal Code*, the *Narcotic Control Act* (Canada) or Part III or Part IV of the *Food and Drug Act* (Canada); and b) family services are necessary to prevent a recurrence; and

ii) the child's parent is unable or unwilling to provide for the child's needs."

For child protection purposes, a definition of **abuse** has been omitted from *The Child and Family Services Act*. The concern is that a legislated definition may be too restrictive or limiting to encompass all aspects of an alleged abuse situation, and therefore, the decision as to what constitutes abuse is left to the judge's discretion.

Working definitions for **physical**, **emotional**, and **sexual abuse** and **neglect** are found in the Saskatchewan Child Protection Policy Manual as follows:

"**Physical Abuse:** Occurs when a parent uses physical means or permits another person to use physical means which result in severe bruising, burns or scalding, broken skin, broken bones or any internal injuries to a child. Chronic bruising or repeated injuries of adolescents by parents is considered to constitute physical abuse.

Physical abuse also includes the feeding of poisonous, corrosive or non-medical mind-altering substances to a child.

Sexual Abuse: Any parental behaviour or behaviour of others permitted or condoned by the parent which may involve erotic touching or posing of a child.

Sexual abuse dealt with by the *Criminal Code of Canada* includes: rape, incest, sodomy and indecent liberties.

Emotional Neglect or Abuse: Is the chronic withholding of affection, the use of threats or terrorism or other chronic parental behaviour which, in the opinion of a qualified human behaviour specialist, is linked to measurable emotional disturbances in a child.

Neglect: Occurs when a parent fails to provide supervision, guidance, medical care, food, clothing or shelter that might reasonably be expected of any parent, and that inadequate provision is associated with:

— unreasonable and unnecessary danger to the child's safety

— severe or chronic health problems

— childhood behaviours that pose a threat to either the safety of the child, or to other persons

— absence from school unresolved by vigorous truancy enforcement efforts

— social ostracism of the child which is significant because of its severity and duration."

Mandatory Reporting of a Child in Need of Protection

Every individual who has reasonable grounds to believe that a child is in need of protection, is obligated to report this information to the Department of Social Services, or a police officer in accordance with Sub-section 12(1) of *The Child and Family Services Act*. In so doing, the individual is protected from civil action provided that the report was not made maliciously and without reasonable cause. Failure to report a child in need of protection is an offence under Sub-section 81(2), punishable by a prison term of six months maximum, a maximum fine of $5,000, or both. Exceptions from the requirement of reporting are made only for situations involving lawyer/client privilege, or Crown privilege.

Investigation of an Allegation of Child Abuse or Neglect

Reports of suspected abuse or neglect come into the system from various sources. A police officer who suspects that a child is in need of protection must immediately report this information to the Department. Conversely, the Department reports all physical or sexual abuse allegations to the police on the premise that criminal acts may have occurred. It is the responsibility of a child protection worker to investigate those cases where there is reasonable cause to believe that abuse or neglect has occurred. A worker must also determine, with the supervisor, the urgency of the investigation, if the child is in immediate danger, and if the child needs to be removed from the home. Depending upon the severity of the alleged abuse and the age of the child, an investigation may be undertaken within the hour, within 24 hours or within 2 days.

In cases of suspected physical or sexual abuse, the worker should determine if the child has been examined by a medical professional in the last 72 hours. If not, arrangements should be made for an immediate examination. If the parent is unavailable or unwilling to give consent, it may be necessary for the Department to apprehend the child and authorize a medical examination.

During an investigation, various forms of intervention may be necessary, including apprehension. Except in emergency situations, the decision to apprehend a child is made jointly between the child protection worker and supervisor. A protection worker does not require a warrant to apprehend a child.

Saskatchewan is developing a family-centred case management model incorporating assessments of risk and of child safety. A policy and procedures manual is currently being developed; training of staff and implementation of the case management model will begin in the Fall of 1993.

Extra-familial abuse refers to abuse inflicted on a child by someone outside the immediate family. The Department has a protection role in cases where the parent is aware of the abuse and does not take reasonable steps to prevent such abuse from occurring. If a parent has no knowledge or control over the abuse, the matter is not a child protection issue but is referred to police for criminal investigation. At this point, the Department may provide assistance to the police in interviewing the victim and may refer the victim and the family to other support services.

When an investigation of abuse or neglect occurs on an Indian reserve, the chief or councillor accompanies the child protection worker and participates in the planning of services, if required.

The Department provides its new personnel with a mandatory three week child protection training program. The course was originally based on the American Humane program and has been modified to meet local and changing needs.

Voluntary Agreements

Depending upon the severity of abuse or neglect and degree of risk to the child, voluntary agreements may be used in abuse or neglect cases where the child can be adequately protected under the agreement. A parent accepting the Department's offer of family services may enter a Family Support Contract which provides for services in the home, or a Residential Care Agreement for children to come voluntarily into the care of the Department.

Services under a Family Support Contract are intended as an intensive short-term form of intervention provided for a three month term with the possibility of extensions to a maximum of twelve months. However, in some cases, less intensive long-term services may be provided for a 12 month term to maintain the family's capacity to care for the child. The Director has the authority to adjust the terms of family support services as appropriate.

Under the terms of a Residential Care Agreement the parent temporarily relinquishes custody, but not guardianship, of the child to the Department of Social Services with the intent of resolving the problems that placed the child at risk initially. For situations where a parent is unable to meet the special needs of a child, a Residential Care Agreement is an appropriate option. This agreement may be made for up to one year and may be renewed for up to another year but shall not exceed 24 months unless the Director rules that it is in the best interests of the child to do so.

Although the legal definition of a child refers to an individual age 16 or less, services may be provided to 16 or 17 year old youth under Section 10 of *The Child and Family Services Act*. According to this provision, agreements may be made to provide residential and/or financial services to youth in need of protection where there is no parent available to assume responsibility for the youth, or the youth cannot be re-united with the family. Under such an agreement, room and board may be provided to 16 or 17 year old youths in need of protection whose parents refuse or are unable to provide for them. Various levels of supervision are provided according to the needs of the youth, and rates are adjusted according to the level of involvement and supervision provided.

Court-Ordered Protection

If an agreement for services cannot be reached and the worker has concluded that a child is in need of protection, an application must be made to the Provincial Court of Saskatchewan (Unified Family Court in Saskatoon) for a protection hearing.

Upon determination that a child is in need of protection, the judge may make one of several orders. An Order to Return the Child to the Parent ensures the child remains with or is returned to the parent with the possible implementation of any terms or conditions deemed appropriate, including an order that the Department supervise the child for a period of up to one year. An Order to Place the Child in the Care of a Person of Sufficient Interest requires that the court designate someone, usually a long-time friend or extended family member, to care for the child for an indefinite period or a time-limited period of up to one year. The judge may grant the parent access to the child during this period, and may order the Department to supervise the child for up to one year.

Under the terms of a Temporary Committal Order, the Minister of Social Services acquires custody of the child for a term of up to six months. Renewal of the term shall not exceed 24 months total, unless a court finds it is in the best interests of the child to grant a further extension. A Permanent Committal Order requires that custody and guardianship of the child, with all parental rights and responsibilities including the right to place the child for adoption, be transferred to the Minister.

Where it is unlikely that a child would be adopted if made a permanent ward (either as a function of age or due to other circumstances), a Long-Term Order to Age 18 may be recommended, placing the child in the Minister's custody until the child reaches 18 years of age. Under this order, the parent retains guardianship but may have access to the youth according to provisions incorporated in the order.

A current or former permanent or long-term care ward who remains in school may enter into an extended care agreement. Services may be extended to age 21, until the educational goal is attained or until marriage, whichever comes first.

If contact between a child and another individual would likely cause the child to be in need of protection, a Protective Intervention Order may be implemented. This prohibits a specific person from contacting or associating with the child for a term up to six months. The order may be renewed for a maximum of 24 months unless further contact would continue to threaten the child's safety.

Child Abuse Register

Saskatchewan does not operate a child abuse register.

Child Abuse and Neglect Protocols

In response to the need for integrated, cooperative and sensitive interaction between various agencies involved in child abuse or neglect allegations, the Department of Social Services has developed several child abuse protocols in conjunction with the departments of Justice, Health and Education. The "Provincial Child Abuse Investigation Protocol" offers guiding principles and procedures to be used by the departments of Justice, Social Services and by the police when investigating cases of suspected child abuse. The Interdepartmental Child Abuse Committee is presently working on expanding this protocol into the area of treatment and follow-up for victims. Within individual communities, the investigation protocol is translated to Local Function Statements providing further detail on the roles and responsibilities of the various agencies and individuals involved in the management of a given child abuse or neglect case.

The departments of Social Services and Education have signed the "Child Abuse Protocol – School Systems", providing policy and procedural guidelines for the reporting of child abuse or neglect and regarding access to children by departmental personnel for the purposes of interviewing at school. These protocols are standard across the province.

Public health nurses also follow a "Child Abuse Protocol" developed by the Community Health Services Branch of the Department of Health which includes basic principles and assumptions regarding child abuse, program objectives and standards plus the assessed effectiveness/impact of following these standards. The protocol is also for use by other disciplines within the Branch and has been circulated to all public health regions.

Statistics

Data presented in this section have been extracted from the Client Index System of the Department of Social Services. The data on children in care and families receiving protection services are shown in table and graph form, as at March 31, 1992.

Protection data counts families with children in need of protection as specified in *The Child and Family Services Act*. Data on children in care counts actual numbers of children who are in need of protection and are in care under the following legal statuses: apprehension, Residential Care Agreement, Agreement for Services to 16 and 17 Year Olds, temporary ward (Temporary Committal Order), Long-Term Order to Age 18, permanent ward (Permanent Committal Order and voluntary relinquishment for adoption) and Extended Care Agreement. Data on natives are included in the statistics.

Due to the limitations noted in Chapter 1, Introduction, these data should not be compared with data for other jurisdictions.

Table 9.1   Families with Children in Need of Protection by Reason as at March 31, 1992

Reason	Number of Families	Percentage
Abuse		
Physical abuse	310	10.2
Sexual abuse	289	9.5
Emotional abuse	32	1.0
Sub-Total	**631**	**20.7**
Physical neglect	691	22.7
Parent/child conflict	379	12.4
Parenting ability	614	20.2
Domestic violence	28	0.9
Non-ward care of child[1]	9	0.3
Investigations[2]	689	22.6
Child under 12[3]	4	0.1
Total	**3,045**	**100.0**

1. Care by person of sufficient interest (usually a member of the extended family or someone else close to the child).
2. Investigation ongoing, reason not determined.
3. Child has committed an offence.

Table 9.2   Children in Care[1] by Legal Status as at March 31, 1992

Legal Status	Number	Percentage
Apprehension[2]	654	26.5
Residential Care Agreement	503	20.4
Agreement for Services[3]	143	5.8
Temporary Ward[4]	236	9.6
Long-Term Order to Age 18	49	2.0
Permanent Ward[5]	835	33.9
Extended Care Agreement[6]	44	1.8
Total	**2,464**	**100.0**

1. Children in care represents children under the legal statuses shown.
2. Matter before the court.
3. Agreement for services to 16 and 17 year olds.
4. Temporary Committal Order.
5. Includes Permanent Committal Order and voluntary relinquishment of child for adoption.
6. Extension of services to 21 years of age for previous permanent wards, or children under a Long-Term Order to Age 18, so that they may continue their education.

Chapter 9 - Saskatchewan   Page 125

Figure 9.1   Children in Care[1] by Legal Status as at March 31, 1992

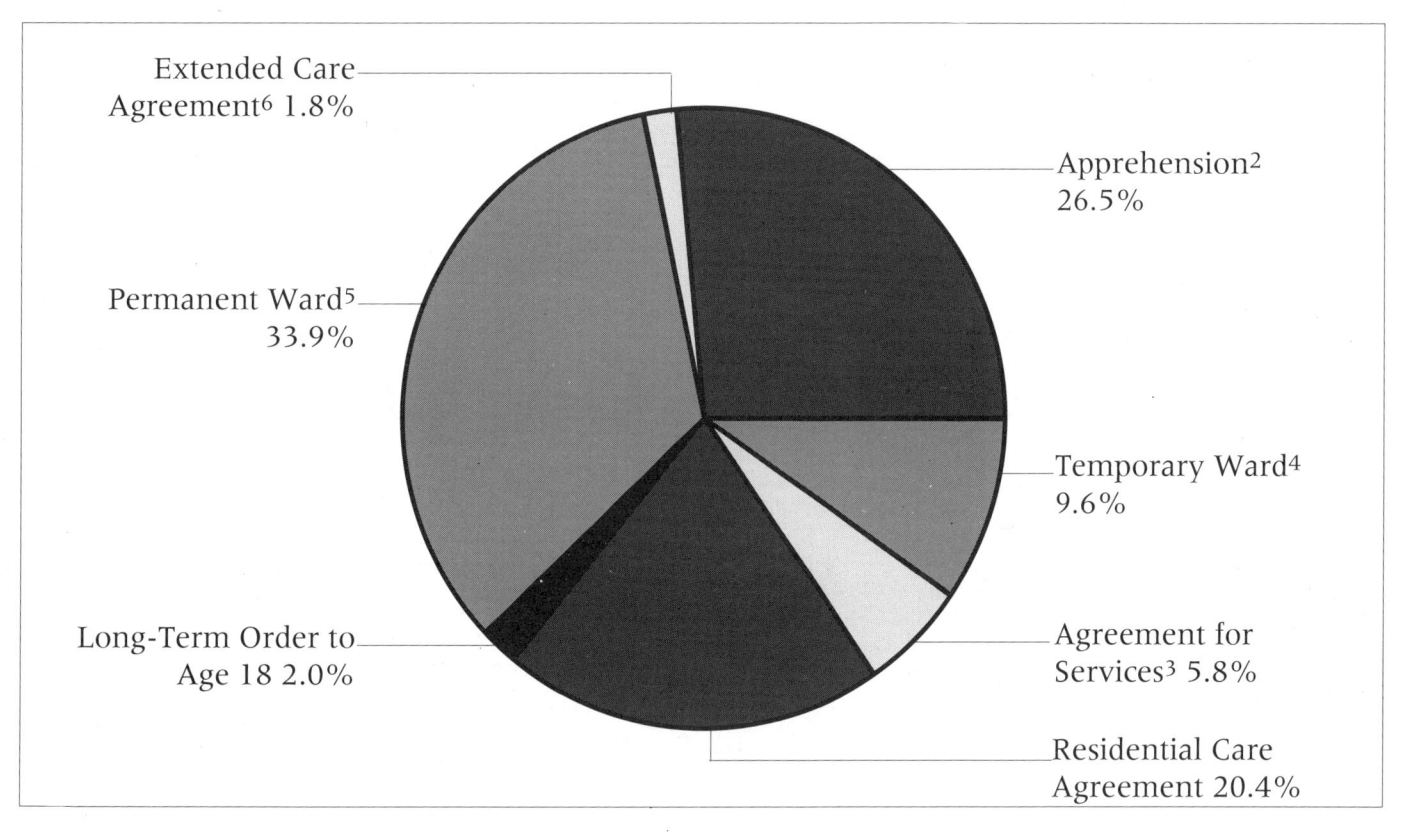

- Extended Care Agreement[6] 1.8%
- Apprehension[2] 26.5%
- Permanent Ward[5] 33.9%
- Temporary Ward[4] 9.6%
- Long-Term Order to Age 18 2.0%
- Agreement for Services[3] 5.8%
- Residential Care Agreement 20.4%

Children in care: 2,464

1. Children in care represents children under the legal statuses shown.
2. Matter before the court.
3. Agreement for services to 16 and 17 year olds.
4. Temporary Committal Order.
5. Includes Permanent Committal Order and voluntary relinquishment of child for adoption.
6. Extension of services to 21 years of age for previous permanent wards, or children under a Long-Term Order to Age 18, so that they may continue their education.

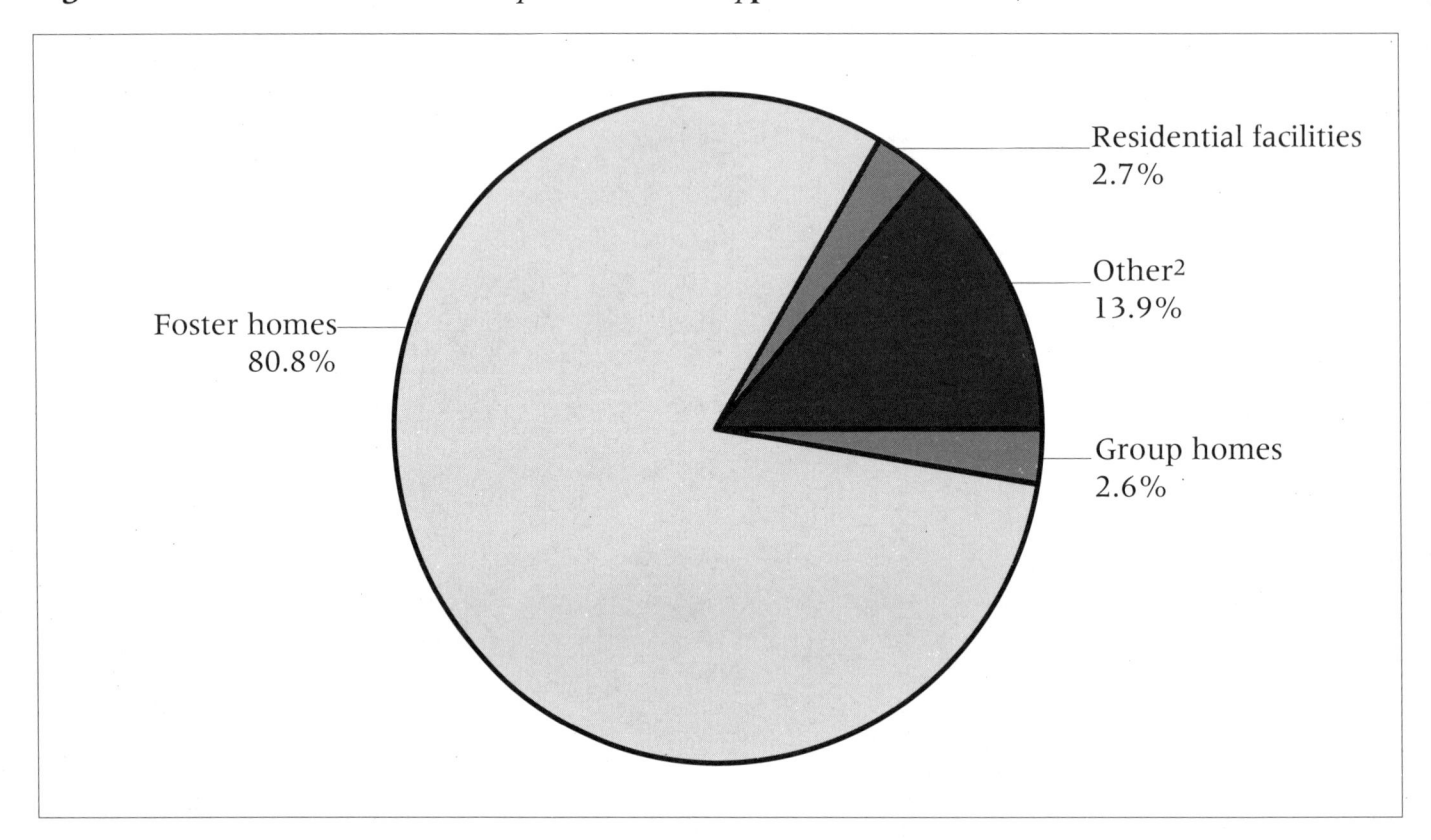

Figure 9.2 Children in Care[1] by Placement Type as at March 31, 1992

- Foster homes 80.8%
- Residential facilities 2.7%
- Other[2] 13.9%
- Group homes 2.6%

Children in care: 2,464

1. Children who are in need of protection and are in care under the following legal statuses: Apprehension, Residential Care Agreement, Agreement for Services to 16 and 17 Year Olds, temporary ward (Temporary Committal Order), Long-Term Order to Age 18, permanent ward (Permanent Committal Order and voluntary relinquishment for adoption) and Extended Care Agreement.
2. Northern child care centres (receiving function), extended family placements, children in care placed in young offenders' open and closed custody facilities, children in care who have been returned home but whose guardianship has not been terminated and older children in care who have left provincial resources.

Resource Material

Legislative Material

The Child and Family Services Act. Revised Statutes of Saskatchewan 1989, C-7.2.

The Adoption Act. Revised Statutes of Saskatchewan 1989, A-5.1.

Reports

Saskatchewan, Saskatchewan Social Services. *Annual Report 1990-91*.

_____. *Quarterly Statistical Report*.

Other Material

Saskatchewan, Department of Social Services. "Child Protection Policy Manual", Regina.

Saskatchewan, Department of Health. "Child Abuse Protocol" (public health), 1987.

Saskatchewan, Department of Education. "Child Abuse Protocol – School Systems", 1985.

Saskatchewan, Department of Social Services and Department of Justice. "Provincial Child Abuse Investigation Protocol", 1987.

Pamphlets, Department of Social Services

"Child Abuse and Neglect – Information for Teachers".

"Neglected and Abused Children".

Chapter 10 – # Alberta

Administration and Service Delivery

Under the *Child Welfare Act*, Alberta Family and Social Services is responsible for child protection services. The Social Supports Services Division, located in Edmonton, oversees the development and delivery of all departmental social support services. These include child and family support services, day care, Native child welfare, services to persons with disabilities, family court mediation and family violence initiatives. Within the Division, the Program Policy Development Branch has program responsibility for all of the above services. The planning and development of child protection services, including those for abused and neglected children, is coordinated through the Support to Families and Children, Resources for Children, and Community Support Native Services units of Program Policy Development. Social services are coordinated through the six regional offices responsible for managing all departmental social services. Social workers in over 50 district offices deliver protective services to abused or neglected children and their families in conjunction with agencies, individuals and residential facilities providing child and family services.

The Native Relations Unit of Intergovernmental Relations liaises with Indians to assist them in delivering their own social services, including child protection services. There are currently three agreements enabling Indians to deliver their own child welfare services; these are with the Siksika Nation, the Lesser Slave Lake Indian Regional Council and the Yellowhead Tribal Services Agency. Where there are no formal agreements, departmental staff are responsible for delivering child protection services on reserves.

The Intergovernmental Committee on Family Violence consists of representatives from Family and Social Services, Health, Education, Solicitor General and Attorney General. It has a broad mandate to examine all aspects of family violence. Within the Department, the Program Advisory Committee assists in developing new programs and policies for all types of family violence, including child abuse.

The *Child Welfare Act* created the position of Children's Advocate, whose responsibility is to represent the rights, interests and viewpoints of children receiving protective services under the Act. The Advocate delegates these responsibilities to regional advocates.

Definitions

Paragraph 1(1)(d) of the *Child Welfare Act* defines a **child** (for both child protection and adoption purposes) as a person under the age of 18 years. Sub-section 33(2) states that care and maintenance of a child may be extended until a child reaches 20 years of age.

Sub-section 1(2) of the Act states that "**a child is in need of protective services** if there are reasonable and probable grounds to believe that the survival, security or development of a child is endangered because

(a) the child has been abandoned or lost;

(b) the child's guardian is dead and the child has no other guardian;

(c) the child's guardian is unable or unwilling to provide the child with necessities of life;

(d) the child has been or there is risk that the child will be physically injured or sexually abused by the guardian;

(e) the guardian is unable or unwilling to protect the child from physical injury or sexual abuse;

(f) the child has been emotionally injured by the guardian;

(g) the child's guardian is unable or unwilling to protect the child from emotional injury;

(h) the child's guardian has subjected the child to or is unable or unwilling to protect the child from cruel and unusual treatment or punishment;

(i) the condition or behaviour of the child prevents the guardian from providing the child with adequate care appropriate to meet the child's needs."

Sub-section 1(3) of the Act further defines emotional or physical injury and sexual abuse.

"(a) a child is **emotionally injured**

(i) if there is substantial and observable impairment of the child's mental or emotional functioning that is evidenced by a mental or behavioural disorder, including anxiety, depression, withdrawal, aggression or delayed development, and

(ii) if there are reasonable and probable grounds to believe that the emotional injury is the result of
 – rejection,
 – deprivation of affection or cognitive stimulation,
 – exposure to domestic violence or severe domestic disharmony,
 – inappropriate criticism, threats, humiliation, accusations or expectations of or towards the child, or
 – the mental or emotional condition of the guardian of the child or chronic alcohol or drug abuse by anyone living in the same residence as the child;

(b) a child is **physically injured** if there is substantial and observable injury to any part of the child's body as a result of the non-accidental application of force or an agent to the child's body that is evidenced by a laceration, a contusion, an abrasion, a scar, a fracture or other bony injury, a dislocation, a sprain, hemorrhaging, the rupture of viscus, a burn, a scald, frostbite, the loss or alteration of consciousness or physiological functioning or the loss of hair or teeth;

(c) a child is **sexually abused** if the child is inappropriately exposed or subjected to sexual contact, activity or behaviour."

Under the *Child Welfare Act*, a child has the following rights: the right to appeal, the right to request legal counsel, the right to apply for a case review, and the right to request the services of the Children's Advocate. In addition, a child over 12 must consent to various agreements or orders concerning his/her custody and guardianship which are made under the Act.

Mandatory Reporting of a Child in Need of Protection

Sub-section 3(1) of the *Child Welfare Act* states that any person who has reasonable and probable grounds to believe that a child is in need of protective services must report this to a director. Any person may be designated by the Minister of Family and Social Services as a director for the purposes of the Act. Responsibility for receiving reports of a child in need of protective services is delegated to departmental social workers. Schools, day care centres and any other community agencies dealing with children must also notify the Department. The only exception to the legal requirement to report occurs in a solicitor-client relationship, where such information is deemed to be privileged. Alberta Family and Social Services also operates the Child Abuse Hotline, which provides a 24-hour service for reporting a child in need of protective services. A person who reports is not liable to legal action unless reporting maliciously or without grounds. Under Sub-section 3(6), any person who does not report is guilty of an offence and is liable to a fine of up to $2,000 or, in default of payment, up to six months imprisonment. Sub-section 3(5) specifies that if a worker believes that a professional has failed to report, the regional director will advise the governing body of the profession accordingly.

Investigation of an Allegation of Child Abuse or Neglect

Each referral received by Alberta Family and Social Services is screened. This process involves deciding whether it constitutes a report of a child in need of protective services and, if so, whether an investigation is warranted. The maximum time permitted for screening is three days. If the worker determines that a protection issue need not be investigated, the caller may be referred to a community resource. If this occurs, the resource must report to the Department if any child protection issue subsequently arises. Valid reports of abuse or neglect require supervisory approval on whether to investigate. Where there are insufficient grounds to proceed with an investigation, the worker must enter relevant information on the Department's Child Welfare Information System (CWIS), where it is retained for 90 days. If a full investigation is warranted, a response time is assigned. In cases where a child is considered to be at immediate risk or injured, the response (including screening) must be immediate; in all other situations a maximum time of ten days from the initial screening is permitted.

Alberta Family and Social Services investigates all allegations that a child's guardian perpetrates, or fails to protect a child from, abuse or neglect. This includes intra-familial abuse, abuse by any person to whom the guardian gives status (for example, a babysitter or boyfriend) and abuse in a child welfare placement facility responsible for the care of a child. The Department does not investigate allegations of abuse against a person to whom the larger community gives status, such as a day care worker, teacher, coach or minister. Where the Department becomes aware of such allegations, it advises the reporter to notify the child's parents and the police. The Department follows up to ensure the police report was made. If the alleged perpetrator is a school staff member, the Department notifies the regional office of the Department of Education. If the alleged perpetrator is a day care staff member, the Department notifies the regional director responsible for day care services. Should the police subsequently report that the guardian is not protecting the child, the Department investigates.

In all situations of suspected physical or sexual abuse, the worker must, after consulting with the supervisor, report the incident to the police. The police will determine whether criminal charges should be laid. Conversely, the police must refer any potential child abuse situation to Alberta Family and Social Services. In either situation, the Department and police proceed with a joint investigation. A child with physical injuries must be visually examined by the worker in the presence of the parent or caregiver. The worker must arrange for a complete medical examination the same day; if a parent refuses consent or is unavailable, the child must be apprehended. The examining doctor must provide a medical report to the Department.

In cases of suspected intra-familial sexual abuse or sexual abuse by a person to whom the guardian has given status, the child and any siblings must be interviewed by a social worker. If the child does not disclose sexual abuse, the worker must interview the parent(s) and assess the need for protective services. If the child does disclose sexual abuse, the disclosure may be videotaped for future use in either criminal or civil proceedings. The worker must arrange for a medical examination as soon as possible to check for evidence of sexual abuse and the presence of any sexually transmitted disease. The worker must interview the non-abusing parent to determine whether the child can be adequately protected; where this is not possible, the child must be apprehended. The Act stipulates that an apprehension order is required to apprehend a child; however, where there is imminent risk to a child's life or health, either the worker or the police may apprehend without one.

Where an Indian child (as defined under the *Indian Act*) is considered to be in need of protective services, the worker must follow any investigation protocol negotiated between the reserve and district office. Where the child needs to be apprehended and time permits, the worker must first seek information and advice from the child's band.

All child protection workers receive mandatory training from the Department within two years of being hired. Topics covered include general orientation (one week), basic child protection training (three weeks), child welfare casework with native peoples, suicide prevention and sexual abuse.

Voluntary Agreements

Alberta Family and Social Services encourages the use of voluntary agreements that provide short-term services to children requiring protective services and their families. These may be used in cases of abuse or neglect if the worker believes that the child can be adequately protected. Under a Support Agreement, the Department provides support services to a family while the child remains in the home. Such an agreement may be entered into by either the guardian or a custodian (alternate caregiver designated by the child's guardian). A Support Agreement lasts for up to six months, and may be renewed indefinitely. Under a Custody Agreement, the child is placed in a departmental resource, such as a foster home or group home. The guardian retains guardianship and the Department assumes temporary custody of the child. The duration of a Custody Agreement may be up to six months, and it may be renewed for up to two years cumulative time in care. In Alberta, a child 16 years of age or over who is living independently and in need of protective services may also enter into either of these agreements.

Part 7, Section 72 of the *Child Welfare Act* states that the parent(s) of a handicapped child may enter into a Handicapped Children's Services agreement with the Department. Under this agreement, the Department assists with the purchase of goods and services required due to the child's special needs. The child may remain in the home or be placed in a specialized resource to facilitate service provision. A handicapped child is *not* defined as being in need of protective services under the Act. Any handicapped child who is determined to be in need of protective services is assisted under the protection provisions of the Act.

A child turning 18 who has entered into either a Support Agreement or a Custody Agreement may enter into a Care and Maintenance Agreement to extend services. An agreement is for up to six months, and may be renewed as needed until the youth turns 20. This may occur when the youth is incapable of living independently, lacks a readily available support network, or the goals of the services provided have not yet been attained.

Court-Ordered Protection

Where less intrusive measures are not feasible or are inadequate, or the child has been apprehended, the social worker schedules a protection hearing in Family Court. If the judge determines that the child is in need of protective services, one of the following court orders is issued. A Supervision Order allows the Department to supervise the family in the home, while providing specified services. An order may not exceed six months, but may be extended indefinitely by the court. A Temporary Guardianship Order is used when the child is unable to remain in the family home, but is expected to return home or become independent within a reasonable period of time. Under this order, custody and guardianship of the child are extended to the Director; however, guardianship is shared with the child's guardian. The initial duration of this order may not exceed one year, but may be extended by the court for an additional year, for a maximum of two years cumulative time in care. It should be noted that the cumulative time a child may be in care under a Custody Agreement, an Interim Custody Order (during court adjournments) and a Temporary Guardianship Order may not exceed two years. However, in special cases, it is possible to obtain a court-ordered extension of up to one more year. A Permanent Guardianship Order is issued when there is little likelihood that the child's guardian will, within a reasonable time, be willing or able to ensure the child's security, survival or development.

Any child who is the subject of a Temporary Guardianship Order or a Permanent Guardianship Order may also apply for a Care and Maintenance Agreement. Such an agreement extends services for up to six months and may be renewed as needed until the youth reaches 20 years; however, the youth is no longer under the guardianship of the Director.

Under Section 28 of the *Child Welfare Act*, a Restraining Order may be issued to prevent any person who has abused or is likely to abuse a child who has either been apprehended or is the subject of any order from residing with or contacting the child in any way. This order may be for a period of up to six months.

Child Abuse Register

The Department of Family and Social Services does not have a formal child abuse register.

Child Abuse and Neglect Protocols

The Department of Family and Social Services has developed, in consultation with related departments and agencies, the following four protocols. These address both the reporting and investigation of a child in need of protective services.

"Protocol and Guidelines for Child Welfare Workers and School Personnel", developed jointly with the Department of Education, provides minimum practice guidelines for schools. District offices and local schools are encouraged to undertake their own initiatives to counteract child abuse and neglect.

"Protocols for Handling Child Abuse and Neglect in Day Care Services" provides guidelines for staff and caregivers in liaising with the Department.

"Young Offender Protocol" was jointly developed with the Department of the Solicitor General to establish procedures for interaction between both departments when dealing with children having joint status. The protocol addresses case management, disclosure of information by both departments, referrals to child welfare and income support, the Office of the Children's Advocate, child welfare investigation of young offender complaints and liaison for ongoing issues.

"Guidelines for Reporting and Investigating Suspected Cases of Children in Need of Protective Services in Women's Emergency Shelters" provides a guide for the development of protocols between individual shelters and district offices. Protocols should outline each other's respective roles and responsibilities in cases of suspected child abuse.

A fifth protocol, "The Protocol Relating to Section 643.1 of the Criminal Code", addresses the videotaping of disclosure statements by child sexual abuse victims. It was jointly developed with the Royal Canadian Mounted Police, the Attorney General's Department and the City of Edmonton Police Department. It ensures statements are suitable for both criminal and civil proceedings, and emphasizes close collaboration between the various agencies involved.

The Department is currently developing a reporting and investigation protocol together with the departments of Health, Education, the Solicitor General, the Attorney General and major stakeholders. The final product will provide a framework for the development of local protocols.

In Alberta, most protocols are developed at the local rather than provincial level. Districts offices are expected to have protocols with both local police and Indian reserves; many also have protocols with hospitals.

Statistics

The following tables and graphs are based on available data from the Child Welfare Information System (CWIS) of the Department of Family and Social Services. All data are for the month of March 1992, with the exception of investigation data which are for the 1991-92 fiscal year. Some terms which appear in the footnotes have not been defined.

In Alberta, all children who are deemed to be in need of protective services as defined in the *Child Welfare Act* are included in the protection data. Although the Act provides for Handicapped Children's Services Agreements for special needs children, these children are not defined as being in need of protective services and are therefore not included in the statistics. As at March 31, 1992, 6,001 children were the subject of a Handicapped Children's Services Agreement.

A child in care is one in need of protective services where there has been a transfer of custody and/or guardianship. Children come into care via a Custody Agreement, Apprehension, Temporary Guardianship Order (including extension to three years), Permanent Guardianship Agreement, Permanent Guardianship Order or an Interim Custody Order (children taken into care during an adjournment of the protection hearing). Not all abused or neglected children who are deemed to be in need of protective services are taken into care: many receive services in the home either voluntarily or under a Supervision Order. As at March 31, 1992, 340 children were the subject of a Supervision Order.

All Indian children receiving protective services are included in these data.

Due to the limitations noted in Chapter 1, Introduction, the following data should not be compared with data for other jurisdictions.

Table 10.1 Investigations[1] Completed by Primary Referral Reason[2], April 1, 1991 to March 31, 1992

Primary Referral Reason[2]	Number	Percentage
Abuse[3]	8,860	34.3
Neglect[4]	5,776	22.4
Parent/guardianship problem[5]	5,143	19.9
Parent/child conflict	3,243	12.6
Child problem[6]	1,716	6.6
Handicapped child	346	1.3
Other[7]	745	2.9
Not coded	7	---
Total	**25,836**	**100.0**

1. More than one investigation was completed for some children.
2. Represents the reason provided by the caller for contacting the Department of Family and Social Services. Only the primary reason is shown (system can record up to three referral reasons per investigation).
3. Includes physical and sexual abuse, exposure to family violence, and abuse pre-1982.
4. Includes physical and emotional neglect, failure to provide medical care, inadequate supervision, unable to care for child and emotional injury to child.
5. Includes abandonment, unwilling to care, physically ill parent, marital conflict, alcohol/drug problem of parent, financial problems/mismanagement, wishing to relinquish guardianship, parent/guardian deceased, and mentally ill parent.
6. Includes emotionally disturbed child, alcohol/drug problem of child, juvenile offence, child/school conflict, truancy, child/community conflict.
7. Includes out of province administrative referral, adoption enquiries, unmarried parent counselling, latchkey child, request for repatriation, private guardianship application investigation, out of province alert, and in province alert.

Figure 10.1 Investigations[1] Completed by Referral Source, April 1, 1991 to March 31, 1992

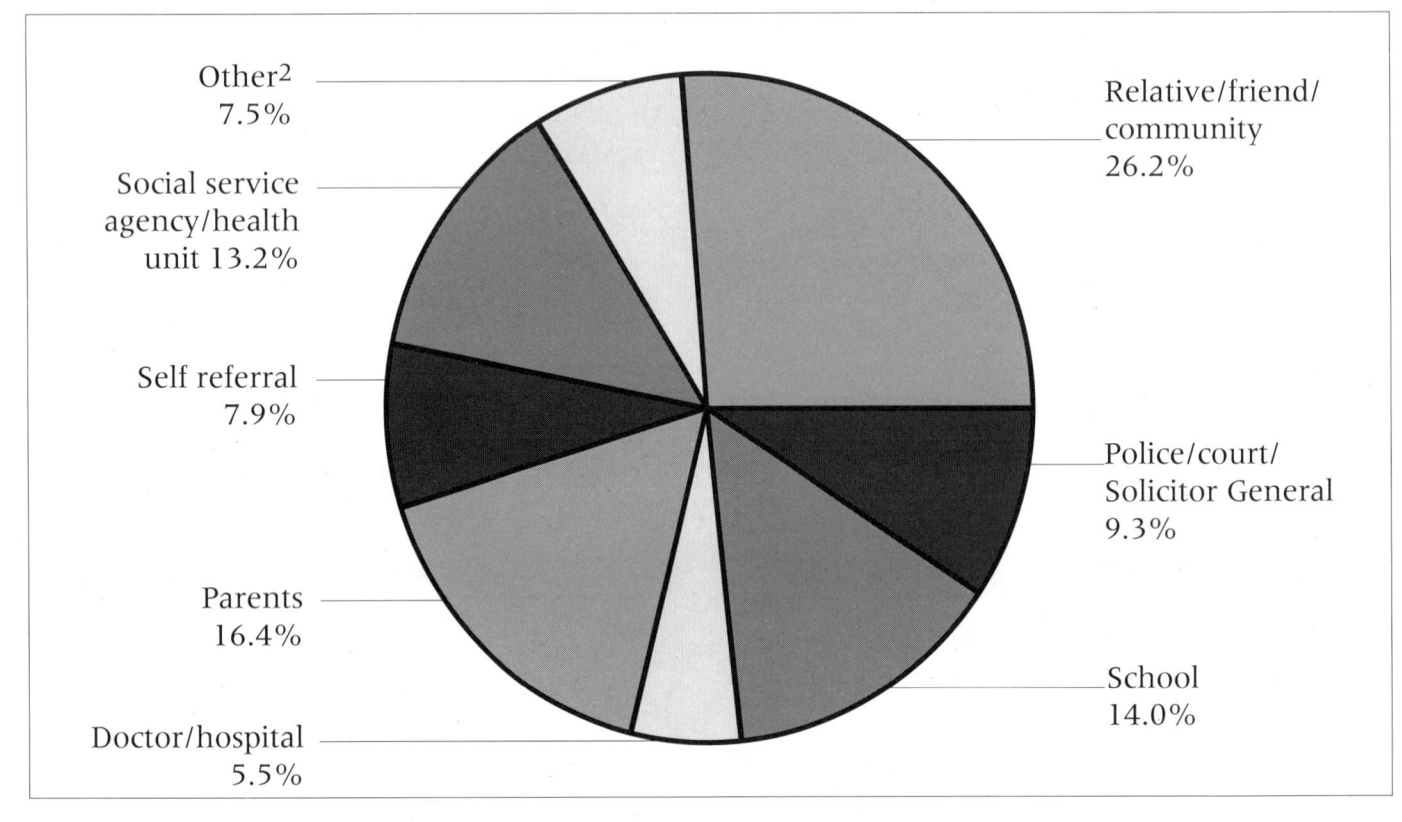

- Other[2] 7.5%
- Social service agency/health unit 13.2%
- Self referral 7.9%
- Parents 16.4%
- Doctor/hospital 5.5%
- Relative/friend/community 26.2%
- Police/court/Solicitor General 9.3%
- School 14.0%

Total investigations completed: 25,836

1. More than one investigation was completed for some children.
2. Includes anonymous and out of province.

Chapter 10 - Alberta

Figure 10.2 Social Worker's Primary Assessment[1] of Investigations[2] Completed, April 1, 1991 to March 31, 1992

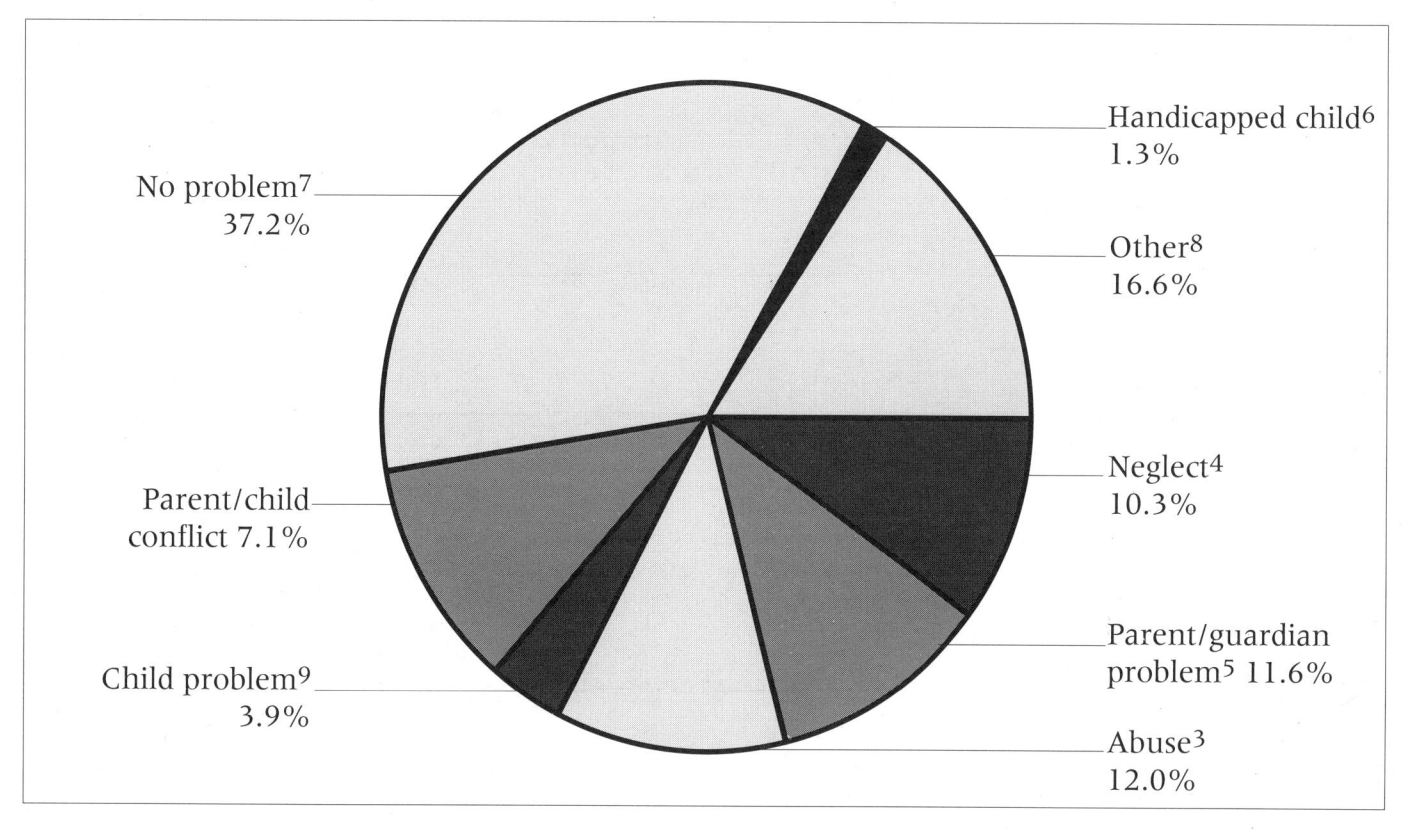

- Handicapped child[6] 1.3%
- Other[8] 16.6%
- Neglect[4] 10.3%
- Parent/guardian problem[5] 11.6%
- Abuse[3] 12.0%
- Child problem[9] 3.9%
- Parent/child conflict 7.1%
- No problem[7] 37.2%

Total investigations completed: 25,836

1. Represents worker's primary assessment of the completed investigation. Currently there are no guidelines for standard reporting by workers; consequently users should interpret these data with caution.
2. More than one investigation was conducted for some children.
3. In all cases where the worker's primary assessment is "abuse", the child is automatically determined to be in need of protective services. Includes physical abuse/ injury, guardian unwilling/unable to protect from physical injury, sexual abuse/exploitation, sexual abuse – extra familial/intra familial/in placement, guardian unwilling/unable to protect from sexual abuse/exploitation and suspected sexual abuse/exploitation.
4. Includes physical neglect, emotional neglect, emotional injury, failure to provide medical care, no caretaker present – inadequate supervision, caretaker present – inadequate supervision, unable to care for child, risk of physical injury, emotional rejection, deprived of affection/cognitive stimulation, guardian unwilling to prevent emotional injury, emergency care in home and emergency care out of home.
5. Includes abandonment, unwilling to care, physically ill parent, alcohol/drug problem of parent, financial problems/mismanagement, parent/guardian deceased, caretaker deceased, exposure to domestic violence, verbal abuse to child, inappropriate expectations of child, guardian unable to prevent emotional injury, emotionally disturbed parent/guardian/caretaker, and mentally handicapped parent/guardian/caretaker.
6. Represents those investigations where the child was handicapped and the parent(s) voluntarily signed a Handicapped Children's Services Agreement.
7. Includes child not in need/truancy/latchkey, malicious, unfounded, no grounds and conveyance only.
8. Includes administrative/out of province, unmarried parent counselling, custody dispute, homestudy in progress, private guardianship agreement in progress, referral to community, referral to income support, referral to mental health, child repatriated and not coded.
9. Includes emotionally disturbed child, alcohol/drug problem of child, juvenile offence, child/school conflict, and child/community conflict.

Table 10.2 Children in Need of Protection[1] by Child's Legal Status and Social Worker's Assessment of Primary Reason[2] as at March 31, 1992

	\multicolumn{7}{c}{Social Worker's Assessment of Primary Reason[2]}
	\multicolumn{4}{c}{Abuse}			
Child's Legal Status	Physical	Sexual	Suspected Sexual	Total	Neglect	Other[3]	Total
Support Agreement	209	324	25	558	415	824	1,797
Custody Agreement	30	36	1	67	84	436	587
Apprehension	6	2	0	8	13	21	42
Supervision Order	47	46	7	100	79	161	340
Temporary Guardianship Order	54	32	5	91	121	307	519
Permanent Guardianship Agreement[4]/Order	89	109	21	219	371	1,533	2,123
Extend Custody to 3 years[5]	1	3	1	5	32	63	100
Extend Care Past 18 years[6]	4	13	0	17	9	83	109
Interim Custody Order[7]	11	8	2	21	46	129	196
Other[8]	44	61	4	109	109	213	431
No legal authority in effect[9]	94	120	7	221	169	475	865
Total	**589**	**754**	**73**	**1,416**	**1,448**	**4,245**	**7,109**
Percentage	**8.3**	**10.6**	**1.0**	**19.9**	**20.4**	**59.7**	**100.0**

1. Represents those children found to be in need of protective services as defined in the *Child Welfare Act*.
2. Represents worker's primary assessment of reason for intervention. Currently there are no guidelines for standard reporting by workers; consequently users should interpret these data with caution.
3. Includes parent/guardian problem, child problem, parent/child conflict, handicapped child, other, no problem and not coded.
4. Voluntary relinquishment of a child for adoption.
5. The cumulative time a child may be in care under a Custody Agreement, an Interim Custody Order and a Temporary Guardianship Order may not exceed two years; this may be extended to three years if ordered by the court.
6. Represents a Care and Maintenance Agreement for youth 18-20 years who were previously receiving protection services.
7. Represents those children taken into care during an adjournment of the protection hearing.
8. Includes related agreements and orders.
9. Represents situations where the child's legal status has expired and has not been extended or changed.

Chapter 10 - Alberta

Table 10.3 Children in Care[1] by Child's Legal Status and Social Worker's Assessment of Primary Reason[2] as at March 31, 1992

| | \multicolumn{4}{c}{Social Worker's Assessment of Primary Reason[2]} | | | |
Child's Legal Status	Suspected Physical	Suspected Sexual	Sexual	Abuse Total	Neglect	Other[3]	Total
Custody Agreement	30	36	1	67	84	436	587
Apprehension	6	2	0	8	13	21	42
Temporary Guardianship Order	54	32	5	91	121	307	519
Permanent Guardianship Agreement[4]/Order	89	109	21	219	371	1,533	2,123
Extend Custody to 3 years[5]	1	3	1	5	32	63	100
Interim Custody Order[6]	11	8	2	21	46	129	196
Total	**191**	**190**	**30**	**411**	**667**	**2,489**	**3,567**
Percentage	**5.4**	**5.3**	**0.8**	**11.5**	**18.7**	**69.8**	**100.0**

1. Children in care represents a subset of protection cases where there has been a transfer of custody and/or guardianship; these are under the legal statuses shown.
2. Represents worker's primary assessment of reason for intervention. Currently there are no guidelines for standard reporting by workers; consequently users should interpret these data with caution.
3. Includes parent/guardian problem, child problem, parent/child conflict, handicapped child, other, no problem and not coded.
4. Voluntary relinquishment of a child for adoption.
5. The cumulative time a child may be in care under a Custody Agreement, an Interim Custody Order and a Temporary Guardianship Order may not exceed two years; this may be extended to three years if ordered by the court.
6. Represents those children taken into care during an adjournment of the protection hearing.

Figure 10.3 Children in Care[1] by Legal Status as at March 31, 1992

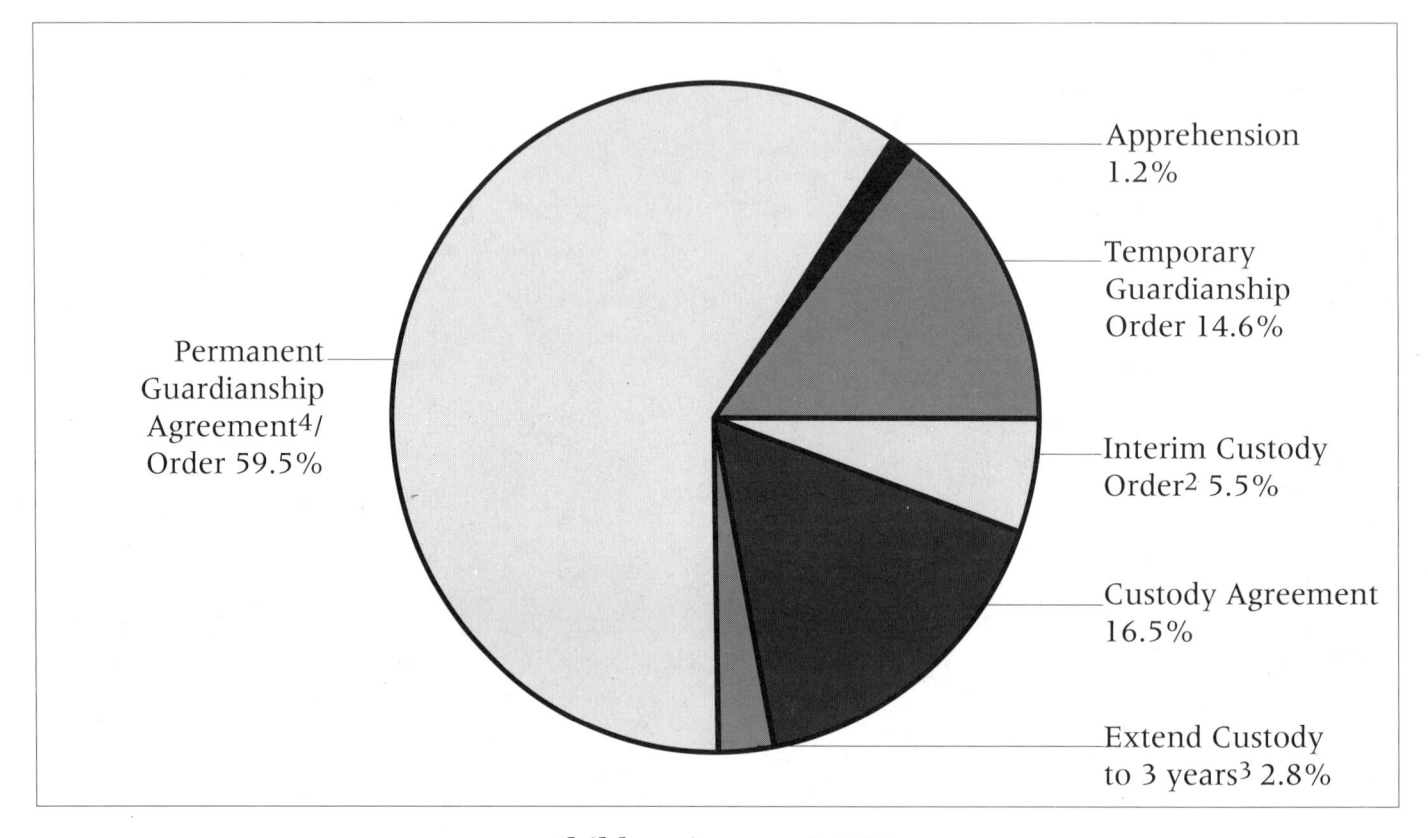

- Permanent Guardianship Agreement[4]/Order 59.5%
- Apprehension 1.2%
- Temporary Guardianship Order 14.6%
- Interim Custody Order[2] 5.5%
- Custody Agreement 16.5%
- Extend Custody to 3 years[3] 2.8%

Children in care: 3,567

1. Children in care represents a subset of protection cases where there has been a transfer of custody and/or guardianship; these are under the legal statuses shown.
2. Represents those children taken into care during an adjournment of the protection hearing.
3. The cumulative time a child may be in care under a Custody Agreement, an Interim Custody Order and a Temporary Guardianship Order may not exceed two years; this may be extended to three years if ordered by the court.
4. Voluntary relinquishment of a child for adoption.

Chapter 10 - Alberta   Page 141

Figure 10.4 Children in Care[1] by Age Group as at March 31, 1992

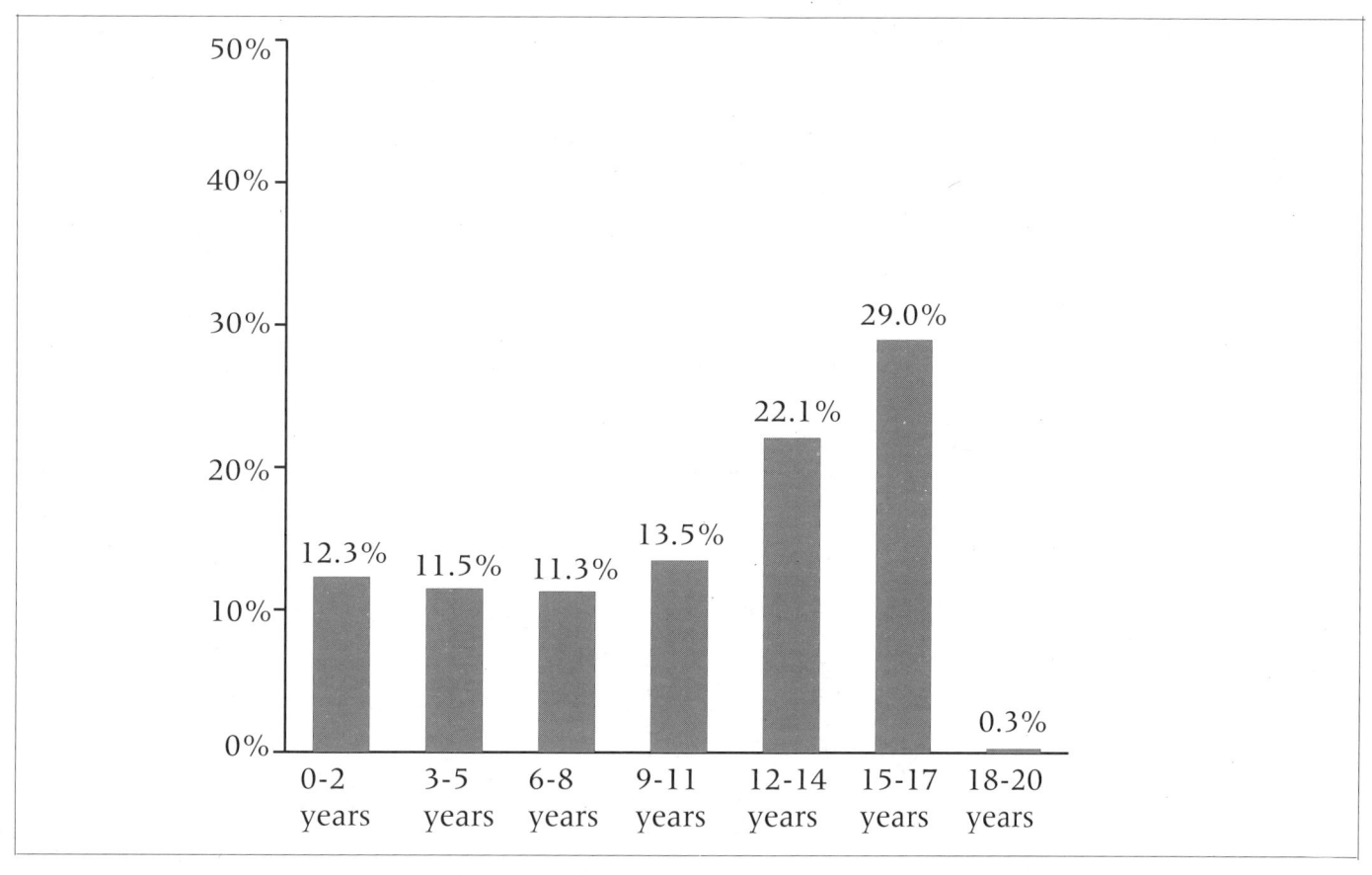

Age Group	Percentage
0-2 years	12.3%
3-5 years	11.5%
6-8 years	11.3%
9-11 years	13.5%
12-14 years	22.1%
15-17 years	29.0%
18-20 years	0.3%

Children in care: 3,567

1. Children in care represents a subset of protection cases where there has been a transfer of custody and/or guardianship. This includes the following legal statuses: Custody Agreement, Apprehension, Temporary Guardianship Order, Permanent Guardianship Agreement, Permanent Guardianship Order, Extend Custody to 3 years and Interim Custody Order.

Table 10.4   Children in Care[1] by Sex of Child as at March 31, 1992

Sex	Number	Percentage
Male	1,911	53.6
Female	1,656	46.4
Total	**3,567**	**100.0**

1. Children in care represents a subset of protection cases where there has been a transfer of custody and/or guardianship. This includes the following legal statuses: Custody Agreement, Apprehension, Temporary Guardianship Order, Permanent Guardianship Agreement, Permanent Guardianship Order, Extend Custody to 3 years and Interim Custody Order.

Figure 10.5   Children in Care[1] by Placement Type as at March 31, 1992

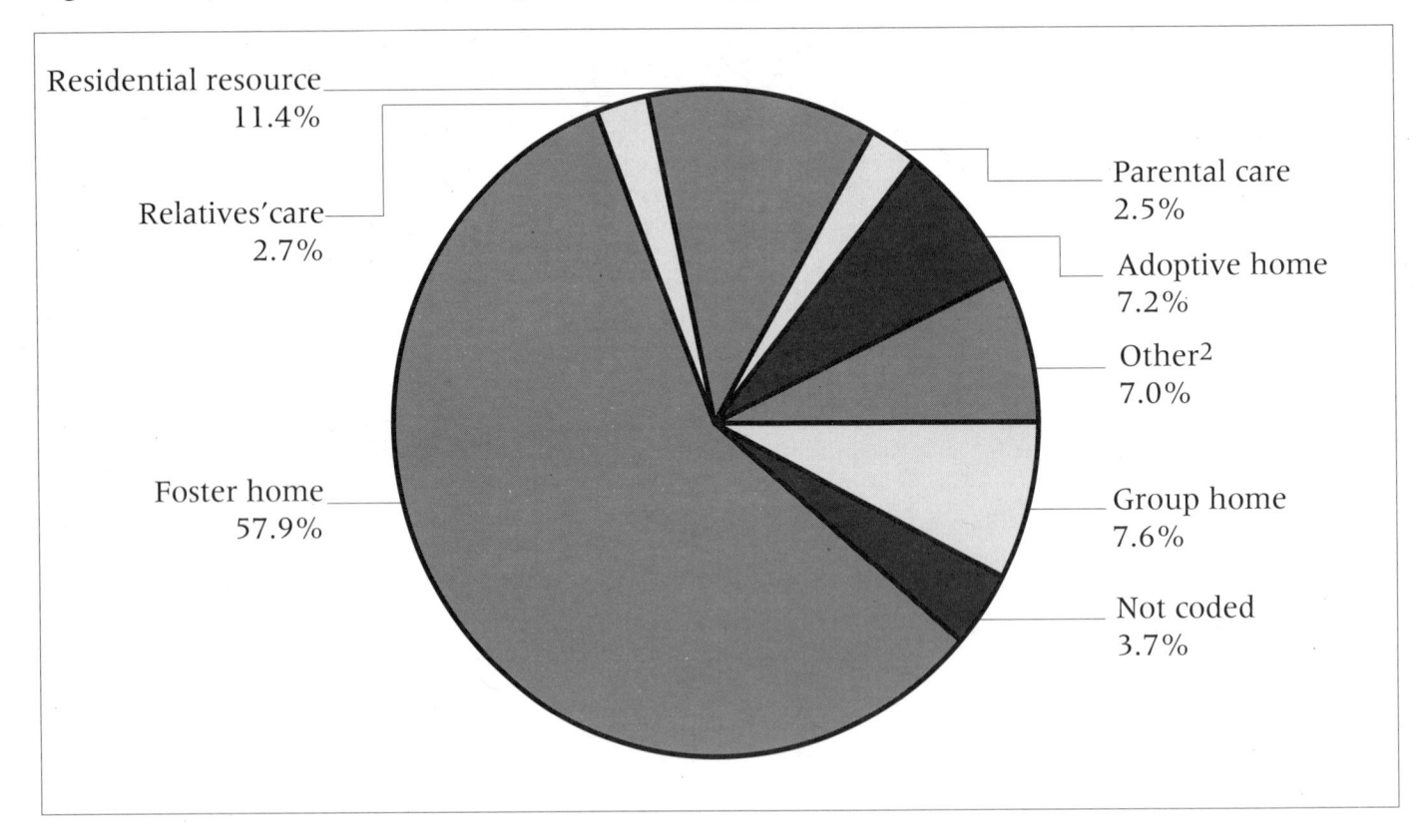

- Residential resource: 11.4%
- Relatives' care: 2.7%
- Foster home: 57.9%
- Parental care: 2.5%
- Adoptive home: 7.2%
- Other[2]: 7.0%
- Group home: 7.6%
- Not coded: 3.7%

Children in care: 3,567

1. Children in care represents a subset of protection cases where there has been a transfer of custody and/or guardianship. This includes the following legal statuses: Custody Agreement, Apprehension, Temporary Guardianship Order, Permanent Guardianship Agreement, Permanent Guardianship Order, Extend Custody to 3 years and Interim Custody Order.
2. Includes compulsory care, detention and other.

Resource Material

Legislative Material

Child Welfare Act, Statutes of Alberta 1984, c. C-8.1, as amended.

Other Material

Alberta, Family and Social Services. "Child Welfare Handbook", Edmonton.

_____. "Child Welfare Program Management Manual", Edmonton.

_____. "Child Welfare Casework Supports Manual" (includes protocols), Edmonton.

Alberta, Department of Family and Social Services and Department of the Solicitor General. *Young Offender Protocol*, November 1990.

Chapter 11 – British Columbia

Administration and Service Delivery

The legislative authority for child protection in British Columbia is the *Family and Child Service Act*. Under the Act, the Superintendent of Family and Child Service in the Ministry of Social Services is responsible for investigating allegations that a child may be abused or neglected. The provincial government is currently reviewing major legislation affecting children and families in British Columbia, including the *Family and Child Service Act*. Extensive consultations with local and aboriginal communities occurred during the first six months of 1992; these formed the basis for two reports which were presented to the Minister in December, 1992. New legislation should be tabled in the Spring of 1993, and proclaimed in the Fall of 1994.

The Family and Children's Services Division, located in Victoria, is responsible for policy and program development, program coordination and monitoring, budget preparation and legislative change proposals. Also housed in Victoria, the Assistant Deputy Minister of Field Operations is responsible for the nine regional offices which oversee the delivery of Ministry programs and services. District offices within these regions have specialist delivery units which focus exclusively on child and family services. While child protection services are a key activity of these units, additional services include family support services, native child welfare, and adoption. In some smaller communities, all Ministry services (including income assistance and services to persons with disabilities) are delivered by integrated units.

Although Ministry social workers provide child protection services, they are assisted by private agencies, companies and individuals providing other related services, such as residential care and family support services. Child protection services to natives vary throughout the province; currently the Ministry has agreements with the Nuu-chah-nulth Tribal Council and the Spallumcheen Band to deliver their own child welfare services on reserves. Agreements are also in place with the McLeod Lake Band and the Carrier-Sekani Tribal Council to provide support services, develop resources and provide cross-cultural training to prepare them to assume responsibility for their own child welfare services.[1] Ministry social workers deliver all services to natives on reserve where there are no formal agreements. In addition, the Ministry's Vancouver region operates the Aboriginal Family and Children's Services Unit for native children in care under 12 years of age.

---

1 In January, 1993, the Ministry signed an agreement with the Cowichan Tribe to take over their own child welfare services. Delegation of authority under the *Family and Child Service Act* will be phased in over a three year period.

The Child and Youth Secretariat was established in 1990, with representatives from the ministries of Social Services, Solicitor General, Education and Health. The Secretariat's purpose is to ensure the efficient provincial coordination and integration of services for children and youth. This involves accessing the full range of services available by other government ministries as well as non-governmental community-based services. The Ministry of Social Services may refer any child and family to such services or purchase services on their behalf. Local Child and Youth Committees, consisting of representatives from all ministries providing services to children and youth, report to the Child and Youth Secretariat.

The Ministry of Social Services is also involved in the Sexual Abuse Interventions Project. This initiative, which is coordinated by the Ministry of Health, is an inter-ministerial approach to providing services to child victims of sexual abuse throughout British Columbia.

Responsibility for coordinating inter-ministerial programs on family violence rests with the Ministry of Women's Equality. A representative from the Ministry of Social Services is responsible for liaison functions.

Definitions

Under Section 1 of the *Family and Child Service Act*, a **child** is defined as a person under 19 years old. Sub-section 15(2) allows for support and/or maintenance to be extended to both current and former permanent wards between the ages of 19 and 21. Section 1 of the *Adoption Act* defines a **child** as an unmarried person under 19 years of age.

Section 1 of the *Family and Child Service Act* also defines a **child in need of protection** as one who is

"(a) abused or neglected so that his safety or well-being is endangered,

(b) abandoned,

(c) deprived of necessary care through the death, absence or disability of his parent,

(d) deprived of necessary medical attention, or

(e) absent from his home in circumstances that endanger his safety or well-being."

There is no definition of abuse or neglect contained in legislation; however, the *Inter-Ministry Child Abuse Handbook: An Integrated Approach to Child Abuse and Neglect* provides the following working definitions, which are applied uniformly across the province by social workers.

"**Abuse** means physical, sexual or emotional abuse.

Physical abuse means any physical force or action which results in or may potentially result in a non-accidental injury to a child and which exceeds that which could be considered reasonable discipline.

Sexual abuse means any sexual exploitation of a child whether consensual or not. It includes touching of a sexual nature and sexual intercourse, and may include any behaviour of a sexual nature toward a child. In determining whether behaviour is of a sexual nature, one should ask whether a reasonable observer, looking at the behaviour in its context, would conclude that it is. This would exclude normal affectionate behaviour towards children and normal health or hygiene care.

Sexual activity between children may constitute sexual abuse if the difference in age or power between the children is so significant that the older or more powerful child is clearly taking sexual advantage of the younger or less powerful child. This would exclude consensual, developmentally appropriate sexual activity between children where there is no significant difference in age or power between the children.

Emotional abuse means acts or omissions of those responsible for the care of a child which are likely to produce long term and serious emotional disorder. This might include effects such as non-organic failure to thrive; developmental retardation; serious anxiety, depression or withdrawal; or serious behavioural disturbance.

Neglect means the failure of those responsible for the care of the child to meet the physical, emotional or medical needs of a child to an extent that the child's health, development or safety is endangered."

Mandatory Reporting of a Child in Need of Protection

Under Sub-section 7(1) of the *Family and Child Service Act*, any person with reasonable grounds to believe that a child is in need of protection must report it to the Superintendent of Family and Child Service; in fact, reports are made to delegated social workers. Professional persons who consider their relationship with clients as confidential are not exempt from the duty to report, with the exception of lawyers (Sub-section 7(2)). Under the *Offence Act*, failure to report may result in a fine up to a maximum of $2,000, a maximum jail sentence of six months, or both. There is no penalty specified in the Act for persons making false or malicious reports; redress would be pursued through civil action.

In situations where an outside agency or institution is the initial contact point for victims of abuse, whether intra- or extra-familial, the Ministry of Social Services must be informed immediately of any potential child protection situation. In addition, any person who reports suspected abuse or neglect to an agency or institution (e.g., the police or a school) is still legally required to report to the Ministry.

The Ministry also operates a 24 hour, province-wide After Hours program to receive reports of suspected child abuse or neglect as well as requests for Ministry services. It consists of the Helpline for Children and the Provincial After Hours Line, for use by professionals and caregivers. Urgent matters are referred for immediate investigation; other reports are handled on the following working day.

Investigation of an Allegation of Child Abuse or Neglect

The Ministry of Social Services has responsibility for investigating reports that a child may be abused or neglected. The child and family services delivery units across the province have teams which deal with child protection cases; in addition, Vancouver, Nanaimo, Kamloops and Kelowna have specialized intake offices which focus exclusively on investigations. Reports received are initially reviewed by a social worker within the same working day to determine whether an investigation is required; decisions not to investigate must be approved by the District Supervisor. All reports received by the Ministry of suspected physical or sexual abuse, whether intra- or extra-familial, must be immediately reported to the police. Where an investigation is necessary, a response time of immediate, within 24 hours, or beyond 24 hours is assigned. Reports of severe physical abuse or neglect, sexual abuse or situations where the family has a history of violence or abuse which could place the child at risk, among others, are investigated immediately. All other complaints are investigated within 24 hours, unless the District Supervisor approves extending the response time beyond this.

If a report is received of child abuse or neglect by a person who is not a member of the child's household, the social worker must also investigate. The social worker must initially ensure that the parent is aware of the allegation(s). If the parent requests help, the child and family may be referred to Ministry or community support services. If the family is unable or unwilling to protect the child, the social worker proceeds with a full investigation and must report any allegation of physical or sexual abuse to the police. In cases of reported abuse in a facility outside the home such as a school, foster home or a child care facility licensed under the *Community Care Facility Act*, the Ministry is also responsible for investigating the complaint. Specific protocols exist for dealing with these situations (see section on Child Abuse and Neglect Protocols).

The actual investigation must ensure that all parties involved (for example, the police, medical health officer and social worker) meet to plan a joint response, with the roles and responsibilities of each party clearly defined. The various investigators must keep one another informed of their decisions and actions. The child should be jointly interviewed as soon as possible following the report or disclosure. Videotaping of the interview is recommended, although there is currently no legislative mandate in the *Family and Child Service Act* which explicitly provides for the admissibility of videotaped evidence. Any siblings of the child victim should also be interviewed to assess whether they are in need of protection. A medical examination is required immediately in cases where physical injuries are present or suspected, and in cases where sexual abuse has, or is alleged to have, occurred within the last 72 hours. Where sexual abuse is substantiated or disclosed, a test for sexually transmitted diseases is also scheduled within 24 hours. All medical examinations require the approval of the child's parent(s); if refused, the child must be apprehended. The social worker must assess risk factors for each child in the family to determine whether the child is safe or is likely to be harmed by abuse or neglect in the near future.

Where there is reason to believe that a child's safety is endangered and cannot be assured by other means, the social worker or police must apprehend the child. If the child is believed to be in immediate physical danger, either may enter the premises, using force where necessary. A warrant is not required to apprehend in either instance; however, if access to a child is denied, a warrant must be obtained. Police assistance is often requested when apprehending a child.

Where no native child welfare agreement exists and the Ministry is investigating a report that a native child on Reserve Lands may require protective services, the social worker should consult with the Band social worker. Where possible, the Band is encouraged to become involved in child protection issues. If it is necessary to take a native child into care, the Ministry will attempt to ensure that the child's cultural, spiritual and linguistic background are respected.

All child protection workers receive basic training which consists of three phases: On-The-Job Training which commences on the first day and continues for six months; Family and Children's Services Core Training, a 4.5 day module which provides an overview of generic social work skills as they relate to the Ministry's family and children's services;

and Protection Core Training, a 4.5 day module focusing exclusively on child protection. Specialized training on investigative interviewing of child abuse complainants and child sexual abuse investigations skills is being developed.

Voluntary Agreements

In British Columbia, voluntary agreements are considered as a support service to the parent. Where the needs and safety of a child cannot be assured in the family home, a parent may sign a voluntary agreement with the Ministry which results in the child being placed outside the home. Under an agreement, custody of the child is temporarily transferred to the Superintendent of Family and Child Service and the parent retains guardianship responsibility. A Short Term Custody Agreement lasts for up to three months, with provision for an additional six month extension. This agreement may be used in child abuse or neglect situations only if the parent acknowledges the need for temporary removal of the child and is in agreement with the plan. The District Supervisor must review the service plan with the social worker to ensure the child's protection needs will be met and must be confident that the parent will follow through with the plan.

The parent(s) of a handicapped child who requires additional support services not readily available may enter into a Special Care Agreement with the Superintendent. The child is usually placed in a specialized resource designed to respond to his/her special needs. The maximum initial term is six months, with provision for indefinite 12 month renewal periods.

A parent may also negotiate for intermittent care under either of the above agreements; this is primarily a respite service for the parent.

Court-Ordered Protection

Where voluntary options are not feasible or successful, or if a child is apprehended, a protection hearing is scheduled in the Family Court. If a child disclosed physical or sexual abuse during the initial investigation phase and the police have determined that charges should be laid, an audiotape or videotape of the child's disclosure may be used as evidence in Family Court. A child may also be permitted to testify in the Judge's chambers. If a Judge determines that the child is in need of protective services, one of the following orders is issued: a Supervision Order, a Temporary Custody Order or a Permanent Order. Under a Supervision Order, the child remains in the family home under the Superintendent's supervision for up to six months. A Temporary Custody Order and a Permanent Order both result in the child being removed from the family home and placed in a resource designed to meet the specific needs of the child. A Temporary Custody Order may be for up to 12 months, with provision for a subsequent six month renewal. During this time, the Superintendent has custody and temporary guardianship of the child. Under a Permanent Order, all parental rights and responsibilities are transferred to the Superintendent.

Under Sub-section 16(4) of the *Family and Child Service Act*, where the Superintendent has custody of a child, a judge may order that an alleged offender not enter a child's residence, or attempt to contact or interfere with the child or person having custody of the child.

Sub-section 15(2) of the Act allows the Superintendent to enter into an agreement with a former or current permanent ward between the ages of 19 and 21 to provide support and/or maintenance. To be eligible for the Post Majority Services Program, the young adult must be accepted into an educational or training program, be terminally ill, or have a serious mental or physical disability.

Child Abuse Register

British Columbia does not operate a child abuse register.

Child Abuse and Neglect Protocols

The *Inter-Ministry Child Abuse Handbook: An Integrated Approach to Child Abuse and Neglect*, stresses the need for inter-ministerial cooperation in dealing with reports of child abuse and neglect. The Handbook was produced by the ministries of Social Services, Health, Education, Attorney General and Solicitor General (Solicitor General has since been merged with the Attorney General). It contains a generic protocol on the investigation of allegations of child abuse or neglect, and details the steps to be taken by persons mandated to investigate and intervene in such cases. The Handbook consists of three parts:

1. An overview which outlines guiding principles in approaching child abuse, a summary of relevant law, confidentiality, working definitions of child abuse and neglect, prevention of child abuse and neglect, mandatory reporting requirements and the integrated response to investigation and intervention;

2. Detailed information on the specific roles of the five ministries; and

3. Specific protocols.

Appendices contain indicators of abuse and neglect, guidelines for interviewing children, the roles of the physician, guidelines for physicians in sexual abuse cases, and the role of Alcohol and Drug Programs.

A committee has been formed to review the Handbook. All protocols will be reviewed and revised as required, and the Handbook will also be revised to reflect the new legislation expected in 1993.

The following specific protocols are contained in the Handbook.

"Protocol 1: Cases with Multiple Victims and Other High-impact Cases" deals with the process to be followed by all ministries and agencies. A committee is formed comprising representatives from the ministries noted above, as well as appropriate agencies (e.g., public health units, mental health services) to plan and coordinate community intervention. This will be further enhanced in 1993 based on research on multiple victim child sexual abuse research being conducted by the Ministry of Health.

"Protocol 2: Investigations of Abuse or Neglect in Child Care Facilities Licensed Under the *Community Care Facility Act* and Provincial Child Care Facilities Regulations" outlines the responsibilities of the medical health officer (primary investigator), the Superintendent of Family and Child Service and the police in responding to allegations of abuse or neglect in a child care facility licensed under the Act.

"Protocol 3: Cases of Abuse or Neglect Allegedly Perpetrated by a School Board Employee" summarizes the responsibilities of the superintendent of schools (primary investigator), the Superintendent of Family and Child Service and the police in responding to allegations of abuse or neglect.

The following protocol and guidelines, which are presently in use, will be included in the next edition of the Handbook.

"Protocol 4: Family Court Counsellors/ Ministry of Social Services Liaison Regarding Family Cases in Common" clarifies the respective roles of family court counsellors and social workers working with the same family to avoid duplication of service, while ensuring that the needs of children and families are met.

"Guidelines for Hospitals" identifies the role of hospitals in child abuse cases and encourages the development of local protocols for the assessment and management of abused children. Suggested areas which should be addressed in protocols are outlined. There are currently no standard protocols for hospitals in place; however, some regions have negotiated their own protocols between regional Ministry staff and the local hospitals.

In addition, protocols being developed for police forces and the Office of the Public Trustee, will be included in the revised Handbook.

The BC Federation of Foster Parent Associations and the Ministry jointly developed the "Protocol for Investigating Abuse Complaints in Foster Homes". This agreement outlines the process, roles and responsibilities of Ministry and Federation representatives in abuse investigations where foster parents are the subject of the complaint.

Statistics

The following tables and graphs, which are for the month of March 1992, are based on data provided by the Research, Evaluation and Statistics Branch of the Ministry of Social Services.

The total children in care population refers to those children who are in the care of the Superintendent of Family and Child Service (temporary or permanent transfer of guardianship and/or custody) under the following legal statuses: Short Term Custody Agreement, Special Care Agreement, under apprehension, Interim Order (in custody of Superintendent during protection hearing adjournment), temporary ward (Temporary Custody Order), permanent ward (Permanent Order), *Adoption Act* ward (voluntary relinquishment for adoption), *Family Relations Act* ward (orphaned child with no guardian) and ward of another jurisdiction. Native children in care, including those who are members of the Native Bands who have negotiated separate agreements with the Ministry, are also included.

It should be noted that a large number of families and children are also receiving Ministry support services in the home, including children who are the subject of a Supervision Order (child remains in home under supervision of the Superintendent); these are excluded from the children in care numbers. As at March 31, 1992, there were 297 children under Supervision Orders.

Due to the limitations noted in Chapter 1, Introduction, these data should not be compared with data for other jurisdictions.

Table 11.1 Helpline[1] Child Welfare Calls by Type[2] during March 1992

Type[2]		Number	Percentage
Abuse			
	Physical	218	13.3
	Sexual	192	11.7
	Emotional	89	5.4
	Multiple	62	3.8
	Sub-Total	**561**	**34.2**
Neglect		413	25.2
Other[3]		666	40.6
Total		**1,640**	**100.0**

1. The Helpline for Children is part of the Ministry of Social Services' After Hours Program which receives reports of suspected child abuse or neglect, as well as requests for other Ministry services. During March 1992, an additional 928 non-child welfare calls were received.
2. Represents caller's allegation.
3. Represents the sum of the following calls: repatriation, guardianship, resource support, other protection.

Table 11.2 Child Protection Complaints[1] Received by Type[2] during March 1992

Type[2]		Number	Percentage
Abuse			
	Physical	683	23.8
	Sexual	537	18.7
	Emotional	125	4.4
	Sub-Total	**1,345**	**46.8**
Neglect		941	32.8
Other[3]		482	16.8
Not coded		105	3.7
Total		**2,873**	**100.0**

1. Complaints received by the Ministry of Social Services under the mandatory reporting provisions of the *Family and Child Service Act*. There may be more than one complaint concerning a specific child. Includes all Helpline calls.
2. Represents caller's allegation.
3. Represents the total of: absent from the home, *Family Relations Act* – Section 29 (orphaned child with no guardian), other, and multiple.

Chapter 11 - British Columbia

Figure 11.1 Child Protection Complaints[1] Received during March 1992 by Referral Source

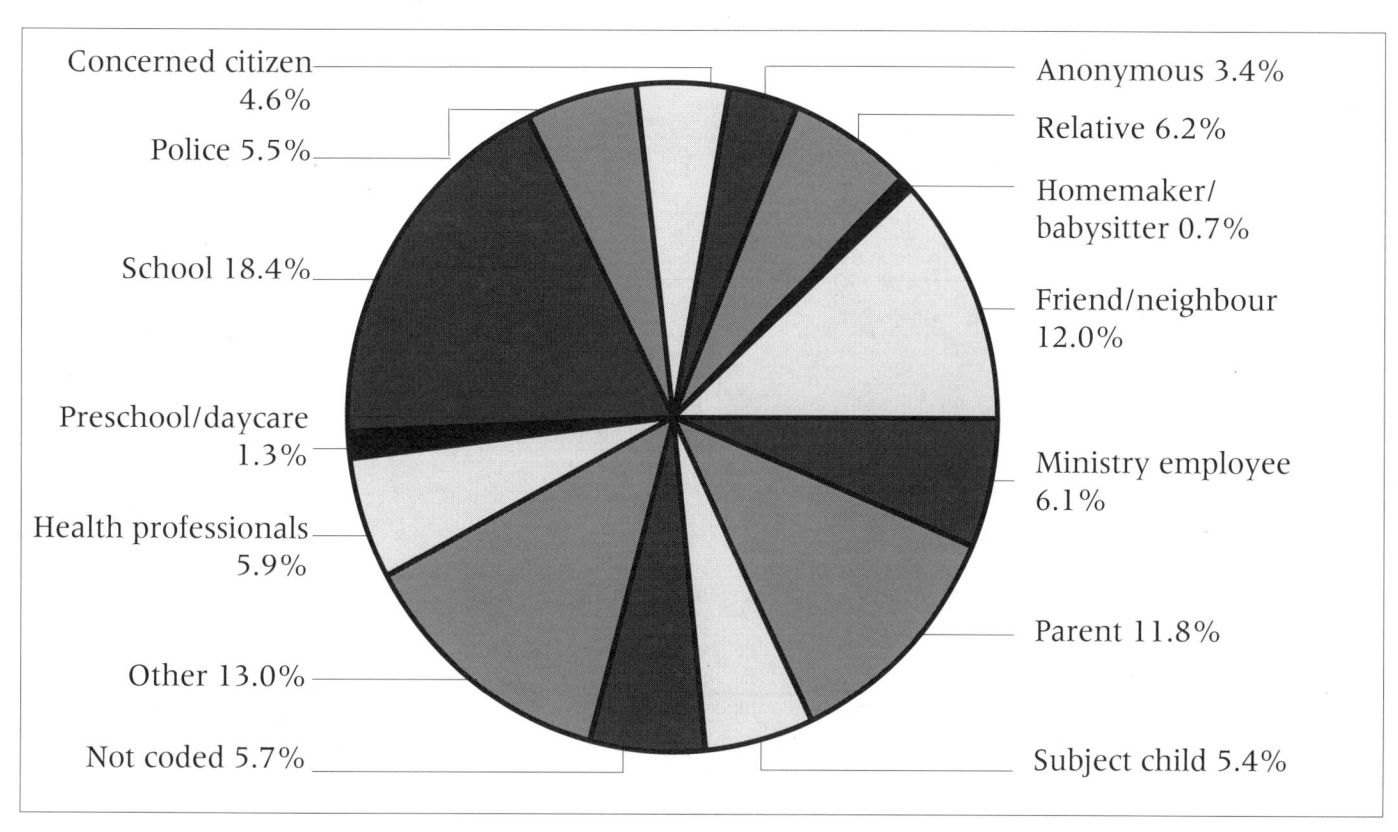

- Concerned citizen 4.6%
- Police 5.5%
- School 18.4%
- Preschool/daycare 1.3%
- Health professionals 5.9%
- Other 13.0%
- Not coded 5.7%
- Anonymous 3.4%
- Relative 6.2%
- Homemaker/babysitter 0.7%
- Friend/neighbour 12.0%
- Ministry employee 6.1%
- Parent 11.8%
- Subject child 5.4%

Complaints: 2,873

1. Complaints received by the Ministry of Social Services under the mandatory reporting provisions of the *Family and Child Service Act*. There may be more than one complaint concerning a specific child. Includes all Helpline calls.

Figure 11.2 Child Protection Complaints[1] Received during March 1992 by Outcome

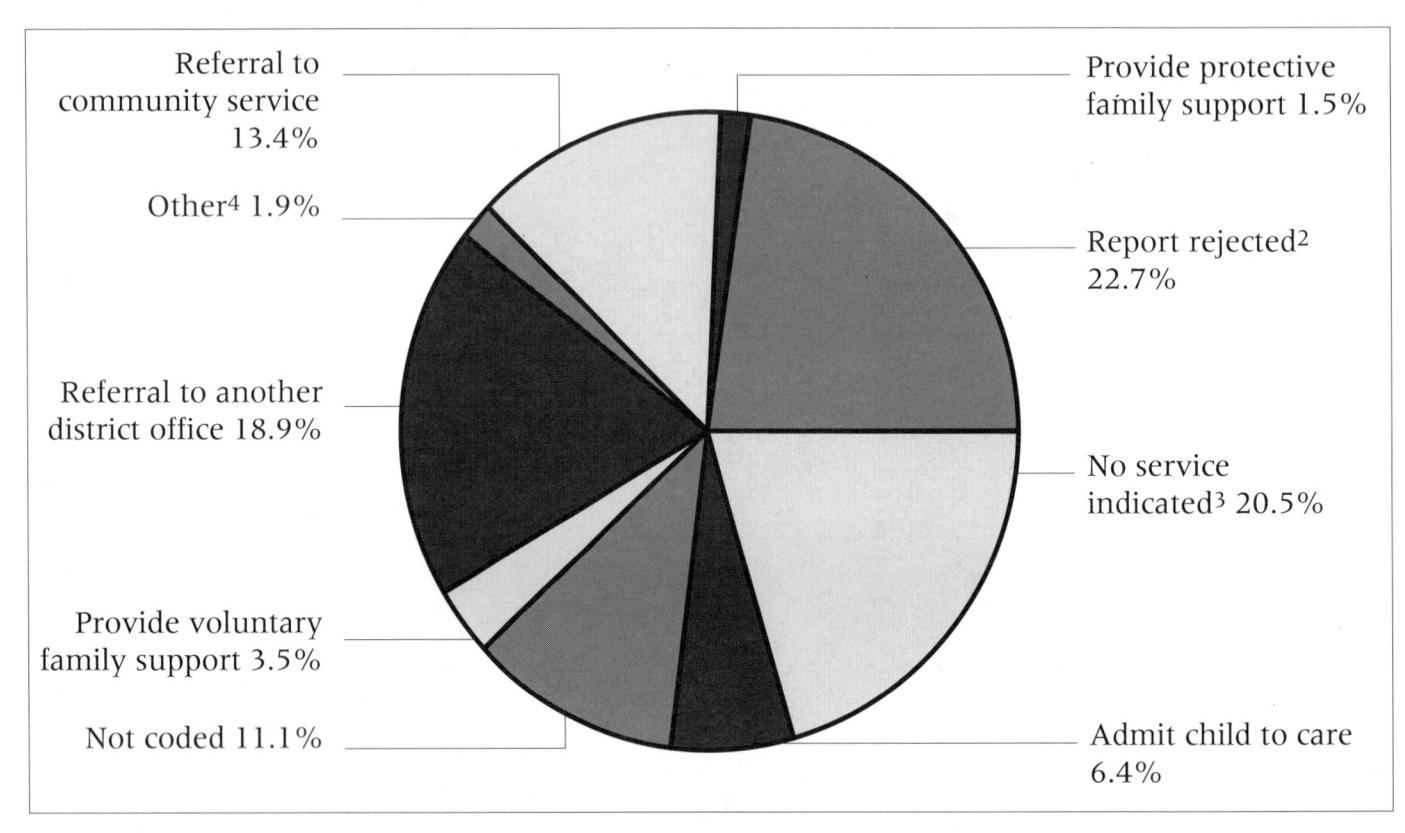

- Referral to community service 13.4%
- Other[4] 1.9%
- Referral to another district office 18.9%
- Provide voluntary family support 3.5%
- Not coded 11.1%
- Provide protective family support 1.5%
- Report rejected[2] 22.7%
- No service indicated[3] 20.5%
- Admit child to care 6.4%

Complaints: 2,873

1. Complaints received by the Ministry of Social Services under the mandatory reporting provisions of the *Family and Child Service Act*. There may be more than one complaint concerning a specific child. Includes all Helpline calls.
2. Initial assessment indicated investigation not required.
3. Investigation indicated no service required.
4. Represents the total of the following: service not accepted, outside family – parent ensuring safety, and repatriation.

Table 11.3 Children in Care[1] by Reason for Admission[2] as at March 31, 1992

Reason	Number	Percentage
Protection Required[3]		
Abuse – physical	429	7.1
– sexual	241	4.0
Sub-Total	**670**	**11.0**
Neglect	544	8.9
Abandonment	426	7.0
Death of caregiver	27	0.4
Absence of parent(s)	196	3.2
Disability of parent(s)	822	13.5
Deprivation of necessary medical care	16	0.3
Absent from home and endangered	225	3.7
Sub-Total	**2,926**	**48.1**
Short Term Care Required[4]	1,368	22.5
Special Care Required[5]	529	8.7
Other[6]	193	3.2
Not coded[7]	1,068	17.6
Total	**6,084**	**100.0**

1. Children in care represents children whose legal status is one of the following: Short Term Custody Agreement, Special Care Agreement, apprehension, interim order, Temporary Custody Order, Permanent Order, *Adoption Act* ward (voluntary relinquishment for adoption), *Family Relations Act* ward (orphaned child with no guardian) or ward of another jurisdiction.
2. Represents the initial reason for a child's admission to care. Reasons are stipulated in the *Family and Child Service Act*.
3. Reasons for a child being in need of protection as defined in Section 1 of the *Family and Child Service Act*. One or more must be proven to the court before a child is committed to care.
4. The child's parent requires temporary assistance in caring for the child and enters into a Short Term Care Agreement with the Superintendent (Section 4 of the Act).
5. The Superintendent and child's parent agree the child requires special care and enter into a Special Care and Custody Agreement (Section 5 of the Act).
6. Includes death of guardian, transfer of guardianship or custody, relinquishment for adoption and request by other province or country.
7. Represents the number of children who were admitted to care under the former *Protection of Children Act*.

Table 11.4 Children in Care[1] by Legal Status as at March 31, 1992

Legal Status	Number	Percentage
Parental agreement[2]	1,214	20.0
Under apprehension	311	5.1
Interim order[3]	359	5.9
Temporary ward[4]	1,111	18.3
Permanent ward[5]	2,666	43.8
Other[6]	423	7.0
Total	**6,084**	**100.0**

1. Children in care represents children under the legal statuses shown.
2. Represents total of Short Term Custody Agreements (549) and Special Care Agreements (665).
3. Child is in custody of Superintendent during protection hearing adjournment.
4. Represents Temporary Custody Order.
5. Represents Permanent Order.
6. Represents total of: *Adoption Act* ward (voluntary relinquishment for adoption), *Family Relations Act* ward (orphaned child with no guardian) and ward of another jurisdiction. These children are in fact permanent wards.

Chapter 11 - British Columbia

Figure 11.3 Children in Care[1] by Legal Status as at March 31, 1992

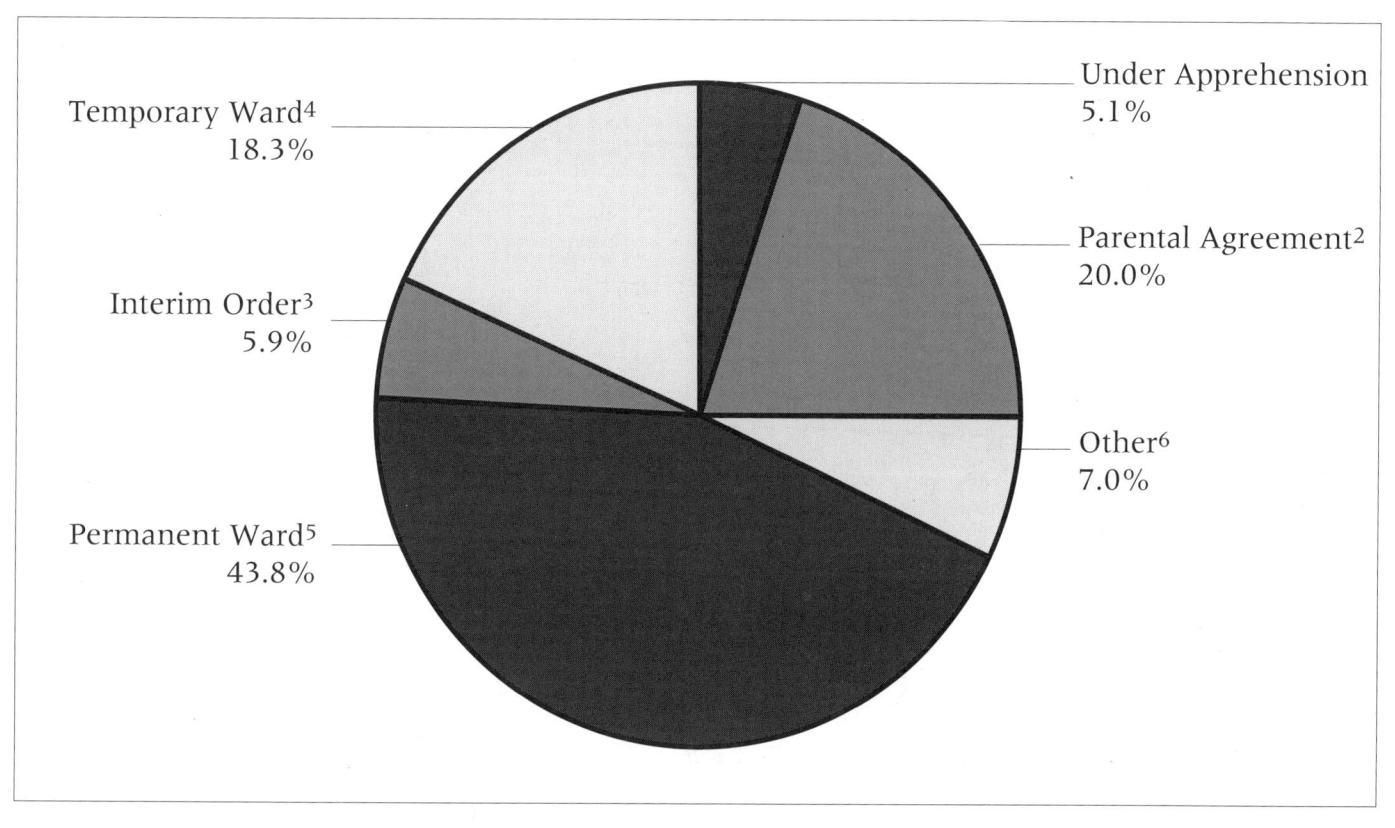

- Temporary Ward[4] 18.3%
- Interim Order[3] 5.9%
- Permanent Ward[5] 43.8%
- Under Apprehension 5.1%
- Parental Agreement[2] 20.0%
- Other[6] 7.0%

Children in care: 6,084

1. Children in care represents children under the legal statuses shown.
2. Represents total of Short Term Custody Agreements (549) and Special Care Agreements (665).
3. Child is in custody of Superintendent during protection hearing adjournment.
4. Represents Temporary Custody Order.
5. Represents Permanent Order.
6. Represents total of: *Adoption Act* ward (voluntary relinquishment for adoption), *Family Relations Act* ward (orphaned child with no guardian) and ward of another jurisdiction. These children are in fact permanent wards.

Figure 11.4 Children in Care[1] by Sex and Age Group as at March 31, 1992

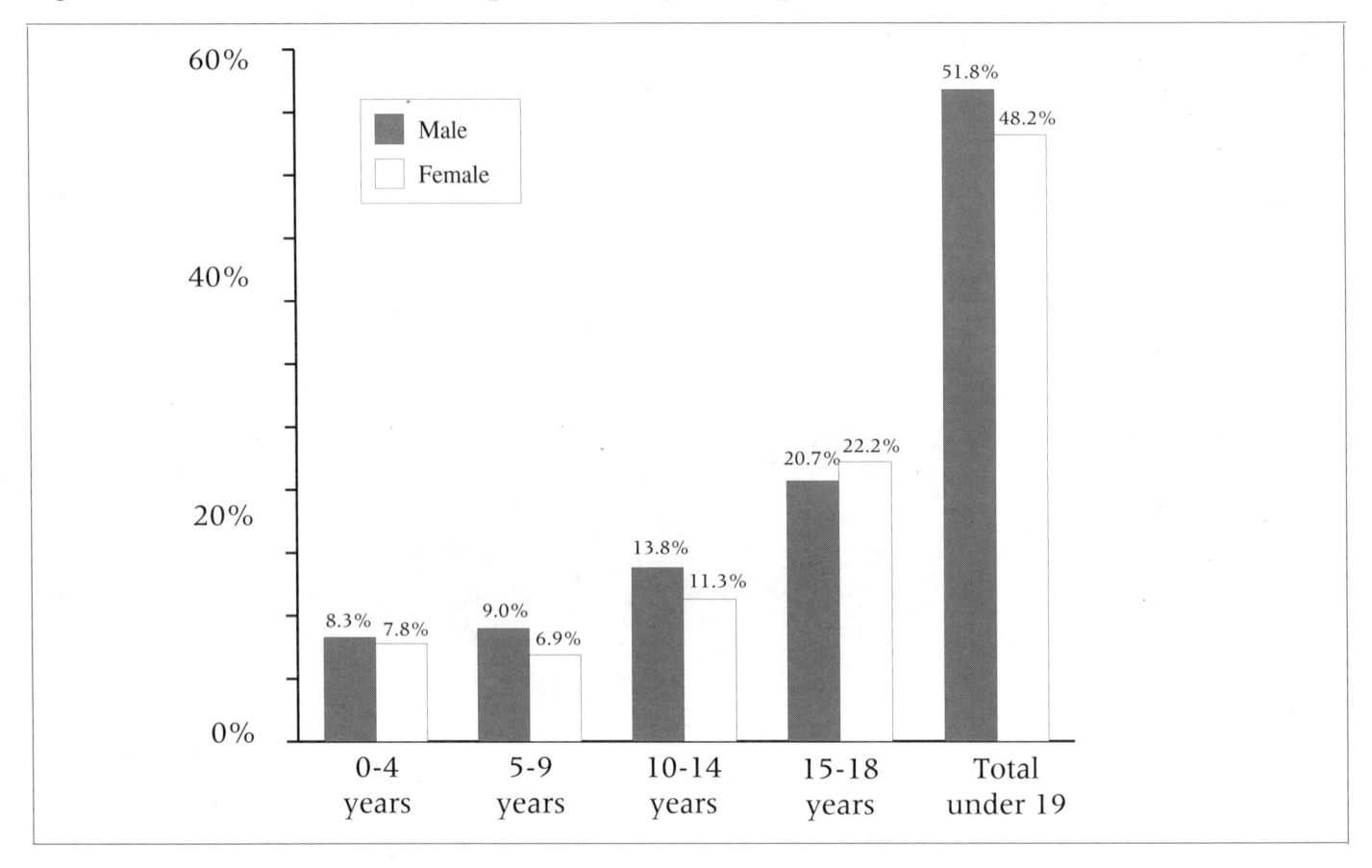

Age Group	Male	Female
0-4 years	8.3%	7.8%
5-9 years	9.0%	6.9%
10-14 years	13.8%	11.3%
15-18 years	20.7%	22.2%
Total under 19	51.8%	48.2%

Children in care: 6,084

1. Children in care represents children whose legal status is one of the following: Short Term Custody Agreement, Special Care Agreement, apprehension, interim order, Temporary Custody Order, Permanent Order, *Adoption Act* ward (voluntary relinquishment for adoption), *Family Relations Act* ward (orphaned child with no guardian) and ward of another jurisdiction.

Chapter 11 - British Columbia   Page 159

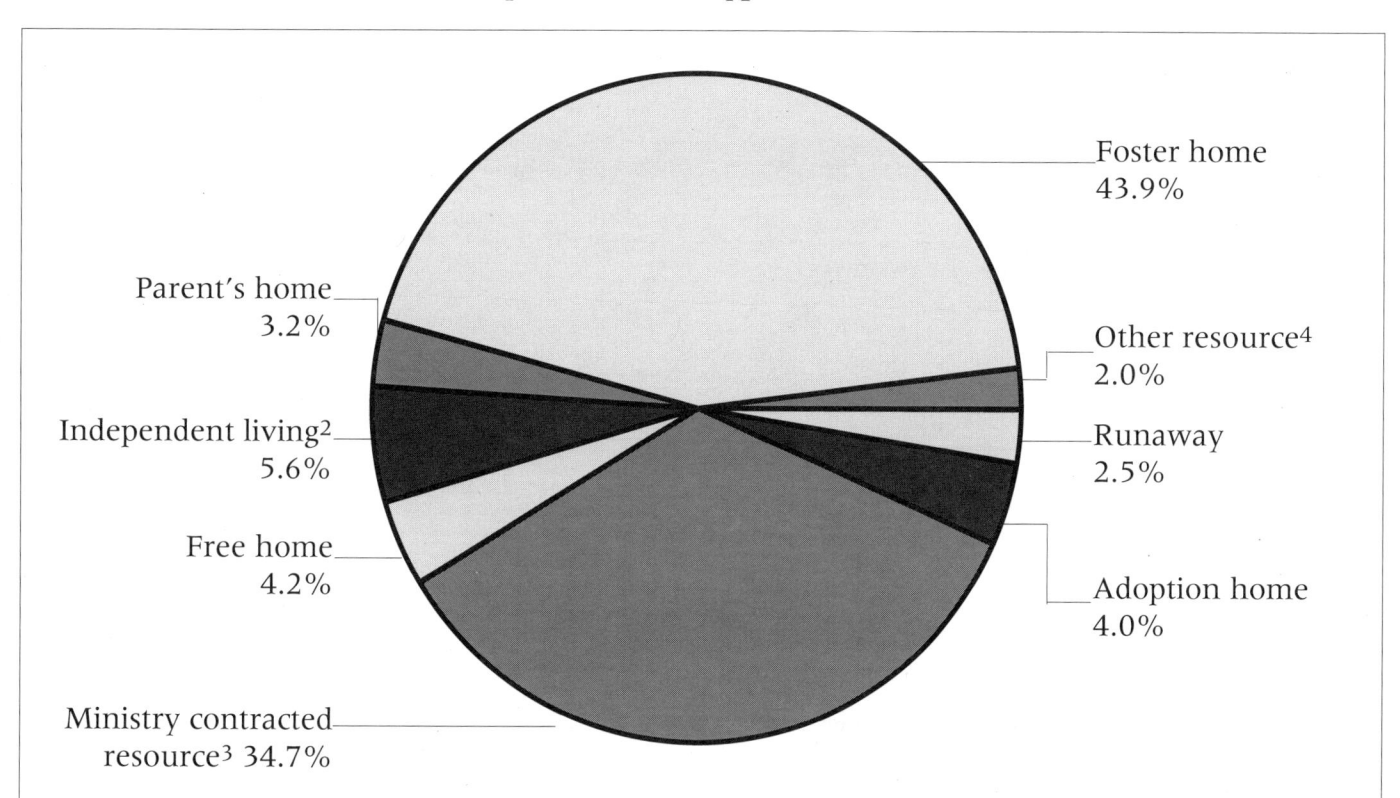

Figure 11.5 Children in Care[1] by Placement Type as at March 31, 1992

- Foster home 43.9%
- Other resource[4] 2.0%
- Runaway 2.5%
- Adoption home 4.0%
- Ministry contracted resource[3] 34.7%
- Free home 4.2%
- Independent living[2] 5.6%
- Parent's home 3.2%

Children in care: 6,084

1. Children in care represents children whose legal status is one of the following: Short Term Custody Agreement, Special Care Agreement, apprehension, interim order, Temporary Custody Order, Permanent Order, *Adoption Act* ward (voluntary relinquishment for adoption), *Family Relations Act* ward (orphaned child with no guardian) and ward of another jurisdiction.
2. Represents independent living and pays own board categories.
3. Includes group homes, special care homes and specialized resources.
4. Includes acute care hospitals and resources of other Ministries.

Resource Material

Legislative Material

Family and Child Service Act, Statutes of British Columbia 1980, c.11, as amended.

Adoption Act, Revised Statutes of British Columbia 1979, c.4, as amended.

Reports

British Columbia, Ministry of Social Services and Housing. *Inter-Ministry Child Abuse Handbook – An Integrated Approach to Child Abuse and Neglect*, 1988.

British Columbia, Ministry of Social Services. *Protecting Our Children Supporting Our Families: A Review of Child Protection Issues in British Columbia*, January 1992.

British Columbia, Community Panel, Family and Children's Services Legislation Review in British Columbia. *Making Changes, a Place to Start*, October 1992.

_____. Aboriginal Committee. *Liberating our Children, Liberating our Nations*, October 1992.

Other Material

British Columbia, Ministry of Social Services. "Family and Children's Services Policy and Procedures Manual – Volume 2", Victoria.

_____. Family and Children's Services Factbook, March 1992

Pamphlets, Ministry of Social Services (and Housing)

"Child Apprehension"

"Sexual Abuse and Your Child"

"Protecting our Children"

"The Child... Everybody's Responsibility"

Chapter 12 – # Yukon

Administration and Service Delivery

The Department of Health and Social Services is responsible for the development and delivery of child and family services authorized under Part 3 – Adoption and Part 4 – Child Protection of the *Children's Act*. Under the Act, the Director of Family and Children's Services is required to ensure the safeguarding of children, to promote family conditions leading to good parenting, and to provide care, custody and supervision to children in need of protection. This includes investigating allegations of child abuse and neglect. The Family and Children's Services Branch, located in Whitehorse, is responsible for policy and program development, coordination of services and service delivery. Within the Branch, the Family and Children's Services Unit and the Placement and Support Services Unit are responsible for the delivery of family and children's services in Whitehorse. Regional Services is responsible for providing these services and a wide range of other departmental services to rural areas through a network of ten regional offices.

The Champagne/Aishihik First Nations are responsible for the delivery of Indian child welfare services for members of their First Nation regardless of where they live in the Yukon. Service funding is provided by the Department of Health and Social Services. Other First Nations receive services directly from the Department of Health and Social Services.

A self-government agreement was completed in June 1992 with the Vuntut Gwich'in First Nation (Old Crow). The agreement, which has not yet been ratified, defines the authority of Vuntut Gwich'in First Nation to make laws and to govern its own land and people. Agreements have also been negotiated with the Mayo, Teslin, and Champagne/Aishihik First Nations. It is anticipated that all 14 Yukon First Nations will be negotiating similar self-government agreements. Once self-government comes into effect, First Nations will have the ability to pass their own child welfare laws that apply to their members wherever they live in the Yukon. Self-government agreements must be ratified by the First Nation, the Yukon Government and the Government of Canada, and then brought into force through Yukon and federal legislation.

Definitions

Under Section 104 of Part 4 - Child Protection of the *Children's Act*, a **child** is defined as "a person under 18 years of age". Under Sub-section 137(1), the Director of Family and Children's Services may extend care and custody to age 19. The age limit of 18 applies for adoption purposes.

Under Sub-section 116(1), a **child is in need of protection** when

"(a)   he is abandoned,

(b) he is in the care of a parent or other person who is unable to provide proper or competent care, supervision or control over him,

(c) he is in the care of a parent or other person who is unwilling to provide proper or competent care, supervision or control over him,

(d) he is in probable danger of physical or psychological harm,

(e) the parent or other person in whose care he is neglects or refuses to provide or obtain proper medical care or treatment necessary for his health or well-being or normal development,

(f) he is staying away from his home in circumstances that endanger his safety or well-being,

(g) the parent or other person in whose care he is fails to provide the child with reasonable protection from physical or psychological harm,

(h) the parent or person in whose care he is involves the child in sexual activity,

(i) subject to subsection 2, *(reference to use of reasonable or aggressive force)* the parent or person in whose care he is beats, cuts, burns or physically abuses him in any other way,

(j) the parent or person in whose care he is deprives the child of reasonable necessities of life or health,

(k) the parent or person in whose custody he is harasses the child with threats to do or procures any other person to do any act referred to in paragraphs (a) to (j), or

(l) the parent or person in whose care he is fails to take reasonable precautions to prevent any other person from doing any act referred to in paragraphs (a) to (j)."

In the "Interdepartmental Protocol on Teacher/Principal Guidelines for Identifying and Reporting Child Abuse and Neglect" (see section on Child Abuse and Neglect Protocols), abuse includes "both familial and non-familial physical, sexual and emotional abuse, as well as neglect". In addition, the following definitions are included:

"**physical abuse**: any act or omission which results in or may potentially result in a non-accidental injury to a child and which exceeds that which could be considered reasonable discipline. It includes, but is not restricted to, physical beating and failure to provide reasonable protection for a child from physical harm.

sexual abuse: any sexual activity involving a child that could be a violation of the *Criminal Code*, the *Young Offenders Act*, or render a child in need of protection under the *Children's Act*. Sexual abuse may include intercourse, molestation, fondling, exhibitionism, sexual assault, harassment, and exploitation of a child for the purpose of pornography or prostitution.

emotional abuse: acts or omissions on the part of a parent or caregiver that result in or may potentially result in psychological harm to the child. The results of emotional abuse may include non-organic failure to thrive, developmental retardation, serious anxiety, depression or withdrawal, and serious behavioral disturbances.

neglect: the failure of those responsible for the care of a child to provide proper or competent care, supervision or control resulting in failure to meet the physical, emotional or medical needs of the child to the extent that the child's health, development or safety is endangered."

Under the *Children's Act*, a child is accorded the following rights: the right to apply to vary or end a custody order; the right to be informed of any protection investigation involving him or her and to be given reasons if he/she is deemed able to understand; and the right for the child's official guardian to determine if the child needs a lawyer at the public's expense. In addition, the child has a right to be in a family.

Mandatory Reporting of a Child in Need of Protection

Under Sub-section 115(1) of Part 4 – Child Protection of the *Children's Act*, a person who has reasonable grounds to believe that a child may be in need of protection may[1] report that information to the Director, an agent of the Director, or a peace officer. Unless the report is made maliciously or falsely, no legal action may be taken against a person who reports this information. If a false or malicious report is made, a fine of up to $5,000 or imprisonment for as long as six months, or both, may result.

A teacher with reasonable grounds to believe that a child is in need of protection is required under the *Yukon Education Act* to report suspicions immediately to the principal and to the Department of Health and Social Services. Where a disclosure of child abuse or neglect is received by school personnel, the Department should be contacted without first contacting the parent or guardian. Principals must immediately report suspicions to Health and Social Services and to the Director or Superintendent of Schools. Day care workers are responsible under the *Child Care Act* to report all suspicions of child abuse or neglect to the Director of Family and Children's Services or to the police.

Investigation of an Allegation of Child Abuse or Neglect

All reports of alleged child abuse or neglect are taken either by a specialized intake worker in Whitehorse or by the social worker/social services worker in rural offices. All calls are screened for urgency or risk. A social worker or a peace officer must investigate all reports that a child may be in need of protection within 24 hours of receiving the report. The person investigating may enter any premises and request any documents or material relevant to the investigation. If access is denied, the worker may apply to a judge for a warrant to enter premises or an order to produce documents if a child is believed to be in need of protection. Although a warrant is generally required, a child may be taken into care (i.e., apprehended) or taken to a place of safety without a warrant if there are reasonable and probable grounds to believe the child's life, safety or health are in immediate danger. When a child is taken into care or to a place of safety, an identification hearing is scheduled to determine (a) the identities of the child and the parent or guardian and (b) whether reasonable and probable grounds exist for taking the child into care. If the judge finds that reasonable and probable grounds do exist for taking the child into care, a protection hearing is scheduled.

If a child is not at immediate risk but the Department has protection concerns, a worker may serve the child's parent or guardian with a Notice to Bring. This is used most often in situations of suspected chronic neglect. A Notice to Bring requires that the parent or guardian and child appear before a judge who will (a) rule whether the child is in need of protection or (b) order that the child undergo medical tests. Where concerns are substantiated by the test results, the child is either taken into care (if at immediate risk) or a protection hearing is scheduled.

---

1 In all other jurisdictions reporting of suspected cases of child abuse or neglect is mandatory.

In cases of alleged familial or non-familial sexual or physical abuse, an immediate medical examination should be arranged by the RCMP officer or the social worker. In cases of less serious physical abuse or neglect, or when the alleged abuse occurred several weeks before, the Department of Health and Social Services requests that a medical examination be carried out as soon as possible. If parental consent for the examination is not received, the social worker must take the child into care before proceeding. In cases of alleged familial abuse, the investigating team should interview the child and the child's siblings as soon as practical. Whenever possible, interviews are audiotaped and videotaped for possible use in Criminal or Family Court.

In responding to allegations of child abuse and neglect, the Department of Health and Social Services encourages cooperation between police and child protection workers in the investigative process. An investigating team comprising a social worker and an RCMP officer responds to reports of child abuse. Each authority advises the other if they are the first point of reporting. Other professionals such as physicians or representatives of the Crown may be consulted, where necessary, at any time during the investigation. With investigations of alleged extra-familial abuse, the lead role is taken by the RCMP, with the Department playing a supportive role. Where the parent can provide for the safety and well-being of the child, the role of the social worker normally ends with the investigation unless the parent requests on-going support and assistance (i.e., information and coordination services during criminal proceedings and/or counselling services).

When investigating alleged cases of child abuse involving First Nations children, the Department has liaison people who live in the First Nations Communities who are involved in all aspects of the investigation. The Department has drafted a child protection protocol with the Ross River Dena Council (see section on Child Abuse and Neglect Protocols). The protocol was drafted to guide the joint investigation of child protection matters between the Ross River Dena Council and the Department of Health and Social Services. Although this Council is the only First Nation with a written agreement, similar guidelines are followed by other First Nations and the Department in daily work with children and families.

Social workers receive training through the Institute for the Prevention of Child Abuse (Toronto), which runs programs in the Yukon on a regular basis. More intensive specialized training is provided in the area of child sexual abuse from time to time.

Voluntary Agreements

As discussed in Chapter One, Introduction, the provision of support services to a child and the family in the home is the least intrusive and preferred form of intervention. If services cannot be provided to the child and family while the child remains in the home, a parent or guardian may enter into a Temporary Care and Custody Agreement with the Director, placing a child under the Director's temporary care and custody. This agreement may be used when the parent or guardian is temporarily unable to care for the child or the child has special needs which cannot be met in the family home. An agreement may last for up to one year, with provision for renewal for an additional year.

Temporary Care and Custody Agreements are generally not used for cases of abuse or neglect. However, there is some discretion delegated to social workers, and where there is not a high risk, agreements have been used to facilitate treatment by parents and alternative care arrangements.

Court-Ordered Protection

When an abused or neglected child is believed to be in need of protection and is taken into care, an application is made to the court for an order regarding the care of the child. A Justice of the Peace or a Territorial Court Judge may issue one of the following orders when a child is found to be in need of protection. A Supervision Order allows the Director of Family and Children's Services, or delegate, to supervise the child while the child remains in the parent's care and custody. The term of the order may vary from 12 months to 24 months depending on the age of the child. If the order is extended, the total duration of the order may not exceed the maxima quoted above. An Order for Temporary Care and Custody temporarily transfers care and custody of the child to the Director of Family and Children's Services for between 12 to 24 months, depending on the age of the child. The order may be extended for an additional two years for children 14 years or older or to age 19 if the child is attending school full-time or has a physical or mental incapacity and is unable to be self-supporting. An Order for Permanent Care and Custody permanently transfers the care and custody of the child to the Director of Family and Children's Services until the child is 18 years of age, or to age 19 if the child is attending school full-time or has a physical or mental incapacity and is unable to be self-supporting. In cases where a family's circumstances have changed, the parent or child over the age of 14 may apply to the court to have an Order for Permanent Care and Custody terminated or varied.

Part 4 – Child Protection of the *Children's Act* specifies that a child taken into care and custody shall be placed with a family of his/her own cultural background wherever this is possible. An official First Nations representative is invited to be involved in the placement and planning of a First Nations child coming into care.

Child Abuse Register

The Department of Health and Social Services does not operate a child abuse register.

Child Abuse and Neglect Protocols

An "Inter-Agency Protocol for the Investigation of Child Abuse and Neglect" has been drafted, with approval by all parties anticipated in the summer of 1993. It is a joint effort between Yukon Health and Social Services, Yukon Justice, Yukon Education, Health and Welfare Canada, Justice Canada, the RCMP, and the Yukon Medical Association. The protocol outlines guidelines for responding to an initial report of child abuse or neglect, interviewing the child, audio/videotaping of interviews, arranging medical examinations of the victim, interviewing the alleged offender, providing support for the child, determining child welfare proceedings and determining criminal proceedings.

An "Interdepartmental Protocol on Teacher/Principal Guidelines for Identifying and Reporting Child Abuse and Neglect" was recently written by the Department of Education and the Department of Health and Social Services and is currently in use. The protocol describes reporting procedures and responsibilities for teachers and principals and outlines indicators of a child's potential need for protection.

The Department of Health and Social Services has recently drafted a protocol with the Ross River Dena Council which is intended to set out guidelines for the investigation of child protection matters under the *Children's Act* between the Ross River Dena Council and the Department of Health and Social Services.

Statistics

The following tables and graphs have been compiled from data collected by the Department of Health and Social Services through their Client Index System. Data reported are as at March 31, 1992.

Children in care include those in the care of the Director of Family and Children's Services under the following legal statuses: Custody Agreement (Temporary Care and Custody Agreement), Apprehension (includes court adjournments), Temporary Ward (Order for Temporary Care and Custody), Permanent Ward (Order for Permanent Care and Custody and Agreement for Voluntary Relinquishment [i.e., for adoption]) and Other (children from outside the territory being supervised in Yukon). Data on natives are included in the following statistics.

Due to the limitations noted in Chapter 1, Introduction, these data should not be compared with data for other jurisdictions.

Table 12.1 Children in Need of Protection[1] by Age, Sex, Ethnicity and Worker's Assessment of Major Reason as at March 31, 1992

		Number	Percentage
Age			
	Birthdates missing	29	9.0
	0-1 year	10	3.1
	2-5 years	63	19.4
	6-11 years	130	40.1
	12-15 years	58	17.9
	16+ years	34	10.5
Sex			
	Male	166	51.2
	Female	158	48.8
Ethnicity			
	Native[2]	124	38.3
	Other	200	61.7
Worker's Assessment of Major Reason			
	Investigation ongoing		
	Neglect	36	11.1
	Physical abuse	8	2.4
	Sexual abuse	9	2.8
	Emotional abuse	1	0.3
	Neglect	115	35.5
	Physical abuse	51	15.7
	Sexual abuse	45	13.9
	Emotional abuse	11	3.4
	Relationship breakdown[3]	20	6.2
	Other[4]	28	8.6
Total		**324**	**100.0**

1. Includes children in need of protection as defined in the *Children's Act*.
2. A native person is a First Nation person who is 25% Yukon Indian and who is eligible for land claims.
3. Includes cases of parent-child conflict with no identified abuse.
4. Includes any other reasons not listed.

Table 12.2 Children in Care[1] by Legal Status, Sex and Ethnicity as at March 31, 1992

	Number	Percentage
Legal Status		
Custody Agreement[2]	31	19.9
Apprehension[3]	15	9.6
Temporary Ward[4]	33	21.2
Permanent Ward[5]	74	47.4
Other[6]	3	1.9
Sex		
Male	76	48.7
Female	80	51.3
Ethnicity		
Native[7]	99	63.5
Other	57	36.5
Total	**156**	**100.0**

1. Children in care represents children under the legal statuses shown.
2. Includes children under a Temporary Care and Custody Agreement.
3. Includes time period when a child is taken into care but has not yet received court disposition (includes court adjournments).
4. Includes children under an Order for Temporary Care and Custody.
5. Includes children under an Order for Permanent Care and Custody or an Agreement for Voluntary Relinquishment (i.e., for the purpose of adoption).
6. Includes children from outside the territory being supervised in Yukon.
7. A native person is a First Nation person who is 25% Yukon Indian and who is eligible for land claims.

Chapter 12 - Yukon

Figure 12.1 Children in Care[1] by Legal Status as at March 31, 1992

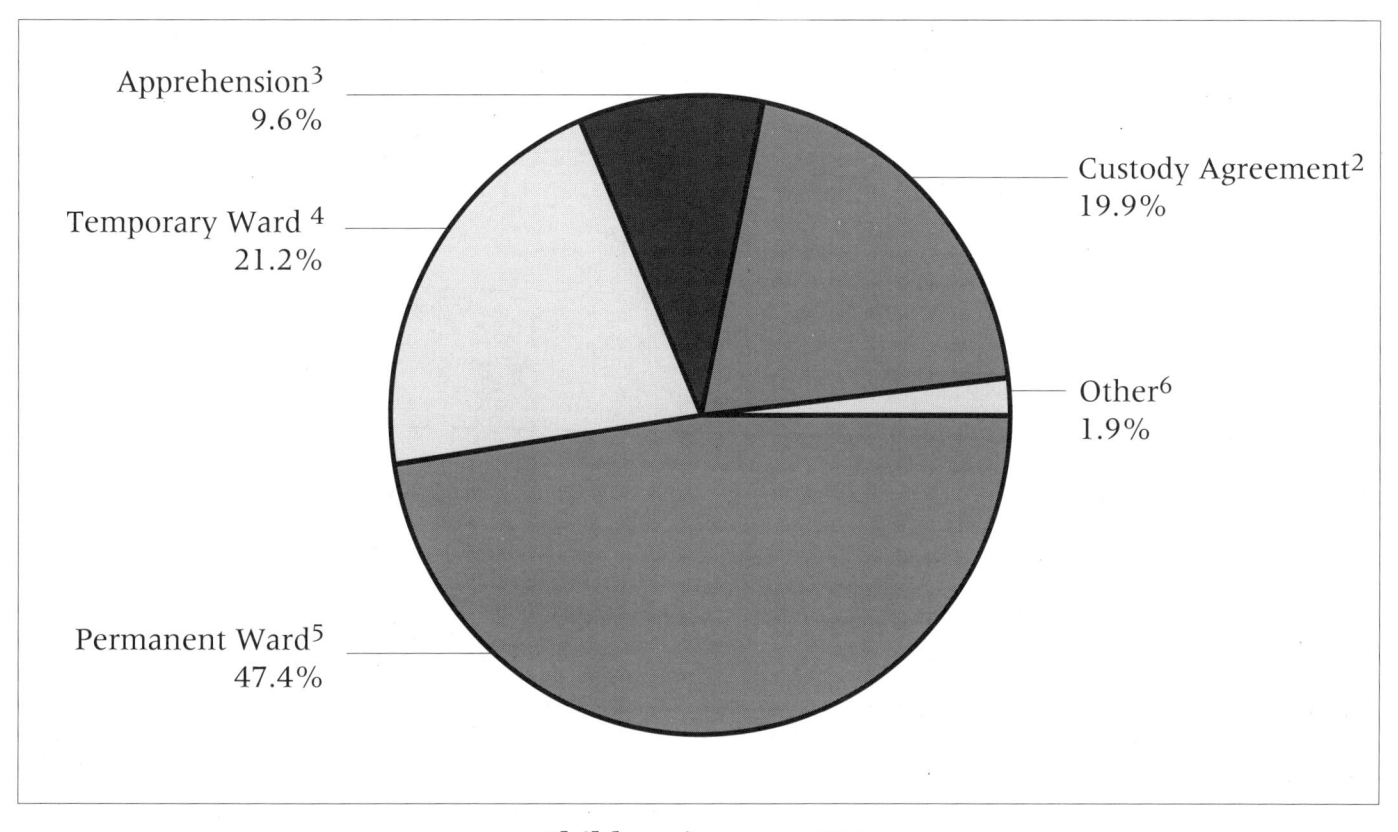

Apprehension[3] 9.6%
Temporary Ward[4] 21.2%
Permanent Ward[5] 47.4%
Custody Agreement[2] 19.9%
Other[6] 1.9%

Children in care: 156

1. Children in care represents children under the legal statuses shown.
2. Includes children under a Temporary Care and Custody Agreement.
3. Includes time period when a child is taken into care but has not yet received court disposition (includes court adjournments).
4. Includes children under an Order for Temporary Care and Custody.
5. Includes children under an Order for Permanent Care and Custody or an Agreement for Voluntary Relinquishment (i.e., for the purpose of adoption).
6. Includes children from outside the territory being supervised in Yukon.

Figure 12.2 Children in Care[1] by Age Group as at March 31, 1992

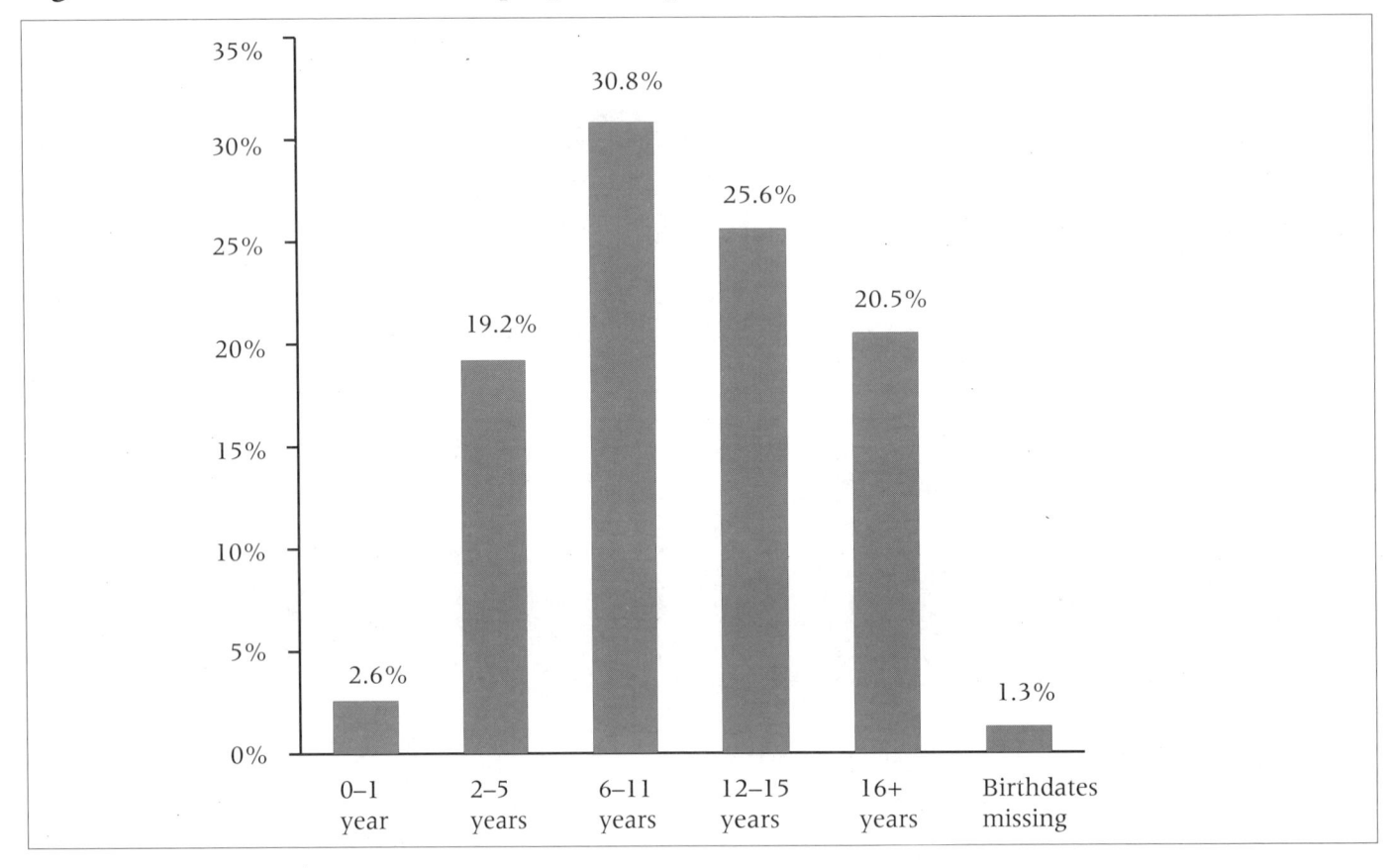

Age Group	Percentage
0–1 year	2.6%
2–5 years	19.2%
6–11 years	30.8%
12–15 years	25.6%
16+ years	20.5%
Birthdates missing	1.3%

Children in care: 156

1. Children in care represents children whose legal status is one of the following: custody agreement (Agreement for Temporary Care and Custody), apprehension, temporary ward (Order for Temporary Care and Custody), permanent ward (Order for Permanent Care and Custody or Agreement for Voluntary Relinquishment [for the purposes of adoption]), and other (children from outside the territory being supervised in the Yukon).

Resource Material

Legislative Material

Children's Act, Revised Statutes of the Yukon 1986, c. 22, as amended.

Other Material

Yukon, Department of Health and Social Services. "Family and Children's Services Manual". Whitehorse.

Yukon, Department of Health and Social Services, Yukon Justice, Yukon Education, Health and Welfare Canada, the RCMP and the Yukon Medical Association. "Interagency Protocol for the Investigation of Child Abuse and Neglect", (Draft) 1992.

Yukon, Department of Health and Social Services, Yukon Education. *Interdepartmental Protocol on Teacher/Principal Guidelines for Identifying and Reporting Child Abuse and Neglect*, 1990.

Chapter 13 – Northwest Territories

Administration and Service Delivery

Under the *Child Welfare Act*, the Superintendent of Child Welfare in the Department of Social Services of the Northwest Territories is responsible for investigating reports that a child may be in need of protection. The reports include allegations of child abuse and neglect. Recently, a family law review was carried out by the Departments of Social Services and Justice, in conjunction with native and other affected organizations. The review will result in important amendments being made to the *Child Welfare Act*.

At head office in Yellowknife, Family and Children's Services Division in the Department of Social Services has responsibility for the development of legislation, policy, and programs in the areas of child welfare, child sexual abuse, and family violence prevention. The Division is also responsible for program financing, staff training, adoptions, and placement of children in facilities outside the Northwest Territories. Child protection and family services are provided by departmental child welfare workers or community workers in a system of five regional offices, two area offices and several community offices. The regional and area superintendents report to the Assistant Deputy Minister of Regional Operations in head office. Some family support services are provided by local agencies.

The provisions of the *Child Welfare Act* apply regardless of the cultural background of a child. It should be noted, however, that the majority of families in the Northwest Territories are native – Inuit, Indian or Métis. Native tribal councils and community councils work with the Department's local offices to provide community programs. The municipality of Iqaluit (formerly Frobisher Bay) on Baffin Island has an agreement with the Department of Social Services to provide child welfare on behalf of the Minister of Social Services and other social services to a largely native community.

The cultural diversity among communities as well as the vast geographic area and small population of the Territories often result in more informal decision-making and lack of access to services than may be the case in other jurisdictions. In most communities, workers are responsible for the delivery of social assistance and corrections services as well as child and family services. Some isolated communities may not have access to any worker on a regular basis but rather only a few days per month. Lack of access to the court system and to medical care are other examples. Native custom adoptions in which children are placed by their parents with relatives or friends without the involvement of the court are an example of a less formal process. Such adoptions are recognized as legal by the Supreme Court of the Northwest Territories. This community approach to caring for children, including those who have been abused or neglected, may help to prevent them from being in need of protection.

In the area of child abuse, an interministerial committee has some responsibilities which complement those of the Department of Social Services. The Child Sexual Abuse Initiatives Coordinating Committee is chaired by the Director of Management Services and includes the Assistant Deputy Ministers from the Departments of Health, Culture and Communications, Territorial Justice and Education as well as representatives from Justice Canada, the Royal Canadian Mounted Police (RCMP), and the Status of Women Council of the Northwest Territories, an independent agency. The terms of reference for the committee include preparation of a coordinated approach to dealing with child sexual abuse (for example, the development of the "Child Sexual Abuse Protocol"), sharing information to ensure consistent integrated practice across the Territories, establishing task/working groups to address areas of concern, and encouraging participation of non-governmental agencies in these groups. A current activity of the Committee is coordinating on-site training of local workers in different disciplines (such as health, education, social services and law enforcement) to encourage them to work together in family violence situations.

Definitions

For the purposes of investigations and the provision of protection services under the *Child Welfare Act*, a **child** is defined under Section 1 to be a person under 18 years of age, including a person under the guardianship of the Superintendent of Child Welfare who is over 18 years of age. Under Sub-section 25(1), guardianship may be extended to age 19 when the child already has been permanently committed to the care of the Superintendent.

For the purposes of adoption, under Section 86 of the Act, a child must be under the age of 19 and not married, although in some circumstances, an unmarried adult may be adopted (Sub-section 98(2)).

Sub-section 12(2) of the *Child Welfare Act* states that a child is deemed to be **in need of protection** when:

"(a) the child is an orphan who is not being properly cared for or is brought, with the consent of the person in whose charge the child is, before a justice to be dealt with under this Part;

(b) the person in whose charge the child is, has delivered the child to the Superintendent for adoption;

(c) the child is deserted by the person in whose charge the child is, or that person has died or is unable to care properly for the child;

(d) the person in whose charge the child is cannot by reason of disease, infirmity, misfortune, incompetence or imprisonment, care properly for the child;

(e) the home of the child, by reason of neglect, cruelty or depravity on the part of the person in whose charge the child is, is an unfit and improper place for the child;

(f) the child is found associating with an unfit or improper person;

(g) the child is found begging in a public place;

(h) the child is or, in the absence of evidence to the contrary, appears to be under the age of 12 years and behaves in a way that, in the case of any other person, would be an offence created by an Act of Canada or by any regulation, rule, order, by-law or ordinance made under an Act of Canada or an enactment or municipal by-law;

(i) the child habitually absents himself or herself from the home of the person in whose charge the child is without sufficient cause;

(j) the person in whose charge the child is neglects or refuses to provide or secure proper medical, surgical or other remedial care or treatment necessary for the health or well-being of the child, or refuses to permit this care or treatment to be supplied to the child when it is recommended by a medical practitioner; or

(k) the child is deprived of affection by the person in whose charge the child is to a degree that, on the evidence of a psychiatrist, is sufficient to endanger the emotional and mental development of the child."

For the purposes of reporting child abuse, Sub-section 30(1) of the *Child Welfare Act* defines **child abuse** to be a condition of

"(a) physical harm in respect of which a child suffers physical injury but does not include reasonable punishment administered by a parent or guardian;

(b) malnutrition or mental ill-health of a degree that if not immediately remedied could seriously impair growth and development or result in permanent injury or death; or

(c) sexual molestation."

Departmental policy specifies the following working definitions of abuse and neglect.

Physical abuse is "any non-accidental infliction of physical injury on a child by a caretaker (guardian, foster parent, etc.). Non-accidental injury includes carelessness and intentional harm." The worker's determination of reasonable punishment is to include consideration of the age of the child.

Emotional abuse means "injury to the emotional or intellectual capacity of a child."

Sexual abuse is "exposure of the child to sexual stimulation inappropriate for his age and role; the sexual exploitation of a child who is not developed mentally or capable of understanding or resisting the contact, or a child or adolescent who may be psychologically or socially dependant upon the perpetrator."

Neglect is "failing to give a child what he/she needs... A lack of attention to the physical and/or emotional needs of a child, and a failure to use available resources to meet those needs". Paragraphs 12(2)(e),(j), and (k) of the definition of a child in need of protection refer to neglect.

Emotional neglect is "A lack of attention to the emotional and social needs of a child to the extent he/she is not able to see himself as a person of worth, dignity and value."

Although a condition of malnutrition is defined in the Act as possible child abuse, it is noted in policy that malnutrition may have causes other than abuse and neglect. A medical opinion is recommended.

Policy also includes examples of neglect and each type of abuse as well as physical and behavioural indicators of abuse and neglect.

Mandatory Reporting of a Child in Need of Protection

Under Sub-section 30(2) of the *Child Welfare Act*, anyone who has information of the abandonment, desertion, or need of protection of a child or of the infliction of abuse on a child must report this to the Superintendent of Child Welfare. In practice, reports are made to a local or regional child welfare or community worker. Under Sub-section 30(3), any professional (excluding a lawyer) who has reasonable grounds to suspect, in the course of his/her professional or official duties, that a child has suffered or is suffering from abuse that may have been caused or permitted by someone who has, or has had, charge of the child, must report it even though the information may be confidential. The penalty for failing to report abuse or for making a malicious report is, upon summary conviction, a fine of up to $500 or imprisonment for a term not to exceed six months, or both (Section 115).

Anyone who reports suspected abuse or neglect to staff of an agency or institution such as the RCMP or a school is still legally required to make a report to the Superintendent of Child Welfare as well.

Investigation of an Allegation of Child Abuse or Neglect

Every report or referral made to the Superintendent of Child Welfare concerning suspected abuse or neglect of a child (intra- or extra-familial) must be investigated by a child welfare or community worker to determine if provision of services is warranted. Follow-up action is to occur as soon as possible. Emergencies, when a child is at risk, must be investigated immediately. During the investigation, the worker must take into account cultural and community norms. The worker must report to the RCMP reports of alleged sexual abuse of a child, as well as situations in which the child has visible physical injuries which the worker believes are due to abuse, or cases where a child cannot be located and the worker believes the child is in need of protection or in real danger. The RCMP may proceed with a criminal investigation.

The "Child Sexual Abuse Protocol" encourages information sharing between mandated agencies during an investigation of alleged child abuse (see section on Child Abuse and Neglect Protocols). The protocol also recommends that in cases which require a criminal and protection investigation, the RCMP and child welfare worker should conduct a joint investigation wherever possible. All reports of child sexual abuse received by the RCMP or an office of the Department of Social Services are to be shared as soon as possible. Special interview rooms are available in Yellowknife, Inuvik and Fort Smith for the interviewing of child sexual abuse victims in a location separate from the investigating agencies. Interviewing is done by child welfare workers and RCMP officers, preferably jointly. A viewing room with video equipment for producing video tapes is located nearby. The "Child Sexual Abuse Protocol" recommends that such video tapes be made when there is purposeful disclosure of sexual abuse and the child agrees to the use of the video taping. The tapes may be useful during the investigation and case assessment and may be used as evidence in criminal court.

Medical examinations are carried out when required, for example, when a child has physical injuries or in cases of suspected sexual abuse. Reports are available to the RCMP and child welfare workers for their investigations. As already mentioned, given the vast geography and small population of the Territories, an immediate medical examination by a doctor is not always possible. Most communities have a nursing station which can provide an initial examination.

At the conclusion of the investigation and assessment of the results, the worker must consult with the supervisor before proceeding with the case. If it is determined that there are reasonable grounds to believe that the child is in need of protection, all efforts to preserve the family through voluntary provision of services have failed, and the child's well-being is endangered, the child may be apprehended. An apprehension may be made by the worker, an RCMP officer, or by anyone delegated by the Superintendent of Child Welfare or the Minister of Social Services. Apprehensions generally occur without a warrant from wherever the child is. The worker may request the assistance of the RCMP.

All workers must complete a child welfare training workshop before they can apprehend a child. In addition, three regions have a child sexual abuse specialist who provides support and training for child welfare workers, the RCMP and medical personnel regarding the identification and investigation of child sexual abuse cases. The specialist also provides individual and group treatment for child victims and adult survivors. The child sexual abuse coordinator in Yellowknife carries out these responsibilities for the remaining regions.

Voluntary Agreements

When a parent is temporarily unable to care for a child, or a youth requires some support, placement with a relative may provide sufficient care. Alternatively, the Department of Social Services offers two types of voluntary agreements to provide help in certain situations. Custody by Agreement may be used to enable parents to give over custody, but not guardianship, of a child to the Superintendent of Child Welfare during which time the child is placed outside the home. This type of agreement may only be used where there is no evidence of abuse or neglect. Special needs children (physically or mentally handicapped) may also be placed through Custody by Agreement. A Voluntary Care Agreement may be used to provide financial and support services to 16 and 17 year olds who are living on their own, are not at risk as defined by the Act and are not receiving any assistance from their families. The parent, however, retains custody and guardianship rights. For either agreement, the initial term is usually six months; the maximum term with extensions is two years. In the case of Custody by Agreement for special needs children, indefinite extensions are allowed to age 18. An agreement ends when the child reaches 18 years of age, either party withdraws from the agreement or the client defaults on the conditions of the agreement.

Court-Ordered Protection

When a child has allegedly been abused or neglected and is believed to be in need of protection as determined by a worker, or has been apprehended, a hearing is held in Territorial Court. The Territorial Court operates on a court circuit which serves several centres, including Yellowknife. If a timely hearing in Territorial Court is not possible, an application for a Temporary Custody Order may be heard by a local justice of the peace. A hearing with respect to a Permanent Custody Order must be heard in Territorial Court. A Supervision Order may be made by either judicial authority.

If a judge determines that a child is in need of protection, one of the following orders may be made. The case may be adjourned for up to 12 months and the child returned, or kept at, home (which may be with a caregiver other than the parent) under a Supervision Order; the case is reassessed in court after the term has expired. Under a Temporary Custody Order, custody and guardianship of the child are temporarily transferred to the Superintendent of Child Welfare. The initial order may be made for up to one year; with extensions, the total term of the order is not to exceed 36 consecutive months. A Temporary Custody Order terminates at age 18. A Permanent Guardianship Order permanently transfers custody and guardianship to the Superintendent until the child turns 18. Permanent guardianship may be extended by the court to age 19 if the child is still in school or is handicapped and requires the Department's support.

Child Abuse Register

There is no child abuse register in the Northwest Territories.

Child Abuse and Neglect Protocols

The "Child Sexual Abuse Protocol" was developed by the Protocol/Interdisciplinary Training Subcommittee of the Child Sexual Abuse Initiatives Coordinating Committee. The subcommittee was made up of representatives of the Departments of Social Services, Health, Education, Territorial Justice, the RCMP and Justice Canada. The protocol was produced to promote cooperation and mutual assistance among professionals in the investigation and management of child sexual abuse cases. The subcommittee also developed a training outline and schedule for all professionals with a legal mandate to investigate child sexual abuse cases.

The mandated agencies which are covered by the protocol are: the Department of Social Services, which is responsible for the protection of children; the RCMP, which has primary responsibility for criminal investigations; Justice Canada, which has responsibility in the Northwest Territories for Crown Prosecutors employed by the Attorney General of Canada in criminal cases; Territorial Justice whose lawyers act as legal counsel for the Superintendent of Child Welfare and conduct child welfare proceedings in consultation with the worker; and health care providers who may identify a case of suspected abuse or be requested to perform medical examinations of the victim. The roles and responsibilities of each agency are specified in the protocol.

A second protocol, "Child Abuse Investigations – Protocol for Social Service Workers", outlines how workers should proceed with an investigation in cooperation with other agencies. These other agencies include the RCMP, schools, the health care system and other community resources. The protocol includes definitions and indicators of abuse and neglect.

Guidelines regarding the reporting of suspected child abuse by education personnel, including teachers, are outlined in "Child Abuse – Procedures for Reporting Suspected Child Abuse". The protocol was signed by the Ministers of Education, Health and Social Services, and Justice. "Draft Scenarios on Reporting Child Abuse" presents two sample situations for teachers and describes the procedures to be followed.

Statistics

The data in the statistical tables presented in this section were provided by the Family and Children's Services Division of the Department of Social Services. Data represent counts during the month of March 1992 except for the child sexual abuse intake reports which are for the calendar year 1991.

Except for the allegations of child abuse and neglect, the data cover children in care who are in need of protection under the *Child Welfare Act* and are in care under the following legal statuses: Apprehension (waiting for court hearing), Supervision Order, Temporary Ward (including temporary wardship status during court adjournments), Permanent Ward (including extension of guardianship to age 19 and voluntary relinquishment of a child for adoption), Custody by Agreement and Voluntary Care Agreement (16 and 17 year olds living on their own). The children may be at home, on their own, or placed outside the home. With the exception of New Brunswick and the Northwest Territories, all other jurisdictions exclude Supervision Orders from their legal statuses for children in care.

Not all abused and neglected children deemed to be in need of protection are taken into care. Many receive services voluntarily in the home of a parent or other caregiver. These children are not included in the data presented in this section.

Due to the limitations noted in Chapter 1, Introduction, these data should not be compared with data for other jurisdictions.

Table 13.1 Intake Reports[1] of Child Abuse and Neglect by Type during March 1992

Type	Number	Percentage
Child Abuse		
Physical[2]	15	19.7
Sexual	13	17.1
Sub-Total	**28**	**36.8**
Parental Neglect	48	63.2
Total	**76**	**100.0**

1. Allegations that were acted upon by a worker and reported to headquarters.
2. Includes physical and emotional abuse.

Table 13.2 Child Sexual Abuse Intake Reports[1] by Sex of Child, January 1, 1991 to December 31, 1991

Sex	Number	Percentage
Male	30	15.0
Female	170	85.0
Total	**200**	**100.0**

1. Allegations that were acted upon by a worker and reproted to headquarters.

Table 13.3 Children in Care[1] by Reason for Admission[2] during March 1992[3]

Reason	Number	Percentage
Child abuse		
Physical	63	14.5
Sexual	10	2.3
Sub-Total	**73**	**16.8**
Parental neglect	134	30.9
Emotional/behavioural problems	55	12.7
Physical handicap	24	5.5
Mental handicap	3	0.7
Parent unable to supervise	56	12.9
Surrender for adoption	10	2.3
Alcohol abuse by parent	17	3.9
Death of parent	2	0.5
Financial need/inadequate housing	15	3.5
Child's conflict with the law	3	0.7
Parent's illness/physical disability	13	3.0
Parent's emotional/mental illness	29	6.7
Total	**434**	**100.0**

1. Children who are in need of protection under the *Child Welfare Act* and are in care under the following legal statuses: Apprehension (waiting for court hearing), Supervision Order, Temporary Ward (including Temporary Custody Order and temporary wardship status during court adjournments), Permanent Ward (including Permanent Guardianship Order, extension to age 19 and voluntary relinquishment of a child for adoption), Custody by Agreement and Voluntary Care Agreement (16 and 17 years olds on their own). With the exception of New Brunswick and the Northwest Territories, all other jurisdictions exclude Supervision Orders from their legal statuses for children in care.
2. Cases of abuse not identified during the investigation but showing up later are missed (child in care for another reason).
3. A child may have been counted twice if a child entered care, was discharged, and reentered care during the month. This happened in a few cases.

Table 13.4   Children in Care[1] by Legal Status during March 1992[2]

Legal Status	Number	Percentage
Custody by Agreement	135	31.1
Voluntary Care Agreement[3]	5	1.2
Apprehension	48	11.1
Supervision Order	66	15.2
Temporary Ward[4]	103	23.7
Permanent Ward[5]	77	17.7
Total	**434**	**100.0**

1. Children who are in need of protection under the *Child Welfare Act* and are in care under the legal statuses shown. With the exception of New Brunswick and the Northwest Territories, all other jurisdictions exclude Supervision Orders from their legal statuses for children in care.
2. A child may have been counted twice if a child entered care, was discharged, and re-entered care during the month. This happened in a few cases.
3. 16 and 17 year olds living on their own.
4. Includes children under Temporary Custody Orders and under temporary wardship status during court adjournments.
5. Includes children under Permanent Guardianship Orders and extensions to age 19, and those voluntarily relinquished for adoption.

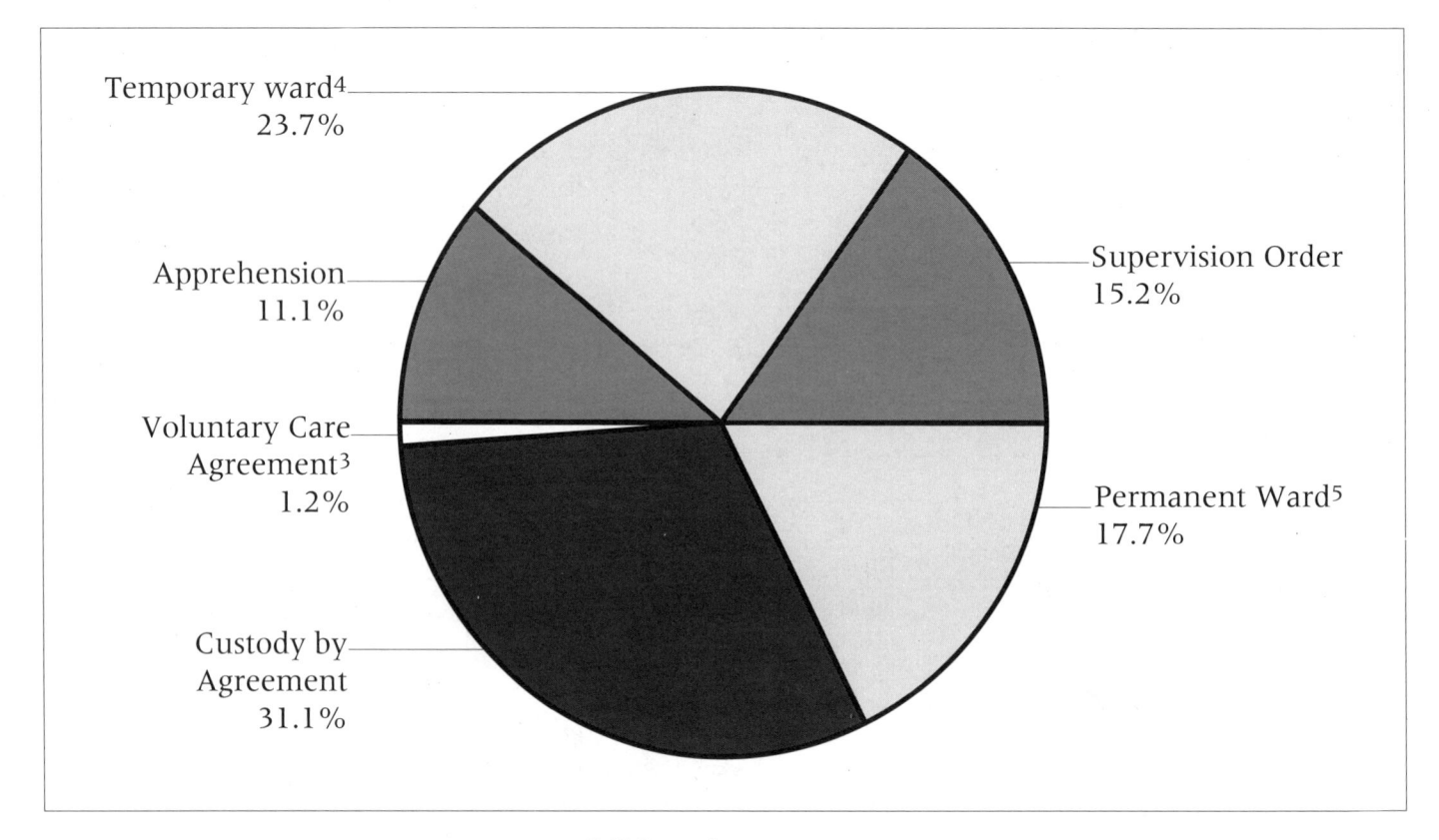

Figure 13.1   **Children in Care[1] by Legal Status during March 1992[2]**

- Temporary ward[4] 23.7%
- Apprehension 11.1%
- Voluntary Care Agreement[3] 1.2%
- Custody by Agreement 31.1%
- Permanent Ward[5] 17.7%
- Supervision Order 15.2%

Children in care: 434

1. Children who are in need of protection under the *Child Welfare Act* and are in care under the legal statuses shown. With the exception of New Brunswick and the Northwest Territories, all other jurisdictions exclude Supervision Orders from their legal statuses for children in care.
2. A child may have been counted twice if a child entered care, was discharged, and re-entered care during the month. This happened in a few cases.
3. 16 and 17 year olds living on their own.
4. Includes children under Temporary Custody Orders and under temporary wardship status during court adjournments.
5. Includes children under Permanent Guardianship Orders and extensions to age 19, and those voluntarily relinquished for adoption.

Figure 13.2   **Children in Care[1] by Age Group and Sex during March 1992[2]**

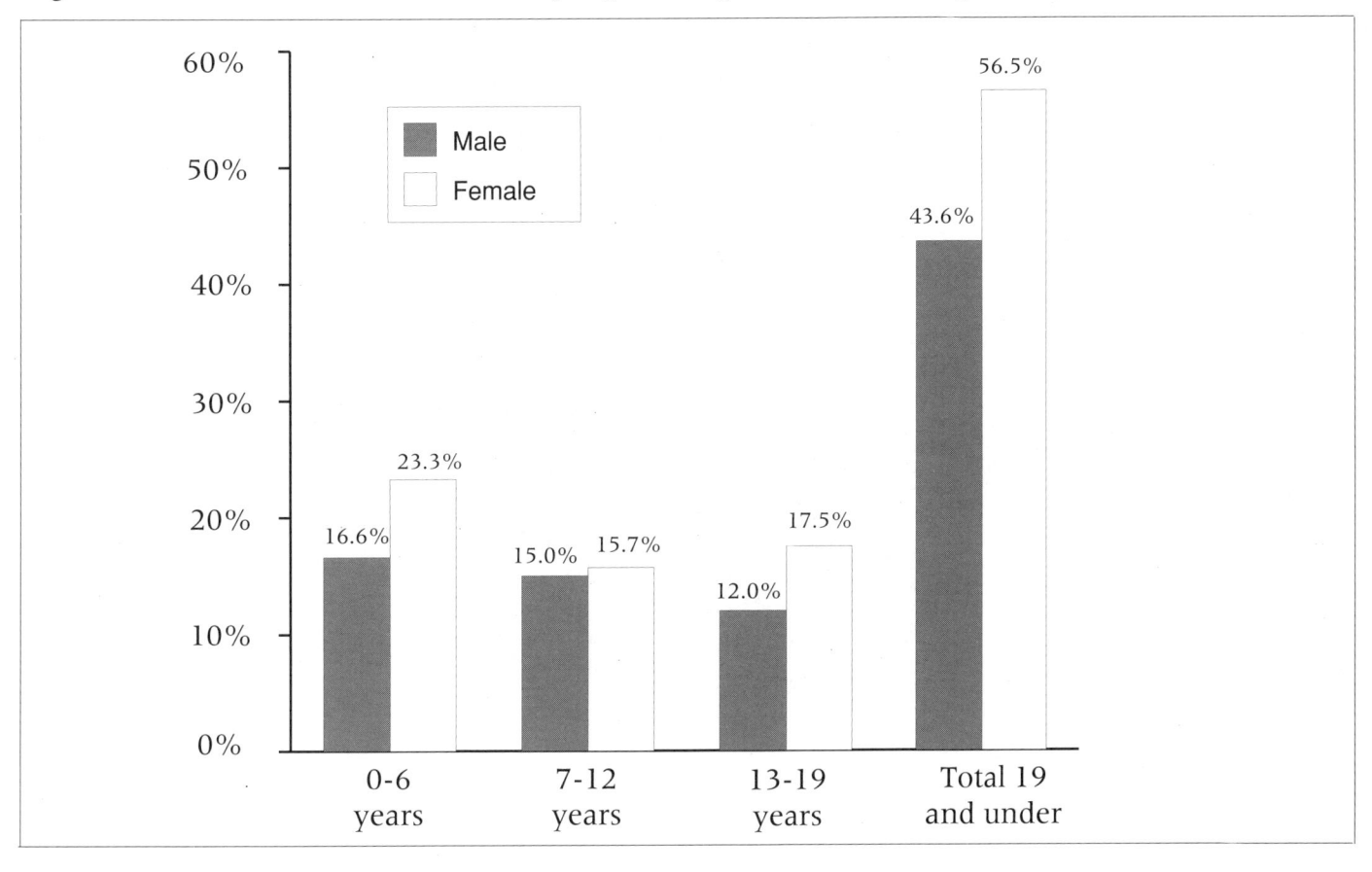

Age Group	Male	Female
0-6 years	16.6%	23.3%
7-12 years	15.0%	15.7%
13-19 years	12.0%	17.5%
Total 19 and under	43.6%	56.5%

Children in care: 434

1. Children who are in need of protection under the *Child Welfare Act* and are in care under the following legal statuses: Apprehension (waiting for court hearing), Supervision Order, Temporary Ward (including Temporary Custody Order and temporary wardship status during court adjournments), Permanent Ward (including Permanent Guardianship Order, extension to age 19 and voluntary relinquishment of a child for adoption), Custody by Agreement and Voluntary Care Agreement (16 and 17 year olds on their own). With the exception of New Brunswick and the Northwest Territories, all other jurisdictions exclude Supervision Orders from their legal statuses for children in care.
2. A child may have been counted twice if a child entered care, was discharged, and re-entered care during the month. This happened in a few cases.

Figure 13.3   Number of Placements[1] of Children in Care[2] by Type during March 1992

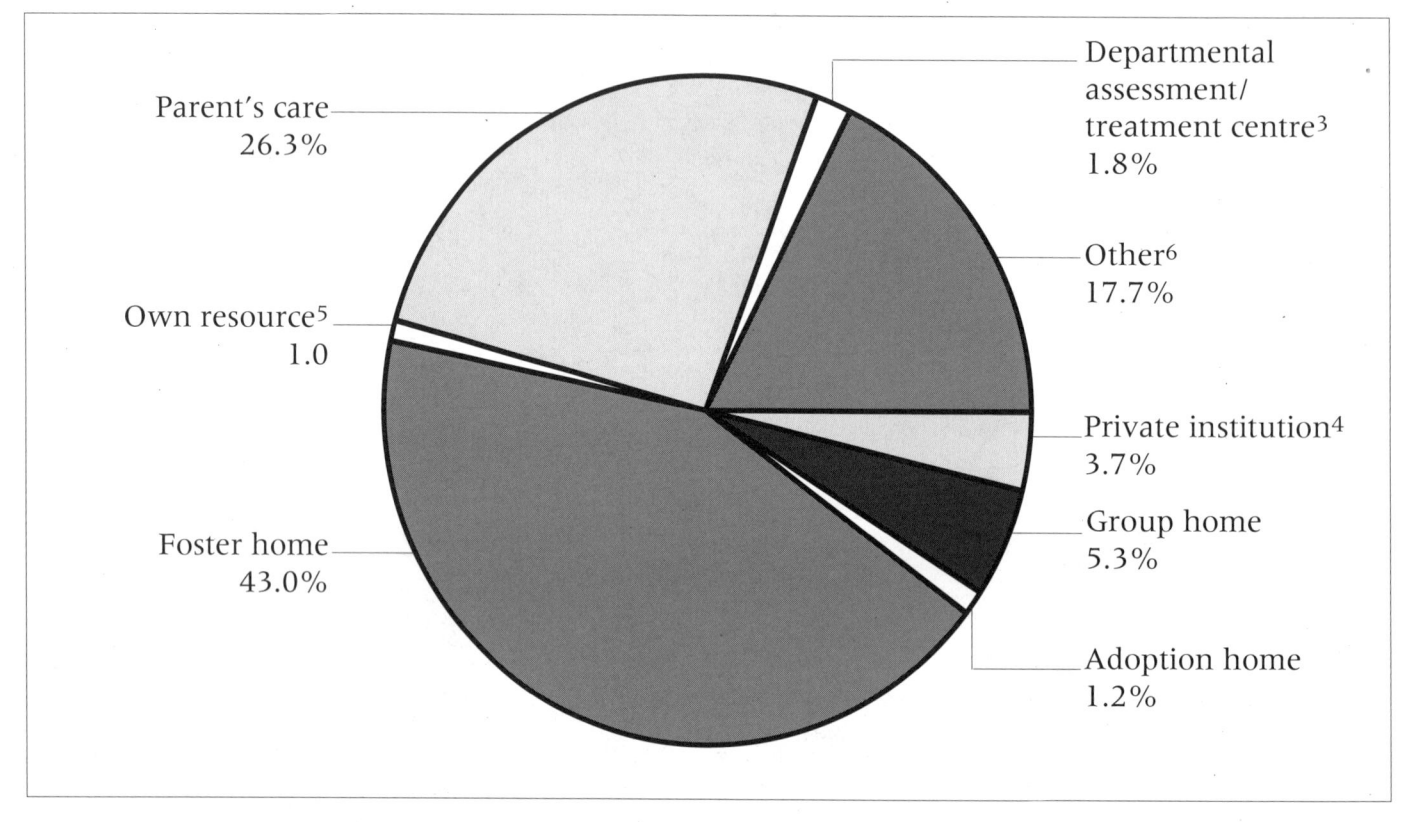

- Parent's care — 26.3%
- Own resource[5] — 1.0
- Foster home — 43.0%
- Departmental assessment/treatment centre[3] — 1.8%
- Other[6] — 17.7%
- Private institution[4] — 3.7%
- Group home — 5.3%
- Adoption home — 1.2%

Placements: 509[1]

1. A child in care may have more than one placement during the month.
2. Children who are in need of protection under the *Child Welfare Act* and are in care under the following legal statuses: Apprehension (waiting for court hearing), Supervision Order, Temporary Ward (including Temporary Custody Order and temporary wardship status during court adjournments), Permanent Ward (including Permanent Guardianship Order, extension to age 19 and voluntary relinquishment of a child for adoption), Custody by Agreement and Voluntary Care Agreement (16 and 17 year olds on their own). With the exception of New Brunswick and the Northwest Territories, all other jurisdictions exclude Supervision Orders from their legal statuses for children in care.
3. Trailcross.
4. Territorial Treatment Centre in Yellowknife and southern facilities.
5. Youth in an independent living situation.
6. Hospital in Yellowknife, student residence and young offenders resources.

Resource Material

Legislative Material

Consolidation of Child Welfare Act, Revised Statutes of the Northwest Territories 1988, c.C-6, as amended.

Reports

Native Women's Association of the Northwest Territories. *Communities Voice on Child Sexual Abuse*. A report on a conference held January 24-26, 1989 in Yellowknife.

Northwest Territories, Government of the Northwest Territories. *Annual Report of the Superintendent of Child Welfare, 1990-1991*.

Other Material

Northwest Territories, Department of Social Services. "Family and Children's Services Program Manual", Yellowknife, February 1987.

_____. "Child Abuse Investigations – Protocol for Social Service Workers".

Northwest Territories, Department of Education. "Child Abuse – Procedures for Reporting Suspected Child Abuse", 1987.

_____. "Draft Scenarios on Reporting Child Abuse".

"Kids in Court in the Northwest Territories – Child Witnesses in Sexual Abuse Cases". Report produced by an Interagency Committee of the Departments of Social Services, Justice, Education, and Health, Royal Canadian Mounted Police and the Department of Justice Canada, February 1991.

Protocol/Interdisciplinary Training Committee of the Child Sexual Abuse Initiatives Committee. "Child Sexual Abuse Protocol: Guidelines and Procedures for a Coordinated Response to Child Sexual Abuse Investigation in the Northwest Territories", September 1990.

Pamphlets, Department of Social Services

"Child Abuse and Neglect Prevention"

"Child Sexual Abuse...Hurts"

"Everyone Should Know About...Reporting Child Abuse"

Appendix A

Table A.1 Number of Children[1] Entitled to Family Allowances[2,3] by Single Years of Age, March 1992

Age	Newfound-land	P.E.I.	Nova Scotia	New Brunswick	Quebec	Ontario
Less than 1 year	7,038	1,934	11,914	9,427	96,770	146,877
1 year	7,554	1,907	12,767	9,824	97,731	148,448
2 years	7,823	1,938	12,497	9,825	93,239	146,350
3 years	7,419	1,909	12,364	9,663	87,646	141,428
4 years	7,615	1,913	12,236	9,816	84,852	139,882
5 years	7,937	1,961	12,359	9,716	85,715	140,878
6 years	8,303	2,051	12,551	10,112	88,158	141,570
7 years	8,686	1,945	12,352	10,205	89,005	141,464
8 years	8,844	1,973	12,508	10,524	90,226	138,733
9 years	9,041	1,972	12,472	10,403	91,045	137,170
10 years	9,145	1,945	12,212	10,363	96,011	134,319
11 years	9,152	1,955	12,171	10,535	97,717	134,144
12 years	9,483	1,918	12,537	10,604	99,871	132,541
13 years	9,416	1,996	12,421	10,525	95,393	130,514
14 years	9,930	1,983	12,261	11,029	95,332	130,790
15 years	10,038	1,968	12,534	11,381	94,803	130,528
16 years	10,539	1,952	12,932	11,357	93,407	132,870
17 years	10,512	1,977	12,742	11,315	90,773	131,027
Total	**158,475**	**35,197**	**223,830**	**186,624**	**1,667,694**	**2,479,533**

1. Children in the care of child welfare agencies or institutions, for whom a Special Allowance is paid, are included; children living abroad are excluded.
2. March 1992 Family Allowances data were used rather than June 1991 Census data to coincide with most data in this report. There is a difference of less than .5% between the June 1991 Census data and the June 1991 Family Allowances data.
3. These data reflect the number of children entitled to Family Allowances during the month indicated, regardless of whether or not payment was actually issued. Payments might be made retroactively due to delays in forwarding and processing information which affects a child's entitlement to Family Allowances. Retroactive changes in entitlement up to December 1992 are included.

Appendix A

Manitoba	Saskatche-wan	Alberta	British Columbia	Yukon	Northwest Territories	Canada
16,943	15,171	41,882	45,046	532	1,594	395,128
17,021	15,742	42,350	45,753	551	1,665	401,313
16,991	16,084	43,288	45,703	504	1,514	395,756
16,600	15,835	41,981	45,584	519	1,532	382,480
16,268	15,731	41,720	45,233	484	1,472	377,222
16,427	15,854	42,264	45,567	485	1,377	380,540
16,514	16,364	42,371	46,596	475	1,285	386,350
16,251	16,235	42,039	46,961	553	1,235	386,931
16,384	16,345	42,533	46,691	513	1,287	386,561
15,720	16,247	41,468	46,222	474	1,186	383,420
15,927	16,023	40,203	45,587	465	1,135	383,335
15,649	15,732	38,981	44,337	417	1,106	381,896
15,637	15,797	38,121	44,092	422	1,108	382,131
15,485	15,381	36,912	43,298	420	1,017	372,778
15,356	15,276	36,905	42,383	344	1,041	372,630
15,513	15,163	36,279	42,249	370	986	371,812
15,980	14,700	35,839	42,054	368	978	372,976
15,828	14,559	34,648	41,056	364	926	365,727
290,494	**282,239**	**719,784**	**804,412**	**8,260**	**22,444**	**6,878,986**

Appendix B

Contacts

A. Directors of Child Welfare[1]

Newfoundland
Ms. Elizabeth Crawford
Director of Child Welfare
Department of Social Services
Confederation Building
P.O. Box 8700
St. John's, Newfoundland
A1B 4J6

Prince Edward Island
Ms. Nancy E. Lee
Director of Child Welfare
Department of Health and Social Services
P.O. Box 2000
Charlottetown, Prince Edward Island
C1A 7N8

Nova Scotia
Mr. George Savoury
Director
Family and Children's Services
Department of Community Services
P.O. Box 696
Halifax, Nova Scotia
B3J 2T7

New Brunswick
Mr. Frank Hand
Director
Family and Community Social Services
Department of Health and
  Community Services
P.O. Box 5100
Fredericton, New Brunswick
E3B 5G8

Quebec
Mme Suzanne Moffet
Chef de service
Services des programmes aux
  jeunes et à leur famille
Direction générale des programmes
Ministère de la Santé et des Services sociaux
1075, chemin Ste-Foy, 12e étage
Québec (Québec)
G1S 2M1

Ontario
Ms. Nicole Lafrenière-Davis
Director
Children's Services Branch
Ministry of Community and Social Services
80 Grosvenor Street
3rd Floor, Hepburn Block
Queen's Park
Toronto, Ontario
M7A 1E9

---

1. As at December 1, 1993.

Manitoba
Mr. Ron Fenwick
Executive Director
Child and Family Support Branch
Department of Family Services
114 Garry St., 2nd Floor
Winnipeg, Manitoba
R3C 1G1

Saskatchewan
Mr. Richard Hazel
Acting Executive Director
Family and Youth Services Division
Department of Social Services
1920 Broad Street, 12th Floor
Regina, Saskatchewan
S4P 3V6

Alberta
Mr. Mat Hanrahan
Acting Assistant Deputy Minister
Program/Policy Division
Department of Family and Social Services
10th Floor, 7th Street Plaza
10030-107 Street
Edmonton, Alberta
T5J 3E4

British Columbia
Mr. Ron Pollard
Acting Director
Family and Children's Services Division
Ministry of Social Services
Parliament Buildings
Victoria, British Columbia
V8W 3A2

Yukon
Ms. Anne Sheffield
Director
Family and Children's Services
Department of Health and Social Services
Box 2703
Whitehorse, Yukon
Y1A 2C6

Northwest Territories
Mr. Andy Langford
Director
Family Support
Department of Social Services
6th Floor, Precambrian Building
500, 4920 – 52 Street
Yellowknife, Northwest Territories
X1A 3T1

B. Working Group on Child and Family Services Information[2]

Mr. Ken Cairnie (Chairperson)
Coordinator, Legislation and Regulations
Child and Family Support Branch
Department of Family Services
114 Garry Street, 2nd Floor
Winnipeg, Manitoba
R3C 1G1

Members: Mr. Bob Creasy
Department of Social Services
Saskatchewan

Ms. Judy Jackson
Department of Community
Services, Nova Scotia

Mr. John McDermott
Department of Family and
Social Services, Alberta

Ms. Marilyn Willis
Human Resources Development
Canada

---
2. Represents the structure of the Working Group during the development and production of this report. As at December 1, 1993, the Chairperson is John McDermott of Alberta's Department of Family and Social Services. Frank Hand of New Brunswick's Department of Health and Community Services has joined the Working Group. Manitoba is no longer participating in the Working Group.

C. Secretariat to the Working Group on Child and Family Services Information

Social Program Information
 and Analysis Directorate
Social Policy and Information Branch
Strategic Policy Group
Human Resources Development Canada
Room 2098
Jeanne Mance Building
Tunney's Pasture
Ottawa, Ontario
K1A 0K9

Members: Ms. Christine Gibson
Ms. Shelley Holroyd
Ms. Liz Nieman
Ms. Anne Tweddle

D. Family Violence Prevention Division

Ms. Elaine Scott
Director
Family Violence Prevention Division
Health Programs and Services Branch
Health Canada
1st Floor, Finance Building
Tunney's Pasture
Ottawa, Ontario
K1A 1B5

List of Tables

Page

Chapter 1 – Introduction

Table 1.1   Age of Child as Defined in Child Protection Legislation   14

Chapter 2 – Newfoundland

Table 2.1   Investigations by Type, April 1, 1991 to March 31, 1992   22
Table 2.2   Children in Care by Legal Status as at March 31, 1992   22
Table 2.3   Children in Care by Sex as at March 31, 1992   24

Chapter 3 – Prince Edward Island

Table 3.1   Children in Care by Legal Status and Age Group as at March 31, 1992   33

Chapter 4 – Nova Scotia

Table 4.1   Child Abuse Register: Recorded Cases by Type, September 3, 1991 to August 31, 1992   45
Table 4.2   Child Abuse Register: Sex of Abusers, September 3, 1991 to August 31, 1992   45
Table 4.3   Protection Cases from April 1, 1991 to March 31, 1992 and as at March 31, 1992   47
Table 4.4   Children in Care by Legal Status, April 1, 1991 to March 31, 1992 and as at March 31, 1992   48

Chapter 5 – New Brunswick

Table 5.1   Reports by Type, April 1, 1991 to March 31, 1992   59
Table 5.2   Outcome of Investigation of Reports Received during March 1992   61
Table 5.3   Protection Cases by Reason for Intervention during March 1992   61
Table 5.4   Children in Care by Legal Status during March 1992   62
Table 5.5   Children in Permanent Care by Reason during March 1992   65
Table 5.6   Children in Permanent Care by Reason, Age and Sex during March 1992   65

		Page

Chapter 6 – Quebec

Table 6.1	Receipt and Processing of Reports, April 1, 1991 to March 31, 1992	78
Table 6.2	Investigations Carried Out by Nature of Decision, April 1, 1991 to March 31, 1992	78
Table 6.3	Youth Protection Measures Undertaken by Type, April 1, 1991 to March 31, 1992	79
Table 6.4	Child Interventions under the *Youth Protection Act* (via Court Order or Voluntary Measures) by Reason, as at March 31, 1992	79
Table 6.5	Child Interventions under the *Youth Protection Act* by Type of Placement Resource as at March 31, 1992	81

Chapter 7 – Ontario

Table 7.1	Allegations by Type, January 1, 1991 to December 31, 1991	92
Table 7.2	Children in Care by Legal Status as at December 31, 1991	92
Table 7.3	Children in Care by Placement Type and Age Group as at December 31, 1991	94

Chapter 8 – Manitoba

Table 8.1	Reports on Alleged Abused Children by Source, April 1, 1991 to March 31, 1992	106
Table 8.2	Reports on Alleged Abused Children by Sex of Child, April 1, 1991 to March 31, 1992	106
Table 8.3	Reports on Alleged Abused Children by Sex of Alleged Abuser, April 1, 1990 to March 31, 1991	111
Table 8.4	Children in Care by Legal Status as at March 31, 1992	113

Chapter 9 – Saskatchewan

Table 9.1	Families with Children in Need of Protection by Reason as at March 31, 1992	123
Table 9.2	Children in Care by Legal Status as at March 31, 1992	124

Chapter 10 – Alberta

Table 10.1	Investigations Completed by Primary Referral Reason, April 1, 1991 to March 31, 1992	135
Table 10.2	Children in Need of Protection by Child's Legal Status and Social Worker's Assessment of Primary Reason as at March 31, 1992	138
Table 10.3	Children in Care by Child's Legal Status and Social Worker's Assessment of Primary Reason as at March 31, 1992	139
Table 10.4	Children in Care by Sex of Child as at March 31, 1992	142

Page

Chapter 11 – British Columbia

Table 11.1	Helpline Child Welfare Calls by Type during March 1992	152
Table 11.2	Child Protection Complaints Received by Type during March 1992	152
Table 11.3	Children in Care by Reason for Admission as at March 31, 1992	155
Table 11.4	Children in Care by Legal Status as at March 31, 1992	156

Chapter 12 – Yukon

| Table 12.1 | Children in Need of Protection by Age, Sex, Ethnicity and Worker's Assessment of Major Reason as at March 31, 1992 | 167 |
| Table 12.2 | Children in Care by Legal Status, Sex and Ethnicity as at March 31, 1992 | 168 |

Chapter 13 – Northwest Territories

Table 13.1	Intake Reports of Child Abuse and Neglect by Type during March 1992	179
Table 13.2	Child Sexual Abuse Intake Reports by Sex of Child, January 1, 1991 to December 31, 1991	179
Table 13.3	Children in Care by Reason for Admission during March 1992	180
Table 13.4	Children in Care by Legal Status during March 1992	181

Appendices

| Table A.1 | Number of Children Entitled to Family Allowances by Single Years of Age, March 1992 | 188 |

List of Figures

Page

Chapter 2 – Newfoundland

Figure 2.1   Children in Care by Legal Status as at March 31, 1992 23
Figure 2.2   Children in Care by Age Group as at March 31, 1992 24
Figure 2.3   Children in Care by Placement Type as at March 31, 1992 25

Chapter 3 – Prince Edward Island

Figure 3.1   Children in Care by Legal Status as at March 31, 1992 34
Figure 3.2   Children in Care by Placement Type as at March 31, 1991 35

Chapter 4 – Nova Scotia

Figure 4.1   Child Abuse Register: Abusers by Relationship to Victim,
                September 3, 1991 to August 31, 1992 46
Figure 4.2   Children in Care and Custody by Placement Type as at March 31, 1992 . . . 49
Figure 4.3   Children in Care and Custody by Age Group as at March 31, 1992 50

Chapter 5 – New Brunswick

Figure 5.1   Reports by Referral Source, April 1, 1991 to March 31, 1992 60
Figure 5.2   Children in Care by Legal Status during March 1992 63
Figure 5.3   Children in Care by Placement Type during March 1992 64
Figure 5.4   Children in Permanent Care by Age Group during March 1992 66

Chapter 6 – Quebec

Figure 6.1   Child Interventions under the *Youth Protection Act* by Reason as
                at March 31, 1992 80

Chapter 7 – Ontario

Figure 7.1   Children in Care by Legal Status as at December 31, 1991 93
Figure 7.2   Children in Care by Placement Type as at December 31, 1991 95
Figure 7.3   Children in Care by Age Group as at December 31, 1991 96

Page

Chapter 8 – Manitoba

Figure 8.1	Reports on Alleged Abused Children by Age Group of Child, April 1, 1991 to March 31, 1992	107
Figure 8.2	Reports on Alleged Abused Children by Type of Trauma, April 1, 1990 to March 31, 1991	108
Figure 8.3	Reports on Alleged Abused Children by Outcome, April 1, 1990 to March 31, 1991	109
Figure 8.4	Reports on Alleged Abused Children by Relationship of Alleged Abuser, April 1, 1990 to March 31, 1991	110
Figure 8.5	Reports on Alleged Abused Children by Disposition of Alleged Abuser, April 1, 1990 to March 31, 1991	112
Figure 8.6	Children in Care by Legal Status as at March 31, 1992	113
Figure 8.7	Children in Care by Placement Type as at March 31, 1992	114

Chapter 9 – Saskatchewan

Figure 9.1	Children in Care by Legal Status as at March 31, 1992	125
Figure 9.2	Children in Care by Placement Type as at March 31, 1992	126

Chapter 10 – Alberta

Figure 10.1	Investigations Completed by Referral Source, April 1, 1991 to March 31, 1992	136
Figure 10.2	Social Worker's Primary Assessment of Investigations Completed, April 1, 1991 to March 31, 1992	137
Figure 10.3	Children in Care by Legal Status as at March 31, 1992	140
Figure 10.4	Children in Care by Age Group as at March 31, 1992	141
Figure 10.5	Children in Care by Placement Type as at March 31, 1992	142

Chapter 11 – British Columbia

Figure 11.1	Child Protection Complaints Received during March 1992 by Referral Source	153
Figure 11.2	Child Protection Complaints Received during March 1992 by Outcome	154
Figure 11.3	Children in Care by Legal Status as at March 31, 1992	157
Figure 11.4	Children in Care by Sex and Age Group as at March 31, 1992	158
Figure 11.5	Children in Care by Placement Type as at March 31, 1992	159

Page

Chapter 12 – Yukon

Figure 12.1   Children in Care by Legal Status as at March 31, 1992   169
Figure 12.2   Children in Care by Age Group as at March 31, 1992   170

Chapter 13 – Northwest Territories

Figure 13.1   Children in Care by Legal Status during March 1992   182
Figure 13.2   Children in Care by Age Group and Sex during March 1992   183
Figure 13.3   Number of Placements of Children in Care by Type
               during March 1992   184

Ministry of Education & Training
MET Library
13th Floor, Mowat Block, Queen's Park
Toronto   M7A 1L2

Ministry of Education & Training
MET Library
13th Floor, Mowat Block, Queen's Park
Toronto M7A 1L2